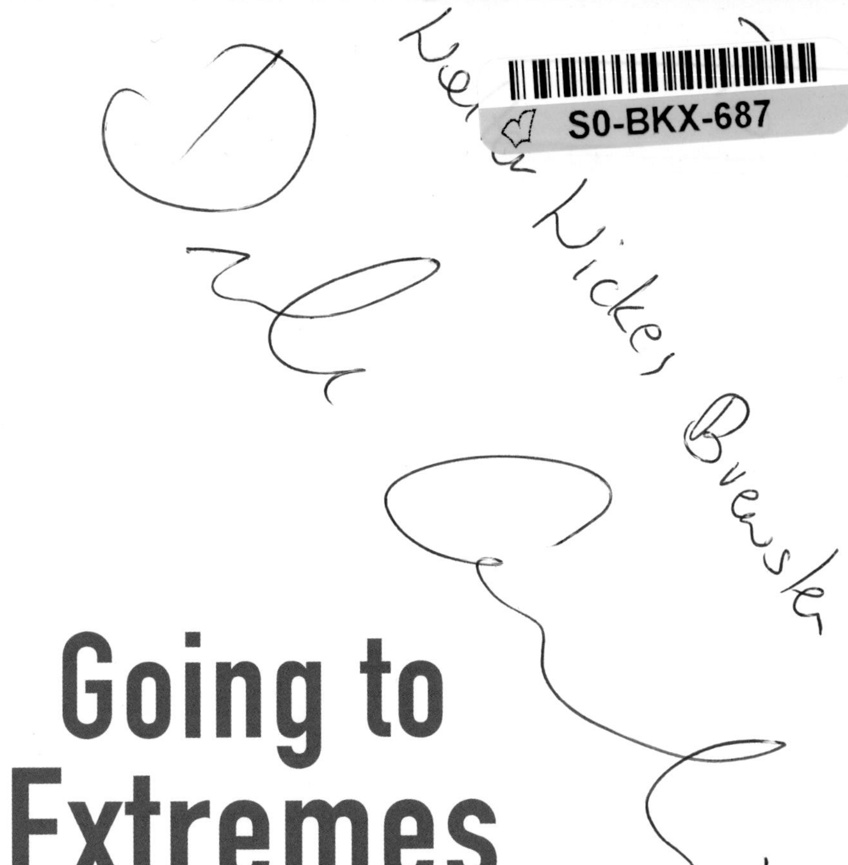

Going to Extremes

Going to Extremes

Adventures in Unknown New Zealand

Derek Grzelewski

To Kennedy,
for everything

NOTE: All these stories, in different and edited versions, have been previously published in *New Zealand Geographic* and *Smithsonian* magazines between 1995 and 2013.

Published in 2014 by David Bateman Ltd
30 Tarndale Grove, Albany, Auckland, New Zealand
www.batemanpublishing.co.nz

ISBN 978-1-86953-826-2

Design: redinc. book design
Photographs: all Derek Grzelewski unless credited otherwise

Printed in China through Colorcraft Ltd, Hong Kong.

Contents

'Fools say that knowledge can only be acquired from books & men . . . and call me a fool & even worse for wasting my life in mountain solitudes. [But] I have now been wandering about the uninhabited parts of New Zealand for over five & thirty years always finding something in nature new to me and the world . . . glimmerings of truth unknown to others. I have never regretted the life I have been leading.'

CHARLIE 'MR EXPLORER' DOUGLAS

•

'Be yourself; everyone else is already taken.'

MAYA ANGELOU

•

'You can live your life like a sheep or you can live like a lion.'

JEAN-MARC BOIVIN

•

'To each, their own Everest.'

MIROSŁAW FALCO-DĄSAL

Prologue

'Sometimes you have to go to extremes just to find room to breathe.'

The soldiers came up in a single file, rifles slung across their backs, their winter-white camouflage turning them into moonlit ghosts against the monochromatic landscape that was all mountains, snow and trees. They must have left their skis on the col below though they had kept their poles for balance and rhythm as they broke a knee-deep trail up the last steep section of their patrol beat. They were climbing hard, their out-breaths thick as smoke. I watched them through a slit in a rock only metres above, sinking deeper into my hiding place as they approached.

I had climbed here a number of times so was well familiar with the place, and had seen the border patrol before and knew this was their turnaround point. Beyond and for many kilometres, there were only crags, bluffs and rocky spires; an outburst of geological extravagance in the usually rolling and mellow Carpathian Mountains, the one section they did not need to guard. The national border was hermetic and only a fool would try to get across it here — a fool or a mountaineer. Still, I was relieved they didn't have dogs. The standard-issue German Shepherds would, at this distance, have sniffed me out regardless of how well I was hiding. My escape plan was sound and carefully prepared, but there were always going to be a few gambles in it, and the presence or absence of dogs was one of the big ones.

It was all a gamble, really, one last all-or-nothing gambit. By all accounts, I should have been one of those soldiers. It was 1986 and the government of Communist Poland and its military certainly did their upmost to conscript able-bodied recruits like me, as I did my damnedest to evade them. We'd played this fox hunt for a few years: me on the run, a fugitive in my own country, trying out one option after another, the hounds of the regime cutting me off at every attempt, slamming shut doors on each of my ways out, confident that, with the borders effectively closed, it was only a matter of time before I gave up my silly antics, as almost all men my age eventually did.

But they underestimated my resolve, my yearning for freedom. Quetzal, the sacred bird of the Mayas, is said to be so adamant about its freedom that it will die if caged. My sentiments, exactly. To me, this yearning for freedom — not liberty, take note, for this can be given or taken away by those usurping the power, but true freedom that is the inalienable birthright of everyone on the planet — was not negotiable. It is as innate as a drowning man's craving for air. No one and no thing can stand in its way. Which is how and why I came to play my last card.

Finally, when even my parents were being hounded by the military police as to my whereabouts, when I had to walk past our home incognito to see if it was safe to come in, when all options seemed used up and all ways out firmly locked, I feigned surrender, a capitulation which was so coldly and patiently expected.

I was issued with a military summons, a one-way ticket to become a red-beret commando, no less, and the honour and distinction of a three-year stint, instead of the compulsory two years' service for 'the country, the people and their Communist ideals'. A weasel of a military bureaucrat, with a cruel smile on his face and wielding what little power he had, assigned me to a garrison furthest away from the town where I lived, no doubt as punishment for the sins of such long evasion.

'No coming home for weekends,' he feigned an apology. 'The trains aren't fast enough to make a round trip before your pass runs out.'

He gave me a week to organise my affairs before commencing my tour of duty to 'serve and protect'. But what that weasel did not know was that I was just buying time. And that one week was exactly what I needed.

• • •

Five years earlier, I had still been a teenager when I'd watched a column of tanks rumble past our home, the soldiers in the hatches stony-faced, inhuman like automatons, avoiding eye contact with those who watched them from the street. On 13 December 1981, unable to contain the groundswell of freedom movements, the Communist cabal, desperate to cling to its power, declared martial law in Poland — in effect a war on its own people. It was a strange kind of war, an invasion from within and, with its imposition, the de facto police state came out of hiding and became official.

The Poles are a feisty and free-spirited lot, with a long tradition of heroic uprisings, but this time around, when they voiced their protest, they were met with an iron fist of uncommon cruelty, something that might have been expected from an outside aggressor, not from a group of your own, supposedly elected, public servants.

Battles flared around the country: workers occupied factories, taking on riot police with lances whose tips were heated white-hot in industrial foundry furnaces; stones and bricks confronted bullets and truncheons; tanks bulldozed impromptu barricades. Stretchers made out of unhinged doors were used to carry the bodies of the fallen, held up as martyrs. Army jeeps blocked intersections while soldiers checked everyone's 'papers' as if in some macabre replay of Nazi Germany, the images still fresh and painful in the nation's collective memory.

This then was the historical background against which I was to serve my time in the army, perhaps one day to open fire on protesters when ordered to do so. But the protesters were people like me, coming of age, and their grievances just. I could no more point a gun at them than I could at myself. This too, like the pining for freedom, was non-negotiable. And so I was about to play my trump card.

• • •

On that mountain pass on the border between Poland and Slovakia, breathing out slowly into my woollen gloves so that the steam of breath would not betray my hiding place, I watched the soldiers I could never become. Huddled in a circle, they stomped their feet and beat their mitts together against the cold, the ear flaps of their fur hats tied tight under their chins. They lit cheap workingmen's cigarettes — filter-less and acrid — and with each drag their faces glowed red with a hint of warmth. They swore, and spat, and checked their watches, stamping around some more, doing what soldiers the world over do best: killing time.

One of them passed around a flask and they all took a swig, and finally, when the requisite number of minutes had passed, the patrol-leader signalled a move-on, and they all filed back down the trail they had broken earlier. On the col below they clipped into their skis, the snapping of their antiquated cable bindings sounding like the metallic clang of closing rat traps. Then they were off, schussing down through the snowy glade from whence they came.

For a long time afterwards I lay still in my rock crevice, listening to the winter silence. If patience is the virtue of a hunter, it is even more critical for the hunted. In a routine learned from winter climbing bivouacs, when staying awake and moving was the only way against cold and frostbite, I clenched and unclenched my fists, one at a time, wriggled my toes ten times each side, to circulate blood to the extremities, to keep them from going numb.

When I finally deemed it safe to come out, I stretched and warmed up with a few callisthenics. Below me, the couloir down into Slovakia — and freedom — was long, steep, snowy and smooth. Tempting.

Coming back from climbs, we had often descended such gullies using a technique known as a snow glissade. This butt-slide, gleeful and fast, feet-first and using the shaft of an ice-axe for both steering and speed control, was a fun way down, until one time my climbing partner ran over a tip of a rock hidden under the snow which nearly took out his tail bone. I've preferred to walk down ever since.

I shouldered my pack and threaded my right hand through the webbing loop of the ice-axe. I thought of the weasel back at the conscription office. I should really send him a note so that he could amend his records. From this day on I was to be considered AWOL. No further notice given; case closed. I could send this to him as a postcard from some stunning exotic island, I thought, a place on the planet where I could get as far away as possible from him and all that he represented. New Zealand, perhaps? Now there was an idea …

I started down the couloir, tentatively at first, stabbing the ice-axe into the snow for safety and balance, punctuating my gait. Then, finding a newer, freer rhythm, opening up the throttle of the soul, I went from small steps to giant leaps and moon-walked down the slope, confident the snow would hold. The Iron Curtain did not have many cracks, but I had just found one and there was no turning back.

Sometimes you have to go to extremes just to find room to breathe.

• • •

How unforeseeable are the workings of life, how mysterious its ways, coincidences, synchronicities. Within less than a year of that Carpathian night I did indeed find myself in New Zealand. There, on the kitchen table in a backpacker's hostel in Auckland, was a torn-out page from the jobs section of the *New Zealand Herald*, days old but with one entry which seemed written especially for me. A high-rise maintenance company was looking for someone with expertise in industrial abseiling, a skill virtually unknown in the country back then, but something which was the only work I'd ever done since leaving school; one which paid enough for an offbeat and expensive climbing lifestyle while also allowing ample time to pursue it.

Within days I had the job and a work permit; within months a residency and my own abseiling business. It would take many years to exorcise the ghosts of the past, the nightmares in which, for some inexplicable reason, I had gone back to Poland and now I would never get out — the dream so predictable and repetitive, yet catching me out every time, making me wake up bolt upright, sweating, breathing hard and checking where I was. But apart from these interludes of bedtime horror, for the first time in my life I felt free, and ready to taste this freedom in all its splendour.

After months of dangling on ropes from the roofs of many of Auckland's high-rises, I bought a mountain bike, still a relatively new invention in those days. I equipped it with saddle bags, a small climbing tent and all the other prerequisites for self-containment, and set out for a year-long tour of my new home, reasoning, after Hemingway, that: 'It is by riding a bicycle that you learn the contours of a country best, since you have to sweat up the hills and coast down them.'

I clocked some 10,000 kilometres on that bike, visited most of the national parks and hiked all the major trails. I spent a semi-Antarctic winter at Mount Cook, largely on my own and in the huts at the head of the Tasman Glacier. I would fly up the névé by ski plane, on standby rate, packing a month's worth of food and books, drag all that stuff to a hut on a kids' plastic toboggan and live there for weeks on end, learning to ski big mountains and learning to write, daily drunk on my new freedom.

People came and went and I joined some of them on their ski tours, but, except for resupply trips, I did not come out until spring. After weeks of sensory deprivation amid the sterility of snow, even the grasses and lichens, let alone flowers and alpine plants, had the pungent intensity of wild thyme snorted straight up, like a drug. I was intoxicated with the country — its varied landscapes so full of potential for adventures, its friendly, laid-back, live-and-let-live people. The space, the clean air and clean rivers, the solitude and the almost unbearable lightness of being free among it all. I saw New Zealand as a place with the diversity of an entire continent — the smallest continent, as I still think of it — one that could take a lifetime to explore and to write about. And so I came back from that bike trip with a plan.

• • •

One grey and drizzly day in 1992, in his Mount Eden office in Auckland, I met the man on whom this entire plan was hinged. His name was Kennedy Warne, and only a few years earlier he had co-founded and more or less single-handedly ran and edited the most illustrious magazine in the country, the *New Zealand Geographic*.

His office was part literary den, part laboratory of some eccentric inventor, strewn with half-read manuscripts dense with pencil annotations, large prints of photographs and mock layouts, trial covers and posters. Amidst this farrago, Kennedy moved back and forth like a whirlwind of creative energy, unable to sit still, forever fetching examples of work, both good and bad.

'See, this is good.' He showed me a stunning photograph of a man climbing a ridge in the Murchison Mountains, radio-tracking a takahe. 'It's good. But it's not good enough. I don't just want to lift the standards; I want to establish a whole new level for magazine writing and photography in this country. We have so many good untold stories here, but they're only worth telling well. Listen to this!'

He read out loud an opening paragraph from one of his favourite stories, in the *Smithsonian*, then another from the *New Yorker*.

'Can you hear it? This stuff sizzles. It's like a sound or a scent wafting from a good kitchen. It draws you in. It's irresistible. It makes you hungry for more.'

I could hear it alright, but whether I could do likewise was another question entirely. I sensed that, like the winter night in the Carpathians, this meeting was another pivotal point in my life. But unlike that time on the border, there was no telling which way things would turn here. This time it wasn't just me who was taking the leap of faith. I had to convince this man to take that leap with me.

I had with me three story proposals, honed to a word like haikus, my only trump cards in this gamble against impossible odds. I had no portfolio, no previous experience. I had only just bought a camera kit sufficient for the job and, hell, English was my fourth language.

But we were both burning with the same fire, the curiosity for life, the treasure hunter's lust to go out into the world and find the nuggets of the best stories, and to bring them home, polish them up as best we could, and offer them for others to experience and, hopefully, savour. It was easy and obvious to see that quality in him, but somehow Kennedy must have recognised it in me, too, for the next day he called me back in, handed me a cheque to cover my travel expenses and a bag of transparency film to shoot my first story.

Within a month I was back at Mount Cook, this time climbing the mountain itself alongside a guide and his client, to write and photograph my first assignment for the magazine, about glaciers, 'Rivers of Ice'.

That was the beginning of an adventure which continues to this day. By my rough estimate, I have done over 70 features for the magazine, and many more for other publications, and, if this has been a wild journey it is because, from the outset, I insisted not just on writing each story well but on living it, too. And so to write about ceramics I became a potter for a time; to learn about the underground world of karst, a cave diver.

I have played the roles of logger and tree-hugger, poacher and ranger, hunter and the hunted, because one of the early and formative wisdoms which Kennedy had impressed on me was that a writer had to 'run with the hares and hunt with the hounds'. And because, from the beginning, I innately believed that for writing to be authentic it had to come from direct experience, and that any writer's block could be overcome by spending more time in the field, gathering experiences, living the story.

I'll spare you that very first piece about glaciers, for it was clumsy and riddled with purple prose, the way ice, though outwardly solid, can turn out to be full of air bubbles and pores when you stab an ice-axe into it. The learning curve of writing and story-telling was vertical for me then, an arduous and foolhardy climb, much like my early mountaineering efforts, the ones from which you come back lucky to have survived to tell the tale. But by the time I wrote 'The Odyssey of Alphonse Barrington', which is included here, the angle of this learning curve had eased off somewhat, becoming a steady, pleasantly steep slope, which it has remained ever since — always a good challenge but never quite such a desperate do-or-die again.

• • •

The narratives in this volume comprise what I consider my best work to date and they will take you to places and people that are as extraordinary as they are unknown, inaccessible, forgotten or just plain surprising. The theme of going to extremes, and the progression from 'elite' to 'ordinary', from speciality interests and a narrow focus to the all-encompassing 'big picture', have become clear to me only in retrospect. At the time of research and writing, I picked the subjects purely because they appealed to me, not really seeing that each choice, adventure and encounter was also a stepping stone on a larger journey of understanding.

By 'going to extremes', I don't just mean outdoor adventures. Any pursuit — saving endangered species, searching for artistic excellence, treasure hunting, maritime rescue or pioneering aviation — can be taken to extremes if instilled with enough passion and commitment, enough inner fire.

The subject matter of these stories is as diverse as my interests, but this collection is at once a record of adventures, a progression in writing life and, above all, an evolution in awareness — my own trial-and-error attempts to 'see a world in a grain of sand . . . And eternity . . .' no, not in an hour, but in that one moment, the Now. Looking for the mystical 'zone' to which the extreme adventurers, athletes, artists, performers and thinkers allude — often in veiled inferences and hushed voices, for the state is as delicate as a soap bubble — and often finding it in the most unexpected places, in the ordinary here and now.

I have always been fascinated with human potential: what we are really capable of, how we act under fire, how seemingly everyday people can become superheroes when faced with a crisis. How, when we are confronted with impossible odds, we can find within ourselves hitherto unrealised reserves, the unused booster tank of clarity, strength, will, energy and resolve that can see us through and out of trouble.

I grew up among people who constantly tested that potential, often to beyond its breaking point. The mountaineering club I belonged to in Poland produced the hardiest and most accomplished bunch of Himalayan climbers ever to walk the earth. Though the most coveted prize in the world of climbing has long been the so-called 'Crown of the Himalayas' — all fourteen of the 8000-metre mountains — the gallant, intrepid Poles, with their 'we can do better than that' attitude, also elected to climb these highest peaks, but in winter! Think Antarctica combined with 'Death Zone' altitude. No surprise that for many years no one else dared to follow, and so the Poles notched the first ten first winter ascents largely by themselves.

Some years later, their exploits became the stuff of global legend after being portrayed in Bernadette McDonald's book *Freedom Climbers* but, at the time, as a teenager trying to make sense of the world, climbing and girls, and soon to embark on my own little freedom climb, I had no idea just who these people really were — Kukuczka, Wielicki, Falco-Dąsal, Hajzer and many others whose names may not mean much to you. They gave their time to the club, teaching us how to use ropes and ice-axes, tie knots and make anchors, then disappeared on far-off expeditions of unspeakable hardships. They pushed the limits of what was possible to such extremes that, over time, most of them did not come back.

Settling in New Zealand and, through my travels and work, getting to know the country, its history and people, I soon became aware that there was no shortage of such heroes here too . . . a more diverse bunch and not so obsessed with mountains, to be sure, but of similar grand calibre: Hillary and Blake, Richard Pearse and Bill Hamilton, Jean Batten and Kelly Tarlton, Don Merton and Arthur Lydiard. Then there was Charlie Douglas, the country's very own Thoreau, and even that old fool Barrington, the accidental explorer, whose journey had been likened to Shackleton's epic crossing to South Georgia, which was also navigated by a Kiwi, Frank Worsley. And they are just the first tier, the avant-garde.

No question then that, for the size of its population, per capita as it were, New Zealand has produced more world-class pioneers, inventors and exponents of the extreme than any other nation. This phenomenon has been globally recognised. It has even caused some pundits to wonder if New Zealanders are endowed with some kind of special 'adventure gene' that is expressed in a greater than usual percentage of the populace. Or if perhaps the land itself, in all its glorious and compact diversity, like some giant magnet or tuning fork, has the ability to activate that adventure gene in those who spend time within it, who hear and respond to its silent song.

I like the second idea better. Nurture over nature, if you like, and away from any implied genetic superiority because, beyond national pride, name-dropping and drawing inspiration from the greats, there is a lot more to consider here.

'Extreme' has become a much overused, almost meaningless word these days, and, combined with an epidemic of celebrity worship, reinforces the idea that any 'going to extremes' is surely the domain of the others — the greats — and never ourselves. Yet the extreme is a highly relative concept. To a Himalayan guide, climbing Mount Everest again may be all in a day's work, but for someone recovering from a heart attack even a short jog can be an extreme effort.

I once spent a day with a Feldenkrais therapist who worked with post-stroke patients, helping them to regain their basic faculties. After their neural network had been partially fried by the stroke — which could erase neuromuscular memories and pathways for even some of the most basic functions — these patients could take weeks, if not months, to re-learn to move their fingers, speak, begin to walk. If that is not going to extremes, what is?

After his fall from Mount Awful, in which he sustained spinal injuries that confined him to a wheelchair, John Nankervis, one of New Zealand's best-known mountaineers, said he now faced the hardest climb of his life, the toughest route. As Falco-Dąsal, one of the 'freedom climbers' wrote: 'To each, their own Everest.'

The most extreme adventures and heroic deeds often happen in our daily lives, unacknowledged and out of sight and they are, more likely than not, overshadowed by empty glam and the fakery of mass entertainment. If you doubt that, ask a fire-fighter, or, better still, join their training programme. It will redefine your idea of 'extreme', as it redefined mine.

Even if our perceptions of what is extreme vary widely, we all innately sense that, if only from time to time, we need to enter this state beyond the comfort zone and, further still, to venture to the edge of what we consider possible.

Why? Because the extreme is where life is lived to its fullest. It is where evolution takes place, where most growth occurs, whether for a lichen or a human body, mind and spirit. It is where the vibrancy of life is refreshed and rediscovered, where we find inspiration and new directions — nourishment for the soul — and we need these as much as we need food, water and air, if not more. There, as we test ourselves in the recurring baptisms of fire, the mundane and the false drop away and only what's real and true is left to shine.

Joseph Campbell, a mythologist and a student of legends and folklore, discovered that all of our stories, the good and memorable ones at least, can be distilled into one essential narrative: a story of going to extremes, and coming back with the goods. The book he wrote about it is called *The Hero with a Thousand Faces*, implying that the story is the same, and only the faces of the heroes and heroines change. The characters may differ, as do the times and settings, but the tale is the same the world over, from the Bible and classical Greek theatre, to indigenous myths and legends, to modern thrillers and movies.

In this archetypal story, the reluctant hero or heroine is thrown out of his or her world of comforts and routines and into a wild adventure, against their will, against all odds and insurmountable obstacles. One after another, things go wrong until, when they could not get any worse, they do. At the pivotal point in the narrative, hounded by fears, enemies, accidents, losses and other misfortunes, the hero reaches rock bottom, down and nearly out.

This is where that booster tank kicks in, when all that was false falls away and the hero finds his or her true strength, and comes through all the challenges and returns to the ordinary world, bringing back a hard-won piece of wisdom, a nugget-like glimmer of larger reality, to share with others.

I am that hero and so are you, because Campbell's one story is the tale of a universal human quest for wisdom and understanding. Our journeys will differ — like fingerprints, no two are the same — but one thing we can be absolutely sure about is that, whether we want them or not, life already has adventures planned for us, and some of them will be extreme.

It has been my direct experience that, unlike Campbell's reluctant hero, it is better to enter the world of adventures voluntarily. This makes for a smoother journey, more engaging and less accidental. And so, here then are some of the favourite treasures I've dug up in my time and brought back to share. May they serve you and inspire your own journey as they have inspired mine.

It's a wild ride, and we are all in this together.

The
Forest Solitaire

'It must be one of the cuddliest of all living things — soft and fluffy, and intelligent — a Persian cat of a parrot, with plumage the colour of fresh moss and carrying the scent of papaya.'

For a moment before it fell down, the helicopter hovered above the water like a dragonfly, straining against gravity, and the three men inside it braced for the inevitable. Their reaction was well-rehearsed: one arm shielding the head, the other hand finding and gripping the doorknob of an emergency exit. The impact was soft as the cabin splashed into the water and briefly bobbed like a buoy. Then, top-heavy with the weight of the engine, it flipped upside-down and began to sink, a bubble of safety turning into a deathtrap for all of its occupants. Through every crevice the water surged in, swirling into froth until the inside of the cabin felt like a washing machine, with a pocket of air rapidly shrinking against the floor that was now the ceiling.

The three men, still strapped to their seats and disoriented by the capsize, were tense with apprehension but they had to wait: outside the cabin the helicopter's rotor would still be scything the water like the blades of a blender. There was a procedure to this sort of chaos and the men remained calm. They took a last gasp of disappearing air, just as the swirling white water blurred their vision. 'One ... two ... three,' they paced their breathless wait, '... four ... FIVE! Push the door open. Unbuckle the seat belt. Go!' They wormed their way out and bolted towards the light and air, now several metres above them, oblivious to the two divers hovering near by in mid-water — their guardian angels holding emergency aqualungs. Two of the men burst to the surface and sucked in lungsful of air, but the third one was remarkably calm. 'That was good, gentlemen,' he said floating alongside them, 'but we'll do it again, just so that you really get it nailed.'

An orange-coloured crane was already lifting the mock-up helicopter out of the training plunge-pool where they were floating, readying it for another simulated crash-landing; on the water's edge, more people in white overalls anxiously awaited their turn. This was not an exercise for military elite forces or the coastguard, not an emergency 'abandon the ship' drill for the workers of the nearby Taranaki offshore oil rigs, though the venue and the instructors were the same.

Yet the fourteen men and women undertaking this punishing Helicopter Underwater Escape Training at the Quantum Safety facilities in New Plymouth were special forces of a sort. By the time their two weeks of aquatic challenges were completed, they would have also learnt how to drive through waves big enough to catapult their inflatables two or three metres into the air, and how to fish each other out of the maelstrom of water, should someone part company with the boat. They would also have endured a run-swim-run ironman-like test to become qualified surf life-savers. And indeed, they were on a life-saving mission of sorts, though it is an odd kind of irony that their SAS-style trials are a preparation to save and protect one of the world's gentlest and most peaceful creatures — a flightless, nocturnal and solitary, hopelessly adorable and totally helpless bird — the kakapo.

It must be one of the cuddliest of all living things — soft, and fluffy and intelligent — a Persian cat of a parrot, with plumage the colour of fresh moss and carrying the scent of papaya. It can show such incredible and endearing trust in people; those fortunate enough to work with them would tell you that it is almost as if the birds know that people are trying to help them. A wild kakapo may clamber up your leg and arm, and sit on your shoulder nibbling gently at your cheek and ears, or preening your hair. It can be playful like a kitten and owlishly wise, its beady chocolate-coloured eyes holding your gaze, then drifting out of focus, looking through you like the stare of a Buddhist monk.

You'd fall in love with a kakapo at the first touch, despite the fact that their claws feel like an animated barbed-wire bracelet. The bird has already stolen the hearts of many. Don Merton, standing still wet at the edge of the training pool, couldn't bear to think that if this helicopter crash happened in real life, he'd most likely have with him on board several cat-boxes, each containing a kakapo, and that he would have to leave them all behind.

• • •

For 40 years, Merton had been a kind of ambulance man and extinction buster for avian kind. He is best known for the rescue of the Chatham Island black robin whose numbers once slumped to five, including only one female, but he also recovered the saddlebacks from the rat-infested Big South Cape Island, and helped a number of other species on the islands of the Indian Ocean: Seychelles, Rodriguez and Christmas. No other conservationist in the world has been directly involved in as many bird rescues as Merton, said Christoph Imboden, director of BirdLife International, a global conservation agency based in Cambridge, England. No other bird, in turn, has provided Merton with as much challenge as the kakapo.

They were once abundant throughout New Zealand, from sea level to the snow line. 'The birds used to be in dozens round the camp, screeching and yelling like a lot of demons, and at times it was impossible to sleep for the noise,' wrote the West Coast explorer Charlie Douglas. On moonlit nights, he went on, you could shake a tree or a bush and the kakapo would fall down like apples.

H. Guthrie-Smith noted that '. . . the diggers lived on them' in the Takaka Valley, praising the delicious and fruity white meat, 'as good eating as a barnyard fowl'. Another writer added, '. . . in Otago during the construction of a certain road, the Night Parrot was slaughtered in great numbers, one bird making a plenteous meal for two men'.

Now, there were only 62 birds left — 26 females and 36 males — each with a name, a radio transmitter, and a long history of medical check-ups. There was no longer a safe place for them on the mainland, and they had been relocated to a few remote offshore islands — Codfish, Pearl and Maud: natural fortresses guarded by the Southern Ocean. Hence the exercises in surf rescue, life-raft scenarios and simulated helicopter crashes, because even getting to these islands can be an adventure. It was a measure of the kakapo's dire straits that the conservation staff responsible for their well-being even engaged in war-games manoeuvres that re-enacted an attempt to kidnap the birds from their sanctuaries. Each bird had become so precious, their caretakers left nothing to chance.

No other creature in the pantheon of New Zealand's natural wonders had ever attracted so much attention, effort or funds, and none is still as critically endangered and vulnerable. Yet for all its ecological charisma and PR glamour, only a few people are likely to ever see a live kakapo, and not just because their sanctuaries are out of bounds to all but key personnel. You could walk their island forests for days and never see a bird. The kakapo evolved with blind and total faith in their perfect camouflage, and they blend into the foliage so well that trying to see them is like picking the shapes out of three-dimensional Magic Eye pictures. Chris Hughes, who worked as a kakapo volunteer in Fiordland in the early 1980s, told me how he once radio-tracked and pinpointed a bird to a single bush, then looked hard until his eyes hurt but still could not see it. And then the kakapo blinked, and the movement betrayed its disguise. The bird was sitting, Hughes recalled, at his eye level, less than an arm's reach away. Its last-ditch defence was to close its eyes. This worked well with eagle-vision raptors, but against the tree-climbing predators that hunt by smell, such behaviour was to be the kakapo's greatest undoing. 'If the bird only knew its powers, it wouldn't fall such an easy prey (to) stoats and ferrets,' Charlie Douglas wrote in his diaries. 'One grasp of his powerful claws would crush either of those animals, but he has no idea of attack or defence.'

There was once a similar bird — similar in circumstances, not in appearance — and it lived in what is now Mauritius, a plateau of volcanic cones roughly the size of Stewart Island, east of Madagascar. Like the kakapo, the bird was highly endemic and a giant of its kind — a solitaire too heavy to fly — and so it walked everywhere, and nested on the ground, leaving its young unguarded because the island was still a garden that knew no Cain. (God first made Mauritius, then modelled heaven on it, Mark Twain would later write.) Like the kakapo, the bird was also numerous, widespread and long-lived, but it was a likewise slow and infrequent breeder, which meant it would not bounce back quickly once its population was severely dented. To its first eye-witnesses, armed with hunting clubs and driven by hunger, the bird was as outlandish as it was fearless, though its fearlessness was not courage but rather an innocent incomprehension of what was coming its way. Like the kakapo, too, the bird was exceptionally good eating and that ultimately led to its demise. It vanished so rapidly and completely we don't even know the colour of its plumage, but we have condensed its sad story into a sound-bite collocation that tolls like an epitome of finality: dead as a dodo.

And so, 300 years later, the story of the kakapo was a case of déjà vu, almost right up to its mournful finale. It could well have been dead as a kakapo, were it not for a handful of dedicated New Zealanders determined not to repeat the dodo story on our shores. For the past four decades, in an effort unprecedented in the annals of conservation, they had been waging a war against extinction of the species. It had been largely a losing battle, with the population of the kakapo remaining stable but aging, and time slowly running out. Recently, however, the tide has turned. And not a moment too soon, according to Don Merton, who has been at the forefront of this effort for the past 30 years. Because, as he said: 'if we can't save the kakapo, our flagship species and the number-one conservation priority, what hope is there for all the other, less glamorous critters?'

To be sure, the kakapo had already once become extinct. Maori hunted them with gusto, and their dogs and the kiore, the native rat they introduced, decimated the kakapo population so that the bird was largely gone from the North Island by the time Europeans arrived. The settlers, and their accompanying entourage of pets and vermin, further accelerated the decline and by the early decades of the twentieth century the kakapo had become extremely rare in the South as well.

Between 1949 and 1973, faced with the imminent extinction of the species, the Wildlife Service (predecessor to the Department of Conservation) organised over 60 search expeditions — some in north-west Nelson and the Tararuas, but most of them in Fiordland. These inaccessible southern mountains — where beech forests cling to vertical rock faces and often, overloaded with rain, peel off like wet wallpaper creating tree avalanches the size of airport runways — had only just yielded the lost species of the takahe and it was apparent that they could be the final bastion of the kakapo as well. In the 1960s, five birds were trapped in the Tutuko Valley near Milford Sound and another one in the Sinbad Gully, under Mitre Peak, but as almost nothing was known about their habits and needs, all but one died in the Mount Bruce Native Bird Reserve in Wairarapa.

It was not until February 1974 that another kakapo was discovered. By then it was confirmed that the birds favoured so-called kakapo gardens — areas where the beech forest was broken up by an avalanche allowing faster-growing berry plants to flourish. In one such place, in the Esperance Valley, Don Merton heard a kakapo calling and managed to record its voice. This scrark call was dubbed on a tape and played back in the garden, and the results were astonishing. A cacophony of rebuttals came back from the forest: shrieks and screams, braying of a donkey and squealing of a pig, rooster's crows and cat-like purrs — all vocalisations of an agitated kakapo. It took another two weeks to trap the bird, who was named Jonathan Livingston Kakapo. He was a sorry-looking thing, old and bedraggled, but it was a find that galvanised the efforts. There followed a period of even more intense searches, with the newly-introduced helicopters, allowing for the first time, access to the eyrie-like forested balconies high on the flanks of the Fiordland mountains.

Three more years of combing for sounds and signs resulted in seventeen birds — and one perplexing mystery. While looking for the kakapo the searchers also found networks of immaculately kept tracks punctuated with half-a-metre wide bowls, their edges trimmed to perfection. It was, one of the finders, Rod Morris, recalled, as if archaeologists had stumbled across the ruins of an ancient civilisation swallowed by the forest. One of those track-and-bowl systems, later named the Kakapo Castle and possibly thousands of years old, was cut into a razorback ridge with 1000-metre drops on either side. Suddenly, Maori lore which told of the Whawharua — a meeting place where each tribe of the kakapo gathered to perform their unusual nightly rituals — began making more sense.

There was one more sound that so far had gone unrecorded, a sound as if someone was blowing across the top of an empty milk bottle, with the power of a fog horn and the regularity of a heartbeat. This was a male kakapo booming — sitting in the amphitheatre of its bowl, inflating itself into a feathered balloon, sending out a pulsing low-frequency love call. The bowls were built in such a way, and in places where the rock walls surrounding them would act as sound-reflectors and amplifiers, as to direct the calls down and across the valleys. Ooooom! Ooooom! Ooooom! The long-wave hum could travel up to five kilometres and bend around obstacles. It carried on like a tribal drum into the Fiordland night.

Alas, the booming went unanswered. All of the eighteen birds found and caught in Fiordland turned out to be males. There were possibly no females left. Technically speaking, the species was extinct. The last booming was heard above the Milford Sound in 1987. Then the kakapo gardens went silent.

Not all was lost however, for in a miraculous reprise the kakapo would get a second chance, a new lease on life. While the Fiordland booming was fading, a 200-strong population of kakapo was discovered in the south of Stewart Island, so far untroubled by introduced predators. In 1977, in the area soon to be known as the Arena Ridge, searchers found a complex of 23 freshly used track-and-bowl systems. This, the biologists concluded, was a kind of a kakapo nightclub where the males would gather — often walking from several kilometres away — to boom, and prance, and display, each in his own manicured dust bowl, hoping to lure in an elusive female, not seen since the turn of the century.

Merton and his colleagues were becoming increasingly alarmed by the strange absence of females in this all-old-boys' fraternity, but then, in 1980, came the long-awaited breakthrough. While searching near the camp, a black Labrador named Mandy picked up a kakapo scent and led her handler, Gary Aburn, to the bird, which was more slender and greener than all others previously caught. Merton examined its primary feathers — a method of distinguishing the sex of the kakapo which he had devised from studying a museum specimen.

The new bird, called Mandy after its captor, did not have the telltale mottling along the tips of its primaries. It was a female! Soon more female kakapo were found, and then their nests and chicks. The fate of the species had finally seemed to turn for the better, but this time too, the jubilations would not last long. Mandy was never seen again and, as the quest for more kakapo continued, it began turning up not only live birds but, more and more frequently, their half-eaten carcasses.

A plague of feral cats had broken out on Stewart Island. Grant Harper, a member of the kakapo team, who also studied the Stewart Island's feral felines, told me that he estimated their population at about 5000. The cats were bush-wise and feisty, and impossible to extract from the dense sub-Antarctic vegetation, which one witness described as 100,000 acres of hedge. Within five years, the cats had halved the remaining kakapo population. Just as in Fiordland, the searchers realised they were riding a bow-wave of extinction. This time, however, they would take more radical measures.

Over the next decade, until 1992, all of the 61 known Stewart Island kakapo were caught and transferred to safe island sanctuaries: Codfish, Maud and Little Barrier. This effectively terminated the last wild population, ending the age of innocence. From now on, constant interisland transfers and airlifting out of trouble would become the norm in kakapo life. While a solution to their predicament was being sought, the kakapo would remain refugees in their own homeland, shuttled from one holding camp to another.

• • •

When you look at the map of Stewart Island it resembles, in an uncanny sort of way, the contours of South America. Paterson Inlet would be its mouth of the Amazon, and the Ruggedy Mountains and the Deceit Peaks could stand in for the Andes, and out to the west, where you'd expect to find the Galapagos, there is Codfish Island. Though it inspired no new evolutionary theory, like the Darwinian Galapagos, Codfish is now also an island of ecological treasures, for it harbours almost the entire world population of the kakapo.

One evening in early April, as the seasons were turning and the winter was already edging in from the Antarctic, I walked with the photographer Rod Morris through the wet rimu forest laced with supplejack, down from the bald summit of Codfish. We each carried a plastic cat-box housing a kakapo. The boxes were heavy, and every few hundred metres we stopped to swap hands and to catch a glimpse of the birds: a youngster named Sirocco in Rod's cage, a female called Hoki in mine. The birds had just been ferried in from Pearl Island, which was their temporary holding station while the 1396-hectare Codfish Nature Reserve was being purged of any remaining vermin. Back in the mid-1980s, all possums were trapped out from Codfish and even the egg-stealing wekas were removed, and now, with the air-drop of 22 tonnes of pellets baited with an anticoagulant brodifacoum, the island was declared a rat-free 'kakaporium' — the safest haven the birds would ever know.

Below the summit of Codfish I opened the grille door of my cage and Hoki stomped out angrily, dragging her brown tail like a baggage trolley, and vanished into the undergrowth. Hoki had been rescued as a starving chick from Codfish and became the first-ever kakapo to be have been successfully hand-reared and later released. New Zealanders may remember her from the endearing media appearances in the early 1990s when she was the charming heroine of a children's book. She was a wild bird now, decidedly shunning human company. But Sirocco, also hand-reared, was in no hurry to leave. Out of his box, he shuffled up a horizontal branch level with my face and stretched jet-lagged limbs in a ballerina-like posture, using his wings for balance. The wings looked fully developed and it seemed as if the bird could fly away at any moment which, of course, he never would, flapping them only to get more climbing momentum or to arrest a jump from a tree.

I reached out slowly with my hand, and Sirocco tasted it with his stubby beak, perhaps checking if it might contain a morsel of his favourite kumara, then unceremoniously leapt on to my arm as if it was an extension of the tree branch, and cramponed up to perch on my shoulder. His flat owl-like face had wide brown discs around the eyes, and the beak was almost lost in the bristle of feathery whiskers. He stretched out to reach the fresh shoot of a creeping fern, then — crrrunch! Crrrunch, chomp! Chomp! — he began to munch noisily. As his sweet fruity scent wafted past my nostrils, I could see why the recovery team was inundated with applications from those wanting to work with the kakapo.

Such is the allure of being with 'one of the most wonderful, perhaps, of all living birds' as a nineteenth-century ornithologist once lusciously described it; such is the competition for a place in the team, even the unpaid volunteers here often had degrees in zoology and ecological sciences. Not that the comparative -ologies were of much use when working with the kakapo. The bird is unique, so incomparable that it has no equivalent in all the animal kingdom, and so saving it had become more like a mathematical riddle, an unprecedented and unpredictable game of numbers, an act of rebalancing the equation so that the birds would breed faster than they died out. But, as the conservationists found out, creating safe-havens and putting all the adult birds together did not necessarily add up to producing more kakapo.

The kakapo are notoriously slow breeders and their courtships and mating are about as infrequent as the Olympic games. The discovery of the track-and-bowl systems in Fiordland led Merton and his then-protégé Rod Morris to propose a theory that the kakapo displayed courtship behaviour known as lekking, similar to that of other better-known examples — birds of paradise and Australian lyre-birds.

Unable to monopolise territories, the males of lekking species gather in prominent and well-established areas and set up miniature courts one next to another. There is a lot of mock fighting, and mucho macho braggadocio. Although no other New Zealand bird shows this behaviour, you are no doubt familiar with the ritual. Every Friday night, you can see it in any major city — the downtown lek of the young bucks, driving around the blocks in souped-up cars, their subwoofers booming out a hopeful techno-beat into the night. The females watch discerningly. Mating takes place shortly afterwards and the pair part company as if they have never met.

One of the few people to ever see a male kakapo lek was Rod Morris, whose sense for being in just the right places at the most opportune times has led him from the ranks of wildlife trainees to becoming a world-class natural-history filmmaker and photographer. One night at Sinbad Gully, lighting his way with a red-filtered torch, Morris stepped into a track-and-bowl system and the kakapo began to dance for him. Morris recounted: '. . . the bird spread its wings like a butterfly, and began waving them slowly. He clicked his beak and started swaying from one foot to the other. He lowered his head, and rhythmically treading the ground on alternate feet began slowly moving towards me, coming closer and closer until he was only about two metres away. Then he began turning around, still coming towards me, only now he was walking backwards! He rocked from one foot to the other until his tail touched my boot and then he just stopped, with his back towards me, his head lowered, and his wings widespread — they were intricately patterned like the wings of a moth or the tail of a peacock.' For the rest of the night the kakapo followed Morris around, dancing again and again, but instantly losing interest in him every time he stepped outside the display area.

Finding out just what triggers the lekking — and breeding — had been at the crux of the kakapo recovery, a brain-twister with many variables. The most consistent prompter for breeding was the intense fruiting, or masting, of plants rich in turpentine: rimu on Codfish, and kauri on Little Barrier (although all kakapo have now been removed from this 3000-hectare island as it is too large and rugged for intensive population management). Supplementary feeding also seemed to play a part and so the birds are now regularly offered sunflower seeds, walnuts and almonds as well as kebabs of fresh kumara and apple skewered on aluminium tent pegs. Then there were the unexpected wild cards.

In early 1999, while in transit on Pearl Island and perhaps succumbing to an island-escape romance, five females nested and produced fourteen eggs. At the same time, Lisa — one of the last kakapo remaining on Little Barrier who had been 'lost' for thirteen years — was rediscovered incubating three eggs. All in all, six juveniles survived, including four females, and so this totally unexpected breeding resulted in the best recruitment in the history of the troubled rescue programme.

Over the years, this programme had been through some shaky times, partly because there are still so many unknowns about the birds, but mainly due to the hobbling properties of bureaucratic red tape which, until only a decade ago, supported a total non-intervention policy. In 1992, for example, breeding did occur on Codfish Island but Merton and his colleagues — then just field personnel without decision-making powers — had to watch the chicks die in the name of hands-off conservation. Only one young kakapo survived that year. It was Hoki — Maori for 'return' — but the return of the species would not really start until three years later when the obviously ineffective management system was revised and the current Kakapo Recovery Team established.

With that move, the total executive power over the budget, strategy, staff and all things kakapo was put in the hands of three people — Paul Jensen, Graeme Elliot and Don Merton — all of whom had clocked up untold backcountry mileage. Jensen, who was the programme leader, had a quietly emphatic manner and the reputation of a man who gets things done, regardless of obstacles or opposition, and Elliot was the team's thinker and tinkerer, responsible for much of the innovative technology employed in the field. Merton contributed his experience and a certain warm-hearted vehemence — after almost three decades he was still so enamoured of the kakapo, his eyes glazed over behind his square gold-rimmed spectacles every time he talked about them. Since 1995 the trio had put the kakapo on the fast track to recovery — well, fast in kakapo terms.

In the avian world, where life is but a flutter, kakapo are the perennial heavyweights, possibly the longest living of all birds. Some of them were first found in mid-1970, already mature adults and, since none has yet died of natural causes, biologists estimate their lifespan at around 60 years, perhaps more. Like the tuatara, they seem timeless, their metabolism so unhurriedly reptilian that they can digest foods containing toxins that would kill us or make us sick, like the berries of the native tutu bush, one of their favourites. Invariably, everything in kakapo life, including its recovery, happens on slow-forward. But still, they keep surprising their caretakers.

Graeme Elliot, in an effort to breathe a little more enthusiasm into the birds' courtship, began injecting selected rimu trees with the hormone gibberellin, inducing them to produce more fruit — so far the most consistent kakapo aphrodisiac known. (He would also develop a boom-box — a portable, weatherproof stereo system which, when placed in a track-and-bowl area, would automatically come on at night blaring out the boom! boom! sound to gather the males up and jump-start their own calls.) And in 1998, the kakapo bred successfully, but it happened on Maud Island . . . without the benefit of the boom-box, and without a rimu tree in sight.

The event on Maud Island was all the more significant for taking place in an extremely modified environment, showing that, despite seeming an ecological anachronism, the kakapo is, in fact, a highly adaptable creature. The 309-hectare Maud, a tip of a mountain flooded by the sea that takes less than an hour to walk around, was once extensively cleared for farming, then garrisoned with defence troops during the Second World War; then, before becoming a Royal Forest and Bird nature reserve in 1975, it was turned into a plantation of exotic pines. And it was the radiata pine that titillated the kakapo into courtship.

By December all four males were booming and soon mating signs — tufts of feathers in the track-and-bowl area — were found. Then, on the island's west-facing slope, where the setting sun dapples through the trees and brown pine needles muffle the footsteps, Merton discovered a nest with three eggs. It was a scratched-up burrow under a stump on a slope so steep that the subsequent track cut to it would be a winding staircase of 140 steps. The breeding was such a momentous turning point that Merton and his colleagues would take no chances with the safety of their charges — the three chicks that hatched were offspring of Richard Henry — the last and the only surviving Fiordland kakapo. 'We've waited twenty years for this nest,' Merton said at the time. 'It must succeed.' And so the intervention began. Every time the mother, named Flossie, left the nest to forage at night, a stealthy construction crew moved in.

First, they cleared the branches around the site and the rocks within it, expanding the cavity of the nest and erecting a plywood roof over it. Then they dug a drain on the upslope to divert any possible floods, and built a safety barrier below the nest to prevent eggs and later the chicks from accidentally rolling down the hill. A piece of plastic pipe became an entrance tunnel, then a black PVC water tank was placed over the nest like a cloche, complete with a viewing porthole and a sponsor's sticker. There was an infra-red sensor, wired to a door chime, across the entrance to monitor the mother's nightly perambulations and video surveillance to keep an electronic eye on the chicks. Then a safe playground area was added, a kind of balcony carved into the slope and reinforced with aluminium profiles. It was as if you lived in a dilapidated shanty, left for a short walk and returned to find a prefab house with a sundeck, and a sandpit for the kids; and as if none of it surprised you at all, for Flossie and the youngsters took the alterations in their goosestep stride. All the while, a roster of bodyguards camped in a tent 80 metres away, ready to dash in in an emergency. This would become a standard procedure with all subsequent kakapo nests.

With such intensive management, twelve juveniles were raised in three seasons, bringing the population tally up to 62 birds, but that was still critically low. Then things went quiet on the kakapo front. Two years had passed since I walked the Codfish forest with Rod Morris to release Hoki and Sirocco. Merton travelled to the Seychelles on another rescue mission: to check up on the echo parakeets and to clear a plague of rats from a sanctuary island, and Elliott was back in his shed, tinkering with hardware. He refined the 'Flossie's burrow' prototype into a portable 'Nest Kit' which, apart from the now-standard non-stop infra-red surveillance, also contained a red panic button in the nest-minders' tent which could set off an explosive charge of smoke and noise to frighten off any potential predator, and — a homely touch — a miniature 'electric blanket' with a thermostat and a fleece pillowcase to cover the eggs, and later the chicks during their mother's long absences. He also devised his pièce de résistance, called Snark, a kind of kakapo radar which individually logged every bird passing within a 10-metre radius. Placed in an active courtship area this mini-computer not only kept track of visiting females, alerting the staff to possible mating, but when positioned next to a supplementary feeding station, also recorded which bird was feeding and how much; and the feeding platform from which a kakapo could reach its favourite morsels operated as an electronic weighing station as well.

Not that all the kakapo gear was so high-tech: Merton's infallible rat poison was a concoction of white chocolate, cereal and brodifacoum, moulded in his wife's muffin tin, and coated with candle wax for waterproofing; and his favourite tool for extracting the kakapo chicks from their burrows was a spaghetti strainer tied to the end of a telescopic ski pole. This balance of the new and the old, a blend of the microchip and the Swannie-and-gumboots approach had been proven to work well, and all the while it was being finely tuned for when the big news broke out. And the news came out of Codfish in August 2001.

A bumper crop of rimu was developing there and the recovery team gathered all the 21 surviving females on the island in anticipation of the best breeding season ever. Supplementary feeders were stocked up and Elliott's boom-boxes would be crooning their love songs. Over 60 extra people had been trained for two-week stints as nest-minders through the critical months between February and May. 'This is our moment of truth,' Merton told me. 'For the first time ever, we have all the odds on our side. We know what to do, and we have the means to do it.' And so, 2002 was to be the year of the kakapo, with Codfish Island becoming one booming maternity ward for the birds. But whatever the outcome of the season, Jensen, Merton and Elliot were already a step ahead.

'Around the world the conservationists keep propping species up, often at a great expense,' Merton explained, 'and there are few better examples of that than the kakapo programme. What we must realise is that this cannot go on forever.' Lots of people had given the kakapo recovery the best years of their lives, he said, but if the continuous rescue efforts were to stop for whatever reason — financial or political — and if the intensive-care unit was unplugged even momentarily, those decades of work, and the bird itself, could simply go to waste. That was why the three-man kakapo junta insisted on finding a lasting solution to their challenge. As Elliott said: 'We are working hard to put ourselves out of work.' And they'd come up with a plan as visionary as it was controversial.

In November, Merton was again flying down to Codfish, to be close to the birds, to double-check everything, and I met him in transit, in the business lounge of the Invercargill airport. The day was sunny and still, perfect for a beach landing on the island, but inside the lounge the monotonous thrumming of many fingers against laptop keys added up to the sound of rain. Against this patter Merton cautiously unveiled the plan.

Kakapo are gone from their natural habitat — in our lifetime they lost their last strongholds in Fiordland and Stewart Island — and there is no way of returning them there, he said. The breeding programme, with Snarks, boom-boxes and all the life-support, was going well and it was fair to expect that the number of kakapo would steadily, if slowly increase, and so Codfish could soon reach its holding capacity. The next challenge, Merton said, was to create a self-sustaining and independent population, one that required little or no management at all. The recovery team looked long and hard and identified an ultimate safe-haven where the kakapo could once again roam free, without human help and interference. This place was Campbell Island, halfway between New Zealand and the Antarctic.

Placing the birds so far outside their natural habitat may seem a form of banishment, Merton told me, but it was in fact like depositing our feathery treasures into a safe offshore bank where no calamity and no cost-cutting or staff downsizing could affect them. It was originally planned to transfer six male kakapo from Pearl Island to Campbell and this was to be a five-to-ten-year experiment to see if they could adapt to living on the island. Campbell is remote and predator-free, it is abundant in megaherbs which would provide a smorgasbord feast for the kakapo; it also harbours a species of snowgrass, *Chionochloa antarctica*, whose fruiting — like rimu, kauri and pine — just might induce the birds to breed. Kakapo, in turn, are cold-weather birds, Merton said. Under their skin, they have a layer of blubber up to one and a half centimetres thick. They love the rain and are totally waterproof. The island and the birds could thus be a perfect match.

Merton talked about the logistics, about the gruelling helicopter crash training the entire team had just completed, about the fixed-wing aeroplane, equipped with emergency life rafts, that would accompany them on the long flight to Campbell. He talked about the Chatham Islands black robin, once the rarest bird in the world, now thriving in a self-sustainable population, without any management at all, and how we absolutely had to do the same for the kakapo — to create a place and a situation where they wouldn't need us any more.

I listened wordlessly and soaked up his radiant enthusiasm, for there was not a shadow of doubt that his lifetime task of seeing the kakapo through its crisis was nearing completion. Later, I walked down with him to his lift, watching this 62-year-old man nicknamed Birdbrain, with a shy smile and a big backpack, going to where he was happiest. Then I drove home and thought of Douglas Adams, the literary galactic hitchhiker, who in 1985 went on a whirlwind tour to see the world's iconic species precariously balanced on the brink of extinction. He wrote a book about his experiences, about the mountain gorillas in Zaire and the Yangtze River's freshwater dolphins — and this book, titled *Last Chance to See*, also contained a chapter on the kakapo.

Adams rushed to New Zealand to see the kakapo before it disappeared, but as it turned out he needn't have hurried. Here, thanks to Merton and his tireless colleagues, the re-run of the dodo story would get a happy ending. 'If you look (a kakapo) in its large, round, greeny-brown face,' Adams wrote, 'it has a look of serenely innocent incomprehension that makes you want to hug it and tell it that everything will be all right.' Now, for the first time ever, we can say that with a degree of honesty.

POSTSCRIPT:

On 10 April 2011, Don Merton passed away, having lost his battle with cancer. He was 72. In his eulogy for this dear friend, Rod Morris wrote: 'Mertie made conservation an adventure for us, and we felt invincible. He loved birds — he wasn't working for the Department of Conservation, he was working for the wildlife. Without him, the kakapo and black robin would probably now be extinct. Rest peacefully, Don, you looked just like every other New Zealander, but you seemed like Superman to us.'

As Don Merton's body was laid to rest, the number of kakapo stood at 131.

The Last Cruise of the *Mikhail Lermontov*

'How do you think he likes his vodka? Straight or on the rocks?'

In Port Gore, three hours' steaming out of Picton on a dive boat named *Sandpiper*, a black buoy rides the Cook Strait swell tugging rhythmically at something deep below the surface. The rope that tethers this bulbous plastic drum is arm-thick from fourteen years of bloating in the water, and feels slimy even through a neoprene glove. But when you descend its length, free-falling into the gloom with half an hour of air strapped to your back, you want to hold on to it, and never mind that it yanks you up and down like a yo-yo. In the soup of silt and ocean nutrients which induce weightless myopia, this rope is your only reference, a handrail to a sunken mystery.

The bottom looms out at fifteen metres, flat and barren, and only as you touch down, kicking up clouds of sediment, does it become apparent that it is not the bottom at all. The surface is unnaturally smooth, and its contours have the regularity of a building. A row of rectangular windows — now hatchways oozing cryptic darkness —

runs off in both directions from where the rope is shackled down. Here you have to let go the handrail, but don't swim off just yet, and whatever you do, don't swim inside! Somewhere in there, perhaps floating limply against a ceiling or a wall, are the bodies of two people who never found their way out. Pause for a moment and try to imagine the size of this thing. Imagine, because you'll never see it all. Not in this murk, not on the clearest of days.

The silt-smothered hulk was once a gleaming ocean liner, a floating island of bargain luxury 155 metres long and 24 metres wide, about the size of a 50-storey skyscraper. It was also a cross-cultural curiosity, a place where the Iron Curtain was temporarily lifted, allowing glimpses of Russian culture against the unlikely backdrop of the South Pacific. On board, you could dine on red caviar and cold-smoked sturgeon to the accompaniment of heart-rending folk songs played on the balalaika, or watch the fiery Moldavian dancers and learn to drink Stolichnaya vodka the Russian way: Do dna! To the bottom! All medical care was gratis and there was, on average, one crew member for every two passengers. Even tipping was discouraged: 'Our smiles are free' the ship's brochure declared. The same brochure also spoke of the 'unlikely event of emergency', though perhaps no one paid much attention. The freshly painted whiteness of the ship implied invincibility; her size created an illusion of safety.

Just why she got where she is now — lying flat on her starboard side, 25 million dollars of past glory turned into a 20,000-ton garbage can stuck in the sandy bottom — is still one of the most perplexing maritime riddles, even more so because the entire incident was promptly sealed off in a cloak of bureaucratic silence, as if it were an embarrassment to be expunged and forgotten, never explained or fully investigated.

But in the South Island's Marlborough Sounds the memory of that February night still lingers, and the ship has become something of a landmark. Divers come from afar to experience the sunken behemoth, and after their adventures may sip cappuccinos at a picnic table in Lifeboat No 10, outside the Mariners' World café. Maybe they joke about the New Zealand harbour pilot who ran her aground. 'How do you think he likes his vodka?' one may quip. 'Straight or on the rocks?'

All things considered, the loss of the ship was a 'lucky' disaster. Only one crew member lost his life, and there were 738 people on board, mostly retired and elderly passengers. Among the many questions and unknowns, one thing remains certain: for an obscure reason the captain never sent out an official Mayday distress call and so no formal rescue operation was mounted. Had it not been for the vigilance and courage of local fishermen and farmers who took the matters into their own hands, or had she gone down earlier or in more exposed water, the sinking of the *Mikhail Lermontov* would have been a tragedy of Titanic proportions.

One of five sister ships built in the Baltic port of Wismar, then in East Germany, she was named after a freedom-loving Russian poet and novelist of the Pushkin era. All her siblings bore equally bardic names because the Russians had a penchant for christening ships after their literary luminaries, particularly those extolling the romantic exotica of the far-off steppes or the pastoral folklore of Rodina, Mother Russia. Consequently, there were the *Aleksander Pushkin* (now *Marco Polo*), *Ivan Franko*, *Taras Shevchenko* and *Shota Rustaveli*, but you wouldn't find a boat named after a bleeding-heart hothead like Mayakovski or an exposé realist like Solzhenitsyn of Gulag Archipelago fame. The ships, furnished with all the splendour and chic that their builders could muster, were the Soviet Union's answer to the Cunard or Norwegian Line's ultra-deluxe, promising a moveable extravaganza of comfort, and escape from everything including mal de mer.

Amid those ocean Edens of credit-card delight, the Russians — always hard-up for hard currency — offered a bon marché deal: affordable holidays for all, a Champagne paradise at rock-bottom prices. The *Lermontov*'s South Pacific cruises were popular, particularly with Australian vacationers; on 16 February 1986, there were over 300 of them on board, their average age around 70.

At 8 a.m. that Sunday, they berthed in Picton after an overnight crossing from Wellington and a dawn entry through the peculiarly narrow Tory Channel where the harbour master and pilot, Don Jamison, impressed the Russian bridge crew with his deft manoeuvring. In port, the ship dwarfed all other boats and ferries. It dwarfed the port itself.

Surrounded by steep and forested hills, Picton is a sheltered haven for mariners, nestled near the end of Queen Charlotte Sound. A tiny town of motels and charter boats, it makes its living from the sea and the passing traffic. Here, the passengers could visit a petite museum displaying relics from the Perano whaling station which they passed earlier that day: jaws of an orca, a Norwegian whaling gun which hurled 85-kilogram harpoons, an enormous black try pot that brings to mind feasting cannibals. Just after 3 p.m., the *Lermontov* left the port on an outgoing tide. She was destined for Milford Sound.

Things seemed to go wrong from the start. While coming out of Shakespeare Bay, Jamison became aware that the ship wasn't turning quickly enough. He ordered full power to the starboard bow thruster to tighten the turn, but nothing happened. With both main engines roaring in full reverse, the ship pulled up at a right angle to the shore, 30 metres short of running aground.

Jamison continued up the Sound, hugging the coast, accelerating up to full manoeuvring speed of fifteen knots. Twice the ship's captain, Vladislav Vorobyov, told him to move further out from shore. Even the yachties among the passengers commented that the pilot was taking her a little too close to the land. But Jamison, an experienced mariner with extensive local knowledge, appeared not to heed the captain's request. He had already demonstrated his piloting skills on the inbound journey, hadn't he? And besides, his job was to show the passengers of this floating belvedere the best of his home scenery, and by keeping a distance of about one boat length from the shore he was giving them a dramatic close-up view.

At about 4.30 p.m., with a safe course plotted, Captain Vorobyov retired to his cabin to catch up on some sleep, and Jamison stayed on the bridge with Chief Navigator Serey Stepanishchev, Second Mate Sergey Gusev and Helmsman Anatoliy Burin. Over the PA system, dinner was announced, and the *Lermontov* was heading out to round Cape Jackson.

The cape, outlining the northern entrance to Queen Charlotte Sound, is an exposed headland running out into a pinnacled underwater reef which terminates at Walker Rock. Some 550 metres out from the cape is Jackson Head — a knife-shaped sliver of rock topped with a disused lighthouse beacon. The winds bend around the headland and the tides surge through the passage. The water on both sides of the reef is some 100 metres deep, and the tidal currents well up and pour over this underwater barricade, often creating a standing white-water rapid.

In the shallows of the cape, under the swaying canopy of leathery kelp trees, lie the remains of the *Rangitoto*, a passenger steamer that foundered here in 1873. Nine years later, the sailing ship *Lastingham* was also wrecked here, with the loss of eighteen lives. Earlier editions of *The New Zealand Pilot*, the mariners' bible, used to carry a warning: 'The tidal streams around Cape Jackson are rapid and there is but little slack water. Several vessels have met with accidents, principally due to the rapidity and the irregular direction of the tidal streams, when using the passage between Cape Jackson and Jackson Head. Vessels should not use this passage.'

But from newer editions this warning has been deleted, perhaps because it's so blindingly obvious. Why try to squeeze between a rock and a hard place when there is enough room in the northern entrance for a ship of the *Lermontov*'s size — a ship of any size — to spin pirouettes or figures-of-eight, bow thrusters or not. The course plotted by Sergey Gusev gave Cape Jackson a wide berth, but Jamison kept favouring the coast, broadcasting a sightseeing commentary on the PA system. Just out of Ship Cove, the place of James Cook's 1770 landing, he bid his audience good-bye and hung up the microphone.

Then, inexplicably, he ordered 'port 10 degrees' and began taking the ship through the gap between the cape and Jackson Head. The Russian bridge crew immediately expressed their concern but Jamison was confident and calm. 'There is no reason to worry,' he replied. 'There is enough water in that place.'

It was about an hour and a half to low tide. Had the visibility been better, the bridge crew might have seen that the gap and distant Stephens Island lined up like a gunsight. Taking the ship along this line, Jamison might as well have been steering into the path of an incoming torpedo.

As with a torpedo, there was a delay. About six minutes. During this time, some of the passengers on deck, sipping whisky and watching the coastline slip by, noticed white water foaming around the ship. 'Any sailor will tell you that white water means danger,' one of them commented later. 'If he doesn't hit those rocks, I'll eat my hat,' said another.

His hat was safe. At 5.37 p.m. the ship suddenly shuddered, groaned and shuddered again, as she slit her iron belly on an underwater pinnacle. Moments later Captain Vorobyov burst through the door onto the bridge.

The thud of the collision was heard some eight kilometres away in the Bakers' family homestead in Anakakata Bay. Tony and Betty Baker had lived here since 1965, farming the finger of steep land jutting into Cook Strait. They had watched the *Lermontov* sail by fifteen minutes earlier.

Tony knew Jamison well and over the VHF radio he marvelled how beautiful the ship looked. She was the biggest vessel ever to pass by their remote outpost. All other liners shunned this side of the sound. He wished the pilot a safe voyage and cleared out. Now came this distant thud.

'He musta hit something,' Tony's son David quipped impishly. It was such an improbable thought!

But soon they knew it was no joke. As they sat down to dinner around 6 p.m., there came a radio message: 'This is a Mayday situation. The *Mikhail Lermontov*. We have struck a rock at Cape Jackson, and we are proceeding into Port Gore . . . We will require emergency assistance. The vessel in danger of sinking. The vessel in danger of sinking. Making water. Proceeding into Port Gore. Over.'

The distress message met with an instant response. The gas tanker *Tarihiko* captained by John Reedman was some seventeen nautical miles away, and it turned for Cape Jackson at full power. Reedman estimated he needed about one and a half hours to get to the troubled ship. Captain John Brew, navigating the interisland ferry *Arahura* also heeded the call. Meanwhile David Baker, his son Jason and cousin Dennis Cox were racing their trail bikes to the top of the hill.

On reaching the bridge, Captain Vorobyov found Jamison white-faced and shaking. The ship had already developed a list, and reports began pouring in from below that water was entering the bulkhead compartments. The captain ordered a general alarm and the closure of all watertight doors. He informed the passengers that the ship was experiencing a 'slight water intrusion'.

In fact, the intrusion was more like a harakiri wound: three gashes totalling almost 25 metres in length. As the ship was still moving forward at speed, the initial surge of flooding was estimated at 63 tons per second — fast enough to fill an average community swimming pool while you read this one sentence.

The pumps, working at full capacity, could each displace about 160 tons of water an hour. Staff Captain Georgy Melnik made a quick calculation: they could take in up to 4000 tons of water and still remain afloat. But when all the damaged compartments were flooded, the ship would be holding almost twice that amount.

Vorobyov realized that his ship was doomed. He ordered the evacuation procedure to get underway and began looking for a sandy place to beach her. She could be then repaired and re-floated. Perhaps it wasn't far to go, or maybe he thought that the crisis was under control. Whatever the reason, at 6.19 p.m. he cancelled the Mayday situation.

That wasn't the way it looked to Dennis Cox who watched the scene from the hilltop lookout: 'We could clearly see the ship with bow down, a starboard list, and the stern quite a way out showing five or ten feet of antifoul. It didn't look good, yet while we waited we could hear (via a handheld radio) the pilot telling Wellington Radio that they did not require assistance.' David Baker added: 'We watched her until about 7.15, stuttering into Port Gore. She had a lot of water aboard and looked in a bad way. She was obviously in trouble but what were we to do? We've never dealt with anything so enormous.'

With the Mayday deactivated, the *Arahura* resumed her course for Picton. Half an hour later, seawater entered the *Lermontov*'s engine room. It sprayed the main switchboard, short-circuiting all pumps and stopping both engines. Silently now, the ship continued its momentum towards the beach.

'Our next instructions were to get life jackets on and to lie on the floor, or hold on, because the captain was trying to run the ship aground,' an Australian croupier recounted. And so they did, hanging on to tables and posts, waiting for the crash that never came. Some passengers felt sure that she touched lightly, and Jamison stated that they stopped about 'a ship's length from the shore'. But, in a decision that still puzzles mariners, the captain did not drop the anchors. He later told the inquiry that he expected the rising tide to take the ship even closer in. It didn't.

As the darkness fell and an offshore wind picked up, the mortally wounded and powerless *Lermontov* began to drift back out to sea.

• • •

Like many backcountry settlers, the Bakers lived an isolated life. Their only contact with the outside world was a twenty-kilometre-long private phone line running over the rugged country to the exchange in Endeavour Inlet. It was notoriously unreliable and required constant maintenance and so, in time, they came to depend more and more on the double sideband radio named Tiki extracted from their boat. Over this radio they would order their groceries, relay medical emergencies, talk to their friends and far-off neighbours. In the maritime community of the Marlborough Sounds they became known as Radio Tiki.

Before long it became the hub of all the radio traffic in the area. Strategically placed in the far outskirts of the Sounds, the Bakers had more reliable news of the Cook Strait weather than the Met Service, whose forecasts they'd still religiously relay. On their busiest day, Betty logged 110 calls and David's wife Sandra used to take a handheld radio when she'd go out to hang the washing. They got to know every boat and her skipper in the area; even the pigeon breeders homed in on their knowledge of the local wind conditions. In 1984, the Waikawa Cruising Club presented them with a VHF set; it was still Radio Tiki to friends, but formally it became Radio Cape Jackson.

Not surprisingly then, on the night when the *Lermontov* was sinking, the Bakers found themselves at the epicentre of the crisis. There was chaos on the air: a Mayday call was sent out, then cancelled. Two tugs were requested by Vorobyov, deployed from Wellington, then recalled as it would have taken them about four hours to get across the strait. The *Arahura* was also recalled. Officially the trouble was over, yet all this time the biggest ship they'd ever seen was sinking in their backyard and no one seemed to be doing anything about it. 'It was lack of communication,' Betty Baker said later. 'I think the captain just didn't want to admit that his boat was gonna go down.'

They thought there was really only one thing to do. Tony and Betty operated the VHF set and the telephone, while David and Dennis Cox readied their six-metre dingy. From about 7 p.m. onwards, Radio Tiki began pulsing out a call for help. Soon a flotilla of small fishing boats was converging on Port Gore.

One man who also didn't believe what he heard was John Reedman, master of the tanker *Tarihiko*. At 6.48 p.m. he too received the 'no assistance required' message but thought it prudent to continue on his course. An hour later, after rounding Cape Lambert, he saw the *Lermontov* with some of her lifeboats in the water.

He radioed an offer of assistance but there came a surprising reply: No, Vorobyov did not wish to use his lifeboats but would the *Tarihiko* come and give them a push ashore? Reedman was dubious. His ship was fully loaded with LPG; he didn't want to add fireworks to the drama.

Instead, he kept safe distance, anchoring within half a nautical mile, readying his own lifeboats. The sea was choppy, with heavy driving rain and a strong southerly. In darkness, he soon lost sight of the *Lermontov* and had to monitor her position on the radar screen.

From 9 p.m. the Russian lifeboats began drawing alongside, offloading passengers. By now, there were some 30 small craft in the bay, and soon the now Wellington-bound *Arahura* also arrived, lowering her lifeboats and using them as lifts to bring the passengers on board, lighting the scene with her powerful searchlights.

The lights revealed an apocalyptic imbroglio building up towards the inevitable finale. The water in the *Lermontov*'s torn bulkheads was reaching critical mass; her list increased to about 40 degrees. There were people hanging from rope ladders, life rafts being swamped, boats spinning out of each other's way to avoid collisions, and the sea was littered with life jackets, floating deck chairs, ropes and other debris. Somewhere among it all, circling the sinking giant, were Baker and Cox in their twenty-foot dinghy.

'We towed some life rafts, but that was easier and more safely done with the bigger boats so we opted for patrolling the starboard side of the *Lermontov*,' David Baker remembered. 'She had such a heavy list that you'd expect people to be falling over that side. Both propellers were above water and we could see that the ship was dying. There was a life raft trapped beneath the stern, water pouring on its roof, and the ship towering above it, about to topple. We were trying to get brave enough to go in and have a look if there was anyone in it, but as we approached, a container broke free from the deck above and hurtled past, breaking glass, bashing through the railings, making a hell of a noise. Then the ship started to sink so fast that we raced off, afraid that she was gonna suck us in. The raft stayed afloat and later we saw that there was no one inside.'

The bridge went under water, and then the funnel, giving out bursts of steam, and the air from inside the ship went up in explosions, lifting up fountains of water ten metres high. Then it all went quiet. At 10.45 p.m. the *Lermontov* disappeared from the radar screen.

Until 2.30 a.m., the search for survivors continued because none of the rescuers knew for sure how many people were on board. They sifted through the floating debris, fishing out every horse-collar life jacket they could find. At least 100 people were feared dead and there was an atmosphere like a lost battle. Not until 11 a.m., after an aerial search and a precise headcount, was it established that only one crewman, a refrigeration engineer named Pavel Zaglyadimov, was missing and presumed dead.

Over the following days and months there was to be much questioning and speculation about what exactly happened that night. But in Port Gore there was a problem of a much more immediate nature: on the surface of the sea, above where the *Lermontov* had sunk, a small oil slick began to appear.

• • •

Malcolm Blair was anchored on *Little Mermaid* in Carnley Harbour, between Adams and Auckland Islands, stuck in foul weather in the company of five other divers when the *Lermontov* went down. On the New Zealand treasure-hunting scene there was Kelly Tarlton and there was Malcolm Blair, and between them they knew almost all there was to know about shipwrecks. Except a few small but vital details, like where exactly lie the remains of the *General Grant* which on 14 May 1866 was becalmed and washed into a large cave in the Auckland Islands' cliff-faced shore, the rising tide apparently forcing her masts against the cave's roof and through the ship's bottom, so that she sank there with a loss of 68 lives and 2576 ounces of gold.

Blair had a focused, problem-solver's face rimmed by a grey no-moustache beard. He wore his wet suit as if it was a second skin, and had evolution been a little faster, he probably wouldn't need to use an aqualung any more. He had been in the diving industry for 22 years, established a highly successful Divers' World retail and training network and participated in the laying of the Cook Strait communication cable. For him and his diving buddies, the sinking of the *Lermontov* couldn't have come at a better time. Searching for the *General Grant* gold was costing them $5000 a day, and after eight weeks and no substantial finds they were all — as treasure hunters often are — flat broke. It was then that they received a radio message requesting their company, the Divers' World Salvage, to retrieve the valuables and to recover the 1500 tonnes of fuel and oil that were still in the *Lermontov*'s tanks.

They started work on 11 March. It was a fat contract, though by no means easy money because commercial diving is no underwater picnic but dirty, cold and inherently dangerous work, with the constant risk of decompression sickness and a multitude of other less conspicuous hazards. They would be spending up to one hour at a depth of 40 metres — the limit of recreational diving — then recompressing in a diving bell or a chamber. They'd be using power tools underwater, including Oxy Arc, go-though-anything gas cutting equipment, highly explosive if accidentally poked into an unseen airspace containing oil. On a previous job eighteen months earlier, their supervisor, Joe Engwirda, had his hearing permanently damaged and both eyes blown out of their sockets by an underwater explosion. Apparently he put the eyes back in himself, igniting an instant cackle of matey jokes: 'You just keep an eye out for us, won't you Joe!'

Blair told me how, on their first big contract (the salvaging of the *Pacific Charger*, a 10,000-tonne freighter that in 1981 sank near Baring Head at the entrance to Wellington Harbour), they had had to use a high-pressure hose to break the surface oil slick so that the divers could get in the water.

The *Lermontov* would prove an even bigger challenge; the oil spill wasn't yet as severe but the enormity of the wreck was overwhelming: The engine room alone was six storeys high. Luckily, the sister ship *Alexander Pushkin* happened to be visiting New Zealand at the time, and so the divers could study her layout and draw up a plan of attack. Still, the job would stretch their abilities and redefine ideas of fear. Blair said: 'One night at the dinner table I asked, "Hands up all those who weren't scared today?" and no hands went up.'

What did they fear? He explained: 'The *Lermontov* was relatively cheaply built, all plastic and aluminium and no brass, and because she's lying on her side there's already a lot of structural deterioration.' Walls and partitions were collapsing. There were also numerous sliding doors, some of them poised open above the passageways which the divers had to penetrate. Touch a door and it could slide down shut like the blade of a guillotine.

Once inside the wreck, the visibility was often so bad they had to work by feel, groping their way through the maze of passages and stairways. Even if they could see, they'd choose to work with their eyes closed; it was good training for the days when you couldn't read the face of your watch.

The divers, wearing full-face masks not unlike the old brass bubble helmets, were always connected to the *Little Mermaid* by their umbilicals — industrial strength lifelines threads and lifelines providing air, hot water to fill the wet suits and communication to guide them. From the *Mermaid*'s control room, where the dive co-ordinator sat in front of a large-scale plan of the wreck, came directions and encouragement:

'Diver One! Go along that wall. Turn left. Go down the staircase. Left again. There should be a door.'

'I'm scared.'

'I know, but you have another twenty minutes. Can you see the door?'

And later:

'Diver One has oil all over his mask. Cannot see. Repeat: cannot see. Has to be escorted out. Diver Two, do you copy?'

• • •

They remained anchored over the *Lermontov* for three months, recovering a safe holding the casino and the duty-free takings, plenty of personal bric-à-brac, repeatedly drilling through the hull and tapping all of the fuel tanks. Then a tanker, *Pacific Explorer*, arrived from Fiji and, like a giant mosquito, it siphoned off all of the *Lermontov*'s bad blood. The residents of the Marlborough Sounds could sleep again and the ship was left to her own fate.

And so she still lies there today, broken like Mother Russia herself was after the perestroika, her infrastructure collapsing, her once-proud hammer and sickle prised off by a Picton souvenir hunter. The crescent-shaped leather couches in the nightclub are still soft and six-packs of fizzed-out Coke and Sprite float dreamily above the bar, but otherwise she is an empty carapace gathering silt, a hideaway for fish and octopus, a destination for divers.

• • •

Our boat, the *Sandpiper*, is a piece of floating Kiwiana, built like many of the vessels that took part in the rescue, slow but solid, with a big cool box in the fore and a dive platform in the aft. Her skipper, Frank Carré, wears a T-shirt proclaiming that 'Beauty is in the eye of the beer holder' and promptly shows me a photo album documenting his and the *Sandpiper*'s adventures. There are pictures of monster crays wearing sunglasses, a pile of dead wild pigs, each with a carry rope around its snout, proud snapshots of men in Swannies and rolled-up balaclavas holding short rods and large fish, gaffed sharks bleeding on the deck. Putting the album away, I notice a well-used cassette with Solid Gold Hits Volume 14. Above hangs a mounted pincer of a giant cray.

A Wellington dive club has chartered the *Sandpiper* for a scuba cruise of the Sounds and so her sides are lined with a palisade of air tanks. There are about a dozen divers — scuba instructors, builders, software consultants, teachers, Malcolm Blair is there too — a hardy bunch wriggling into their cold wet suits, filling them with hot water against the bone-chilling southerly and the 13°C sea. It's a long weekend, a chance to get away from the city, to bring home some crayfish and scallops. The *Lermontov* is to be the highlight of the trip.

I team up with Ross Marett, a Wellington builder, who offers to show me around the wreck. From the buoy we drop down along the anchor line and follow the row of windows towards the propellers. After the heavy spring rains the visibility is so bad that at times all I can see are Ross's fluoro-green flippers wagging in front. It's dark down here at 30 metres below and fuzzy shapes appear out of the murk just before you can touch them. The wreck feels like a graveyard swathed in thick fog.

Our second dive takes us to the fore and the bridge, from where Jamison issued his momentous 'port 10' command, and where another team of divers have now rigged up a penetration line. Because the ship lies flat on her starboard, visiting the bridge resembles swimming up a chimney, that is if you can convince yourself to enter its narrow 'fireplace' end.

For a long while I float outside this rectangular black hole, wrestling with fear. Once inside, there is no visibility at all and so it makes no difference whether you keep your eyes open or shut. There is only the gurgle of exhaled bubbles, faster now than ever before, and the rope leading up into the gloom.

At 30 metres underwater, claustrophobia and blindness are a heady cocktail. You are at a constant threshold of panic, where fear dries your throat to a rasp and the slightest snag seems a death trap. Groping for obstacles, moving upwards in a tight spiral, you pull yourself along, tugging at the rope as if to sound an invisible bell.

For whom would this bell toll? Perhaps for Pavel Zaglyadimov, who perished here during the sinking, though some good-hearted gossip has it that he may have jumped ship and be living in a quiet bach someplace. Maybe for Erica Lowe, a Wellington diver who in May 1987 became disoriented and drowned, and whose body was recovered more than a year later. And the 40-year-old Barry Evans who swam away from his guideline and was later found floating unconscious in the restaurant area, and who was brought up on to the deck of the diving boat where no amount of first aid would resuscitate him. Lastly, though probably not finally, for a Blenheim boy named Martin Greig, a nineteen-year-old petrol station attendant, who one July day in 1989 was looking for artefacts at the bottom of the nightclub with his buddy, Deane Armstrong. The silt rose around them, thick like a sandstorm, and when they could no longer see, they signalled each other to surface and swam up. They had no guideline and on the way up they separated. Only Armstrong returned to the boat.

'Greig must have ascended at a slight angle and instead of the roof he hit the entranceway and followed it looking for a window,' Kevin Bailey, owner of a Blenheim dive shop would later tell me. 'Thinking that he was getting out he was in fact swimming further into the wreck. Deep inside the water is still and often clear. At that depth he wouldn't have much air left by then. Maybe he saw sunlight coming through one of the windows and bolted for it like a bat out of hell.'

But most windows still have glass in them, thick, solid glass, unbreakable for a diver with nothing but a knife. The last few moments were probably a fit of exponential panic. The following day Bailey dived the nightclub and the entranceway which leads to a huge spiral staircase. Police divers continued the search inside the wreck for two more days, and reported carpets floating off the floor and curtains poised like fishing nets — one of them had to cut himself free from such entanglement. Greig's body was never found.

Out through another window, the rope leads me back into the open where Ross Marett waits hovering like a ghost. We fin back to the anchor line and up to where, at five metres below the *Sandpiper*'s bow, a safety stop-tank rigged with regulators is bobbing up and down like a caricature squid. The closer to daylight, the friendlier the sea becomes. Only later do we learn about the drama that took place behind us.

Kirsten McGhie, a parliamentary clerk in her twenties, stands on the deck on still trembling legs while her friends help her to de-kit from a tangle of diving gear. On the way to the bridge she got stuck in a narrow swim-through, snagged by her regulator hose. There was a sudden surge of panic but she managed to fight it off. Her buddy, Anna Barker, was right there, holding her hands, calming her down. Still, Kirsten has bitten off the rubber mouthpiece of her regulator. Now her voice breaks and a sobbing laughter shakes her body, venting out suppressed tension. On her face the shape of the diving mask is still imprinted, and big tears roll down her cheeks. Or maybe it's just sea water.

As the day ends we steam towards the shelter of the Sounds, and like many divers before us, we try to solve the riddle of the *Lermontov*. What possessed Don Jamison to take the ship through the gap at Cape Jackson? 'He was really tempting fate out there,' I recalled David Baker saying. 'You know, you could take a ship through the passage, there is enough water there, but the fit between the pinnacles is impossibly tight. It was like playing Russian roulette with three bullets!' But why didn't anyone stop him, countermand his order? Did the whole bridge crew, like a pod of pilot whales, experience a collective lapse of navigational reason?

Those who know Jamison say that he was just too good a navigator to commit such a blunder, and this, combined with the tail end of the xenophobic Cold War paranoia of the mid-1980s, and the governmental hush-up that followed the sinking, only fuelled airheaded speculation. Was the sinking an insurance put-up job, or was the *Lermontov* really a gigantic spy station disguised as a cruise liner? Did the pilot, in the end, do us all a favour by cleanly chopping off a tentacle of Soviet communism creeping into the South Pacific? If so, he did a thorough job of it. As it was quipped at the time, New Zealand was the only country in the world to have sunk a Russian ship of that size since the end of the Second World War.

Only Jamison knows and he's not telling. Since his written statement during the inquiry he has gone silent, refusing to comment or explain. But can you blame him? Over the past two centuries some 2200 ships and boats have foundered in New Zealand coastal waters, splintered on rocks and reefs, pounded by heavy seas after grounding on shifting sandbars — a hefty price for settling and living on oceanic islands. Of all these, the *Lermontov* was the largest, the luckiest and the most avoidable, and consequently Jamison has become a kind of anti-hero, a subject of barroom mockery. In the maritime nation that wins the America's Cup and the Whitbread race, where kids learn to sail before they can drive, where how you back the boat trailer down a launching ramp still speaks more of your manhood than any amount of sea-dog braggadocio, it must be hard to be Don Jamison.

With strange irony, a sort of prophetic double entendre, the best-known work of Lermontov the writer is called *A Hero of Our Time*, its last chapter titled 'The Fatalist'. It's a tale of duels, intrigue and kidnapping set against the lofty panorama of the Caucasus, a cloak-and-dagger romance without daggers, but with plenty of gunfire. Lermontov never quite made it to the top of the Russian literary echelon. His prose remained crude and stuttering; his translator Vladimir Nabokov, the author of *Lolita*, called it dry, drab and inelegant. But he had potential, he had the élan, the gift. After Pushkin was shot dead in a duel, Lermontov was heralded to become his literary successor. He never did.

One July day in 1841, in the spa resort of Pyatigorsk, and as if re-enacting a scene out of his novel, he became engaged in a trivial argument with a fellow officer. The following day, in an act of totally avoidable and nonsensical waste, Lermontov was shot dead in a duel, from a distance of six paces. He was 26 years old.

Inside Queen Charlotte Sound the water is smooth and, as the darkness falls, lights begin to twinkle in the windows of homes scattered along the shore. Gathered on the deck of the *Sandpiper* we are toasting life, reliving our dives, making plans for the next day's adventures. What we don't know is that we wouldn't dive the *Lermontov* again, not on this trip. The following day the Cook Strait wind would gust to 50 knots causing the Met Service to issue a storm warning. We would not get around Cape Jackson.

Later, in a bout of sea-dog machismo, Frank Carré would tell me that, of course, he and his boat would handle it just fine but for us passengers it would have been damn miserable. Deck-hosing material. And who was to argue? On one hand, Frank has to live up to the size of the crays in his photo album; on the other, he doesn't want to turn his boat into another diving destination.

In Cook Strait, one of the roughest sea passages on the planet, humbleness is a mariner's greatest virtue.

Tales from the Underworld

'... the walls seized my upper body with the firmness of a hydraulic press. My feet dangled in the air and I could no longer turn my head as the helmet became wedged as well.'

In Motueka — a small town near Nelson known for its fruit, house trucks and organic hippies — the stress level was undetectable. Along the main road muscle cars lazily rumbled for attention and somewhere a child was hammering out the daily chore of piano scales. The town felt safe and friendly, like a place where nothing can ever go wrong. But that was an hour ago. Now, as fear wells up inside me, I begin to wish I have stayed in town.

Only ten kilometres away, I am in a world so different I could well be on another planet. Underground and underwater, inside the bowels of a marble mountain, I am finning against the almost imperceptible current of the Riwaka River. My hand slides along a nylon rope strung out by my guide. All I can hear is my breath hissing in and gurgling out through the mouthpiece of my air supply, Darth Vader-like. The steel air cylinder strapped to my back hits the rock ceiling with a metallic clang. In this silent, liquid gloom the slightest sound has the intensity of a Chinese gong.

My torch-light zigzags across the grey walls, revealing an austere and surreal landscape, as if a railway tunnel, hewn out of solid rock, has been flooded with clear spring water. The passage — its walls as cold as glacial ice — slants down and narrows, then, at a depth of ten metres, turns upwards and opens like the wide end of a horn. I surface next to my guide Sean Mitchell, resting on a pile of boulders, and take a gasp of moist cave air.

We are in a chamber the size of a circus tent. When we turn off our lights, the darkness is absolute, so thick I can feel it pressing against my face. These walls have never seen sunlight! And yet we have only passed the entrance sumps, flooded siphon-like passages . . . a kind of Lewis Carroll mirror-gate into another world. Ahead, through chambers and tunnels smothered with yellow-brown clay, through twisting squeezes which corkscrew down like deformed keyholes and through yet more sumps, the cave continues and no one knows how far.

Sprawled on the riverside rocks in total darkness — monsters with black wet suit skins and flippered feet, faces distorted by hoods and masks — we may well look a part of this world but we feel quite the opposite. For caves make you feel alien in a way that no other earthly landscape can. They are black holes in our knowledge and imagination; they bring to mind cold, eternally dark places teeming with creepy, slithering creatures, where early explorers found themselves involuntarily slicing the air with crosses and mumbling paternosters. They've come to epitomise almost all our fears: of tight, claustrophobic passages, darkness, unfathomed depths and, ultimately, the fear of the unknown.

Since ancient times, caves have been considered the domain of death and suffering, and if the mountains, with their grand vistas and open skies, embodied the spirit of romanticised freedom, the dungeon-like caves became the symbol of hell. Here was the kingdom of the dead ruled by Hades and guarded by three-headed Cerberus. Here lived bloodthirsty bats and dragons, trolls and goblins, the Greek Minotaur and the Austrian Tatzelwurm; in fact, most of the monsters and nasties any folklore has ever produced. Occasional discoveries of prehistoric mammoth-size bones and skulls only strengthen such beliefs. Proteus, a blind, pale-pink, 30-centimetre-long cave salamander found in Slovenia, was said to be the freshly hatched offspring of a dragon, soon to be spitting fire, terrorising villages in search of toothsome virgins. How else could you explain the unearthly adaptations of a creature which had both lungs and external gills, could detect light and scents through its skin, change colour when brought into the daylight and survive without food for up to three years!

It must have been a place similar to the Riwaka where Bilbo Baggins traded riddles with Gollum: 'Is it nice, my precious? Is it juicy? Is it scrumptiously crunchable?' In here, I could feel Gollum eyeing me in the dark. 'If precious asks, and it doesn't answer, we eats it, my precious. If it asks us, and we doesn't answer . . . We show it the way out, yes!' I flick on my torch to dispel the monsters. Sean flashes his beach-boy grin at me; he's no Gollum and I don't have to bargain for my life. We dive into the gloom and follow our rope towards the sunlight.

● ● ●

Around the world caves are almost as common as mountains, but because of their very nature, we hardly know of their existence. 'Under the earth's crust, in absolute darkness, there exists such an enormously great world, that we can with some justice speak of a new continent,' wrote Swiss speleologist Alfred Bögli. But even venturing underground, with our vision confined to only what the myopic lights can reveal, we find the extent of caves staggering, their dimensions difficult to comprehend.

Under Mount Api in northern Borneo there is the Sarawak Chamber, large enough to accommodate seventeen football fields clustered side by side. Entering this world so strange that 'no writer of fiction could invent it', one of the cave's original explorers — an accomplished and well-travelled speleologist — suffered an acute attack of agoraphobia, paralysing fear of open spaces.

Caves are mostly found in limestone and marble, sedimentary rocks formed from the calcium-rich shells of dead molluscs and crustaceans which over millions of years have been compressed and solidified. Although in New Zealand there are caves in almost every part of the country, the deepest, longest and possibly the oldest cave systems are to be found within the 90-kilometre-long belt of Ordovician marble arching from Collingwood towards Murchison, across the Kahurangi National Park, bordering Golden Bay at the top of the South Island.

This belt of marble is not continuous but resembles — geologically speaking — a chain of chunky, steeply rising islands. The highest of them are Mount Owen (1875 metres) and Mount Arthur (1795 metres). Their bald, ice-scoured tops are an otherworldly landscape of bulging rock slabs cut by rifts and crevices, dotted with shafts and craters, as if a glacier had been showered with red-hot meteorites and then petrified.

The rock, sharp as coral, is weathered by heavy rainfall, but these rugged marble tablelands have the dry air of a desert about them. You can walk for hours and not find any surface water. But water — streams and rivers, waterfalls and pools — is there in abundance, deep underground.

Landscapes like these, collectively known as karst (after a region in Slovenia), usually indicate extensive subterranean labyrinths, 'plumbing systems' draining entire mountains. In one such area, at the northernmost tip of the marble belt and bordering Abel Tasman National Park, is Takaka Hill, I've come to see the 176-metre-deep entrance shaft to Harwood's Hole.

In the picnic area at the end of the Canaan Road I meet my caving guides: no-nonsense West Coaster Kerry Silverwood, and his happy-go-lucky son, Neil. Together they make a good team: youthful daredevilry tempered by practical wisdom and the kind of resourcefulness that sees you carrying your toolbox with you at all times.

The Hole has the rough shape of an hour-glass and the long descent begins just above its narrowest part. Here, Neil and Kerry rig up a 200-metre-long rope; its weight — close to twenty kilograms — makes it stiff like a wire. As I inch my way into the abyss, fear creeps in again and my imagination throws up phantasmagoric scenarios of disaster: the rope snaps with the twang of an overextended rubber band and there is a moment of no gravity, and then an endless fall, a fall where you suffer from motion sickness long before you reach the bottom. But it is the titanic size of Harwood's Hole that overwhelms all other emotions. The mind has no reference points for such grandeur, everything seems out of scale.

Abseiling on a rope this long has its finer points too. Go too slow and the harness will cut the blood circulation so effectively your legs will be numb before you reach the bottom. Go too fast and the abseiling rack can overheat until it's too hot to touch.

'Don't stop at the bottom,' Kerry warned me. 'Keep walking down the slope as you untie the rack or it might melt through the rope.'

If you speed out of control, it is virtually impossible to stop or even slow down. The last accident here happened just like that; the victim suffered severe rope burns and a fractured thighbone. The rescue, herculean in its scope, took nearly twelve hours.

During the first part of the descent, life is abundant all around me. Bonsai-like trees reach out for sunlight from their cracks in near-vertical rock; layers of spongy moss absorb the water constantly dripping from above. Swallows dart towards their hidden nests; there is a multitude of insects taking advantage of this unique ecological niche. But further down, as the daylight recedes, so do the plants and animals. Finally, I can see nothing but bare rocks with an occasional hint of algae.

At the bottom, in a chamber some 50 metres across, Neil explains the techniques of efficient caving: 'Forget all about grace, about trying to stay clean and dry. You have to move quickly and safely but without unnecessary aesthetics. Think ferret: it would make a good caver.'

We're all wearing standard caving attire: meat-workers' white gumboots, one-piece overalls with layers of fleece underwear, a harness with an abseiling rack, and a carbide light generator, backed up with two or three electric torches. The generator is one piece of equipment which cavers both love and hate. In a pint-sized pressure-proof container worn on a waist belt, calcium carbide is mixed with drip-fed water thus producing a burnable gas (acetylene) which is channelled via a hose to the front of a helmet and lit with an in-built lighter. It's like carrying a miniature welding torch on your forehead. The entire contraption can be temperamental and prone to malfunctions, but it also produces pleasantly warm and powerful light far outlasting any electric counterparts. On long caving escapades — which can last 20 to 25 hours — carbide is still the only practical light source.

We climb down a slope of loose rocks, then follow an underground river, our hands and legs spread out X-shaped against the tubular walls of the passage. The floor is usually a crystal pool of water so clear it's impossible to judge its depth. The pools cascade into one another and we abseil through the resultant waterfalls, climbing down or jumping smaller steps and chutes.

'I'm not much of a swimmer,' Kerry admitted before setting out, 'So I've brought a few of these.' He produced an impressive range of empty soft-drink bottles. 'You put them inside your overalls; three or four will make a fellow float quite well.'

What today is the deepest natural shaft this side of the equator began as a bowl-shaped pond littered with rotting vegetation. In the presence of carbon dioxide (from decomposing organic matter), water forms a corrosive carbonic acid, which chemically dissolves the rock-hard marble and limestone. As the carbon dioxide-rich water seeps towards the underground water table, it corrodes its way down the lines of natural weakness — cracks and hair-line fissures — widening them until, many thousands of years later, they become tunnels and chambers of astonishing shapes and sizes.

Cold temperature, heavy rainfall and sharp vertical relief of the land are all accelerating factors. In the Riwaka Basin, scientists estimate that during one year, around 100 cubic metres of marble can be dissolved from each square kilometre.

As long as the water continues to percolate from above, the cave is alive and constantly changing. Dripping, trickling, chiming, roaring, the underground water tirelessly wears away the obstacles in its way, creating a remarkable complexity of passages. Caves themselves become underground watersheds. There are rivers and tributaries, white-water rapids, waterfalls and crystal lakes so still that, like caves, they too seem made of stone.

Further into the cave, the pools grow deeper and occasionally Kerry inflates an extra bottle and adds it to his already bulging bust. The walls around us become bristled with stalactites and stalagmites. Some are fragile, like spun glass, others solid like Greek columns. Sometimes they join together to form intricate chandeliers, curtains and 'dwarfs' beards' — waterfalls of white rock frozen in mid-air.

With the regularity of a pendulum, water drips from roofs and arches and thin rings of crystallised calcium carbonate build around each droplet like stains from evaporating saltwater. With time, the stacked-up rings form hollow tubes called soda straws. These tubes eventually disappear under new growths of crystals and become stalactites. The water dripping from their tips releases still more calcium carbonate as it hits the floor, forming stalagmites, sometimes mirror images of the stalactites above. This process, repeated in its infinite variations, can produce an exquisite cave decor, a display of beauty comparable perhaps only to the artwork of hoarfrost.

Towards the end of the cave we leave the increasingly narrow streamway and climb up towards the exit known as Starlight Cave.

Suddenly, we find ourselves in the middle of a Hans Christian Andersen fairy tale. Awoken by our lights, the walls, the stalagmited floor and the ceiling thick with stalactites — this entire shark's jaw interior — glitter with delicate stardust, minute crystals embedded in the rock. Through the last waist-deep pool we wade into the daylight. After four hours in the cave, never warmer than 4°C, the outside world greets us with the air of an overheated sauna, pungent smell of the forest and blue, blue sky.

• • •

Every year towards the end of December the most enthusiastic cavers from all over the country gather for a sort of Black Christmas at Bulmer Lake in the Mount Owen karstfield. This wild and inhospitable place combines the harsh climate of the South Island's alps with heavy West Coast rainfall. A trip up here is always an expedition requiring military-style logistics and helicopter transport. On occasions, unable to cross the often-impassable Owen River, cavers have been trapped for several days in their flood-prone base camp.

Within the karstfield lies a vast cave complex: the Bulmer Cavern. Since its discovery in January 1985 over 40 kilometres of passages have been explored and surveyed, making it the longest cave in New Zealand. Still, there are so many new 'leads', so many question marks on the cave's mural-size map, that, as Lindsay Main, the expedition organiser told me, it is rare to go into Bulmer and not find at least a few hundred metres of unexplored passages.

The cave comprises Upper and Lower Levels, which could almost make separate systems if not for the 100-metre-deep connecting shaft known as Lion's Den. Climbing up this underground equivalent of Harwood's Hole at the end of a twenty-hour exploration blitz is a daunting prospect even for the most experienced cavers and so a shortcut into the Lower Levels has been eagerly sought.

One rather mysterious possibility, tenderly referred to as 'The Dig', is a narrow, horizontal fissure filled with sediment, about two hours from the main entrance. If unearthed, it could bypass Lion's Den and its less daunting but decidedly awkward extension, the 200-metre-long Castration Corridor. Cavers got down on their knees and began to dig.

Digging is the darker side of caving and probably not your idea of adventure. Not mine either. You kneel or lie flat in a constricted squeeze, gnawing at it with a sawn-off shovel and filling up a heavy-duty rubbish bag with the debris. When the bag is full, you crawl out backwards pulling the bag as you go. With a bit of luck, there is someone to take over, but not always.

'Once I spent five days on The Dig,' Neil Silverwood told me as if recalling a nightmare. 'Sometimes the dust was so thick, you couldn't see your hand in front of you.'

At last measurement The Dig was over 40 metres long, with no breakthrough in sight. Meanwhile, an extremely tight bypass of Lion's Den, christened Memory Lane — only 100 metres long, it takes 40 minutes to traverse — was discovered and so The Dig was abandoned. The new bypass revealed that another 100 metres of digging would have been required to make the connection.

But why dig, you could ask, if there are so many big caves nearby? Indeed, of the 30 deepest caves in New Zealand, the depth being the difference in altitude between the cave's entrance and its lowest point, only one — Aurora in Fiordland — does not lie within the Mount Owen-Mount Arthur-Takaka Hill karst. At minus 889 metres the Nettlebed under Mount Arthur is our deepest cave known so far and, incidentally, 24 of its 25 kilometres were found on the other side of a successful dig. The nearby Ellis Basin System is 28.7 kilometres long, 775 metres deep and growing rapidly. Yet all this seems a mere reconnaissance, for the surrounding mountains are percolated with caves, resembling blocks of Swiss cheese.

'The vertical relief of the Mount Arthur and Mount Owen karst indicates potential for caves 1500 metres deep,' Lindsay Main told me. 'That would make them some of the deepest in the world. For example, we know that Nettlebed cave contributes only one-eighth of all water which comes out at the Pearse resurgence, the river draining the side of Mount Arthur. If you translate the remaining seven-eighths into caves, it means systems totalling over 100 kilometres.'

But there is no illusion about caves giving up their secrets easily. Many high-altitude cave entrances — often deep and narrow shafts — are permanently choked with snow which, accumulating year after year, becomes a kind of underground glacier. The low altitude entrances are overgrown with bush and access to them may require abseiling down the forested bluffs.

Although cave prospecting and exploration happen both in expeditionary outbursts of activity and quiet weekends of pot-holing, major discoveries still take everyone by surprise. In 1990, four years after my little 'freedom climb' when the Iron Curtain was just a rusting shadow of its former self, a group of determined Czechoslovakian cavers arrived in Nelson. Nursing their hard-won Western currency, avoiding Motueka pubs at all costs, they set out on a methodical, military-style search for a major cave system on the south side of Mount Owen.

'We steered them away from our own leads and sent them where we thought it was safe,' one Nelson caver told me. 'They went off and, on a shortcut between two campsites, found Bohemia, over seven kilometres long and, at minus 662 metres, the fourth deepest cave in New Zealand. We had walked past the entrance many times. No one ever thought of looking in there.'

Some of the local cavers, still licking bush-thorn wounds from their own searches, cursed not loud but deep. It was as if the Trinidad and Tobago rugby team had come and thrashed the All Blacks. Possessed and possessive about their caves, some of the Kiwi troglophiles (cave lovers) turned out to be fiercely territorial and surprisingly nationalistic, passively opposing if not being altogether hostile to foreigners exploring in New Zealand.

Chris Pugsley, the editor of the *New Zealand Speleological Bulletin*, explained: 'Unexplored caves are a limited national resource; why should we let someone else come and explore them for us? If you inherit a cellar full of good wine you don't throw a big party and drink it all at once. So with the caves, you want to savour the experience of exploration, a little bit at a time.'

The liberals among cavers think that there are plenty of caves for everyone. 'In New Zealand you can still wander off into the bush and find a completely new cave — YOUR cave, a place where no one has been before!' said an excited British expat. 'You can name it, explore it, map it, all the Captain Cook stuff. I guess we're all explorers born a couple of centuries too late.'

Too late to discover new islands and mountains perhaps, but just in time to explore caves in our largest systems, like the upper levels of Bulmer, which are in the last stage of their geological lifespan. When the water, constantly seeking the most direct way down, recedes to the lower levels, the caves begin to dry out and collapse. The once-smooth passages fill with the rubble of boulders peeling from the roof. The weakened underground structures slowly give way causing implosions and slumping on the surface. The remaining carbon dioxide escapes into the atmosphere reducing the acidity of water and slowing down any cave making which may still go on in the lower levels. Finally, after millions of years of incessant erosion, the caves are filled and smothered flush with the ground as though they were never there.

• • •

Fortunately, we are talking in geological terms here, where a millennium is but an eye blink and a million years a handy brick-size unit to build the past with and extrapolate the future. In our reality caves seem frozen in time. There is no danger of them disappearing just yet and that can turn them into valuable pieces of real estate.

What would you do if you suddenly found a cave under your property? According to the Roman land law in place in New Zealand, you own everything, except minerals, within the boundaries of your land and the centre of the earth, including caves. So it would be YOUR cave! If it was small, you could turn it into a wine cellar, something the French call *la cave*, a cool and musty place full of bottles carrying the patina of age. But what if the cave was huge and complex, a labyrinth encrusted with candelabras of stals and perhaps only partly explored, an asset of unknown value and possible business potential? Would you let cavers come and go as they please, build a ticket booth and charge tourists for looking at your cave, or would you just bolt the entrances and keep the cave safe?

This is a dilemma faced by over twenty landowners farming the Waitomo karst, in the Waikato region west of Rotorua. They call their land — the green hills cratered with sinkholes — 'rolling country', meaning it's easy to roll a farm bike here! The underlying caves are mainly horizontal, often with steep entrance shafts known as tomos (wai means water, tomo a hole in the ground). They are warmer than their South Island counterparts and usually well decorated. Located near major population centres, they have been the cradle of New Zealand caving.

When the New Zealand Speleological Society (NZSS) was formed in 1949, Waitomo was its first playground and the following two decades yielded the milestones of underground exploration, caves like the twelve-kilometre-long Gardner's Gut, Waipuna and Lost World. Here, most cavers learnt to crawl before walking into the more challenging marble caves of the northern South Island. But now, all this is a thing of the past. A few years ago, caving in Waitomo took a deep and sudden dive.

On a steamy day one late February I met the man whose decision brought this dive about, a farmer named James Haggas. He was carving slabs of raw meat from a cow's carcass and throwing them to his work dogs. He stood up, retiring the knife to a hip sheath, and eyed me defiantly while I explained my business. The carcass at his feet was instantly mobbed by flies.

'The cavers really shot themselves in the foot,' he explained. 'They overstayed their welcome.' He told me how, on a busy weekend, some 50 people would be wandering around his paddocks making nuisances of themselves: gates were left open, stock scattered, a calf died a horrible death after swallowing a forgotten container of spent carbide. He started charging five dollars a head to make up for the inconvenience: 'Not a fortune, you agree?' But some cavers were unwilling payers. There were two rescues and plenty of scope for more; and there was a threat of the caves becoming a liability.

Then came the final straw, James's own visit to one of his caves. He was shown the damage accumulated over the years: broken stals, mud smeared over pristine flowstones, carbide refuse and broken glass. All this in HIS cave! That was the day when James Haggas had had enough. There would be no more of 'them cavers' on or under his land, he declared. He leased exclusive rights to three of his caves and all his worries to a commercial caving company. They took care of the caves and safety, their clients are thrilled and asking for more and James pockets a handsome commission. The only party left out of the deal are the cavers themselves.

All this would seem a storm in a teacup if not for the fact that the Haggas property contains about ten significant caves, some say the best caves in the North Island. Their closure was a shock to the caving community. These were, after all, THEIR caves too! They found, explored and mapped them. They took the access for granted, true, but this is how it's always been. They pleaded and begged, then slyly offered to help James fence off his tomos. All to no avail. When the dust of the dispute had settled, James Haggas stood unmoved by his gate like a bouncer, arms across his chest. His caves remain off-limits to recreational cavers.

• • •

The first to explore Waitomo caves and their tourist potential was Taane Tinorau of the Maniapoto tribe. In late December 1887, accompanied by an Englishman, Fred Mace, Taane drifted through what would become the Glow-worm Grotto in a raft made of korari (flax flower stalks). Before their two candles burnt out, he had seen enough of the cave to realise that it was a profitable discovery. A year earlier the eruption of Mount Tarawera obliterated the world-renowned Pink and White Terraces of Rotorua; now the glow-worms could steal the limelight. And steal they did.

Tourists have been pouring into Waitomo ever since and paddling a boat through the cave, under the firmament of glow-worms, has become a world-class attraction. Recently, with the advent of 'adrenalin tourism', more challenging ways of seeing the caves have evolved. Almost anyone can now abseil into the 100-metre-deep entrance shaft of Mangapu Cave (better known as the Lost World), raft underground rivers in a truck's inner tube, walk along keyhole streamways, squeeze through low passages half-filled with water, to experience real caving without becoming a caver, to see the underworld wonders without the months of training. All this has made Waitomo a major stopover for foreign tourists, like Milford Sound or the Westland glaciers. During the day the village resembles a giant parking lot filled with cars and buses. Their passengers are invariably underground.

On my own tour of the Glow-worm Grotto — the world's great wonder and Waitomo's highlight for over a century — I was sandwiched between one busload of Japanese, grumpy because they couldn't use their cameras here, and another of French, who strolled around with a cool dignity usually reserved for the halls of the Louvre. We walked through the cave, lit discretely like a church, and its interior — Gothic in grandeur and sparsely baroque in decor — exuded the presence of a cathedral that makes you involuntarily hush your voice. Then we boarded a flat-bottomed boat which the guide pulled along a tension rope. The lights petered out and we drifted into the perpetual cave night.

I sat next to a little French girl, cuddled up to her mother. 'Regarde ça, Maman!' I heard her whisper. 'Tellement d'lumiere! Ils sont comme les etoiles!' Gliding through perfect silence, we found ourselves in one of Antoine de Saint-Exupéry's night flights, mesmerised by the light of galaxies. The cool, green lights were clustered so close together it was impossible to group them into imaginary constellations. It was as if the Milky Way had spilled across the entire sky.

• • •

While caving, I've always had a guide — a professional, a friend, sometimes both — for entering caves without experience and local knowledge can be a risky venture. In caves, my sense of direction, not infallible at the best of times, would leave me, as it were, in the dark. But getting lost is only one of the potential perils. Cavers have been strangled by the chin straps of their own helmets jammed in vertical squeezes, poisoned by carbide making its way into food or drinking water, burnt by an exploding carbide generator and knocked unconscious by a rock thrown down a shaft by tourists experimenting with gravity. In wet caves, drowning and hypothermia are constant threats and there is always a danger of ropes wearing through by constant rubbing against sharp rocks.

Less hazardous but no less intimidating are the squeezes. Exiting Hollywood Cave, on the northern fringe of Paparoa National Park, we had come to a cul-de-sac with a narrow rift cleaving the ceiling. Without hesitation, Neil Silverwood had weaselled his way up with a mixture of brute force and uneasy contortions. There was much panting and grunting as his gumbooted feet wriggled violently above my head. I could hear the rasping of Cordura against the rock. Minutes passed; the panting and grunting intensified. Then I heard his muffled voice:

'I'm through; come on up!'

I made two metres of upward progress, then the walls seized my upper body with the firmness of a hydraulic press. My feet dangled in the air and I could no longer turn my head as the helmet became wedged as well. I assessed the situation, remembering all too well an incident in Waitomo's Rumbling Gut, where a woman caver got so severely stuck in a squeeze, known as the Last Minute Crawl, it took nineteen hours of drilling and chiselling to get her out.

'Undo your helmet buckle first,' Neil volunteered a piece of advice. 'Breathe out and then push your chest through one rib at a time.' I did. Five centimetres ... ten ... twenty ... Slowly the walls receded and I was through. 'Thin people around 60 kg can usually squeeze through a letterbox 180 mm high,' I read later in a 'caving made easy' book by British caver Ben Lyon. 'For those near 80 kg the limit is likely to be around 225 mm.'

Think about it: it's about the height of this book you are reading!

Always, when facing a particularly uninviting squeeze, I follow Neil's pointers closely for his expertise is unrivalled. He learnt the hard way. One of these squeezes nearly cost him his life. It was the first time he made national news.

Some years ago, he was prospecting for new caves in the dense bush near Charleston, on the West Coast of the South Island, with local teacher and novice caver Chris Manuel. They found a steep-sided sink-hole with a small opening at the bottom and Neil, eager to scoop the glory of being the first explorer, lowered himself feet-first into the hole. He was about a metre in, his head already below the floor, when suddenly the sides caved in and he was wedged in a vertical squeeze.

Both his hands — he'd kept them above his head to streamline the body — were jammed between the crumbling walls and his helmet. He tried to wriggle himself out, but his feet were treading only air and with every movement his body sank deeper into the squeeze, turning the chin strap of his immobilised helmet into a tightening snare, so that he could barely breathe.

Without a knife to cut the strap, Chris Manuel was helpless. The sides of the hole were loose and his attempts at rescue only brought down more debris which cemented around Neil. There were two hours of daylight left. They both agreed that Chris should go and find help.

Through the trackless bush he set out towards the road, only a kilometre away, marking his way with strips of orange tape. The going was hard for the bush-covered karst is full of traps: sudden cliffs, ravines and holes camouflaged with thick vegetation. An hour and a half later, he was still in the bush, and he had run out of tape.

It began to rain. Neil's sink-hole was soon flooding and more debris was being washed down. 'I couldn't move and the water was pouring down the funnel and along my body,' Neil told me. 'I was stuck in the middle of a stream. It got very cold and I wasn't sure if Chris would ever make it back. I had to constantly fight off panic and despair. I thought of all the reasons for living, all the things I still wanted to do, all the people I love. I really wanted to live!'

Eventually, Manuel reached the road and stirred up a full-scale rescue, but in the darkness, bush and pouring rain, he could not find his way back to the hole. For eight hours Neil remained buried while some 30 rescuers combed the bush for bits of orange tape. Shortly

IN BARRINGTON COUNTRY

'Exploring is delightful to look forward to and back upon, but it is not comfortable at the time, unless it be of such an easy nature, as not to deserve the name.'
EREWHON, SAMUEL BUTLER

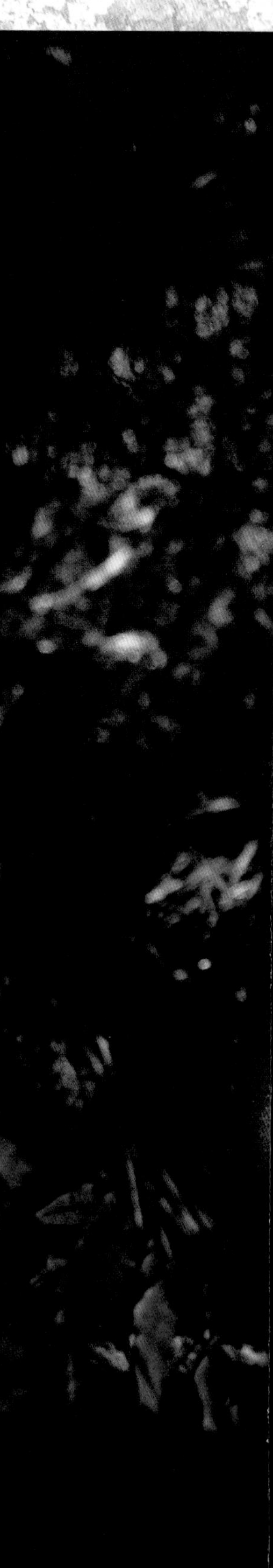

BIRDBRAIN

Don Merton's lifetime work with the kakapo (top & right) has helped to bring the unique forest parrots back from the edge of sure extinction. Their 'booming' (bottom left) is now heard regularly in their Codfish Island sanctuary.

(PHOTOS: ROD MORRIS)

AMARANTHINE BEAUTY

Though resembling a snowflake, this fist-sized cave rose would have taken eons to reach this size. Growing in perfect darkness, it has only ever been seen by a handful of dedicated underground explorers.

EARTH'S WOMB

'Ahead, through chambers and tunnels smothered with yellow-brown clay, through twisting squeezes, which corkscrew down like deformed keyholes and through yet more sumps, the cave continues and no one knows how far.'

ABSEILS AND SQUEEZES

Descending on ropes into cathedral interiors and worming through flooded keyhole passages are the two extreme aspects of caving. Mud, darkness and cold take their toll too and consequently the sport has only a handful of active but uncommonly passionate exponents.

MOUNTAIN MAGIC

Chris North and Guy White pause to unrope after the second complete ascent of the Kaipo Wall, New Zealand's largest rock face in the Darran Mountains in Fiordland.

In memory of Guy White. Rest in peace my friend, you have climbed the highest mountain.

SNOW AND FIRE

Barrington's 'worst country in the world' is today a playground for well-equipped adventurers. Mick Hutchins, a former Oxford scholar in Icelandic mythology and a Mount Aspiring National Park ranger ponders the meaning of it all while drying off after a storm.

after midnight they found one and Neil's father, Kerry, was the first to reach the hole. All he could see were his son's fingers sticking out of the mud.

'You still there, son?' the old man asked reaching for the lifeless fingers.

'Dad? DAD!' came a sobbing reply.

Kerry frantically scraped away the dirt, reached down and, with his pocket knife, cut off the helmet strap. It took another two hours of digging to remove the debris stone by stone, until the rescuers could place a sling around Neil's shoulders and pull him out to safety. 'These things make you grow up real fast,' Kerry told me. Today Neil is one of New Zealand's most active and experienced cavers and one of the country's best adventure photographers; he was only sixteen at the time.

• • •

Perhaps the most extreme way of exploring underground is cave-diving. According to an American cave-diving manual, regardless of fitness or experience, 'anyone can die at any time on any cave dive'. The balance between acceptable risk and sheer madness is so fine, most of the fatalities result from divers simply scaring themselves to death. Even diving guru Jacques-Yves Cousteau, the co-inventor of the aqualung, described his cave-diving as the 'worst experience in five thousand dives'.

The history of cave-diving reads like a book of horrors, where scenarios of disorientation, entanglement in safety lines, out-of-control panic and subsequent drowning repeat themselves in predictable patterns and where an occasional happy ending comes as an unlikely surprise. But it is also a remarkable account of human ingenuity and endeavour.

In 1934, twenty years before the invention of aqualungs, Jack Sheppard and Graham Balcombe braved the sumps of Swildon's Hole in Somerset, England, armed with motorcycling goggles, nose clips, bicycle pump and twelve metres of garden hose. The one who was going to dive held the hose in his mouth like a pipe, while the other used the pump as a compressor above ground. Pioneering the most daredevil adventure yet invented, they could not possibly imagine that 50 years later, their followers would look more like astronauts on a spacewalk than cavers. In Australia, riding torpedo-like underwater scooters and trailing sledges loaded with a dozen air tanks, modern-day aquanauts found the end of the Cocklebiddy Cave, 6090 metres from the entrance. Long considered a world record, this feat has been overshadowed recently by the exploration of the Nohoch cave system in Mexico, which has yielded many kilometres of underwater passages resembling flooded metros.

The more caves I visited, the more it became apparent that an ideal caver would be a cold-blooded, spineless midget contortionist, equipped with gills and webbed feet and, like a glow-worm, generating their own light. This, as one enthusiast assured me, was not all that impossible. 'These things take time. Caves took eons to make and you can't expect evolution to produce an overnight miracle,' he explained, unfolding his theory. 'Cavers often marry cavers and if their children become cavers too, they are well on their way towards such adaptations.' The new golden age of caving may be only a few generations away.

• • •

So far, ferreting around New Zealand caves, I'd always followed someone else's more or less trodden path. The caves I had visited were explored and mapped. Some, like the by-permit-only Hollow Hill in Waitomo, received only a handful of visitors a year; others were frequented more regularly; others seemed as busy as pedestrian subways. Finally, one clear autumn day in April, I took part in the most rewarding and passion-stirring form of caving: an exploration of a new system.

As our heavily-laden helicopter croaked above the Heaphy River, in the north-western corner of Kahurangi National Park, Neil Silverwood pointed out a huge opening gaping in the forest. It was during a similar flight in 1994 that he had found this entrance and a cave which he named Megamania. The fervent exploration that followed revealed over fifteen kilometres of passages, making the cave the fourth longest in the country. Still, as Neil assured me, there were plenty more yet to be found.

For the next five days we lived in the cave, just beyond the edge of daylight, and every morning I shook out my overalls and gumboots to shoo out spelangulas, local cave spiders as big as the palm of your hand. Day after day, we explored the maze of known passages hoping to find some new ones. We abseiled down tomos, pushed through muddy squeezes and ran along tubular tunnels that could have accommodated a narrow country highway.

Every night we came back, tired and dirty like miners after a long shift, to sleep under the false firmament of glow-worms, lullabied by the roar of an underground river. Carbide torches were our daylight and mud, like darkness, became an inseparable part of our life. This wasn't the countryside mud of wet dirt roads or farm paddocks, which merely soils your gumboots, but the primordial ooze that threatens to swallow you whole and makes you leave a desperate trail of Yeti-like footprints. You taste it in food and water, feel it inside your sleeping bag and find it smeared on your face when you wake in the morning. It could drive you crazy, this muddiness; like a fosse, it was the cave's formidable line of defence.

Although the names of Megamania's passages betrayed the awe and excitement of their discoverers: Great Wall, Mega Blast, Goldrush, Fake and, true, Orgasmia; at the time, the cave was determined not to give away any more secrets. Neil had previously undertaken a lengthy dig and found only 150 metres of new cave. Another caver, Dave Harmer, found a new tomo, but its bottom was choked by a rock fall. This time, it seemed, we had to settle for what was already known.

For me, that was still plenty and occasional glimpses of unearthly beauty made me instantly forget all the mud and discomfort. In one calcite room, bristled with straws like a hedgehog's wardrobe, I was told to lie down and peep in between the stalactites that, having grown into the floor, formed a natural low-roofed cage. Inside, there was a garden of crystal flowers, petrified white roses hanging up-side-down on long, slender stalks, glistening as if they were made of diamonds. Their beauty seemed ironic and unfulfilled for they were doomed to exist in perpetual darkness, like an old master in the safe of a private collector. This was a rare moment when the vault's door was briefly open. You can look but not touch and I looked for as long as I could hold my breath.

In the end, the craving for daylight got the better of us and we left the cave and made a beeline for the Heaphy Track. There was little doubt that the cave would eventually surrender a few more kilometres of passages and who-knows-what calcite jewels, but finding them will require much perseverance and many more expeditions.

Poring over cave maps full of question marks, trying to make out which way the cave may 'go', is like solving a three-dimensional puzzle where you not only don't know the entire picture, but neither do you know the shapes nor the sizes of individual pieces. The missing links are often predicted long before they are found. 'In Takaka Hill, seemingly so thoroughly explored, we still haven't found the main cave system,' leading Nelson caver and palaeontologist Trevor Worthy told me. 'The entire side of the hill drains into the Gorge Stream. We know that the cave is there, but we just can't find an entrance.'

And so the caves remain an open frontier and finding the Big One is every caver's dream. Even in a country as compact as New Zealand, a casual caving trip can result in the discovery of a completely new system, perhaps larger than all those known so far, the geographical equivalent of finding a mountain higher than Mount Cook or a glacier larger than the Tasman.

A day after our Megamania expedition, I was idling with Neil and Kerry Silverwood in their cosy home, just north of Westport. Their dog, Silver, was fast asleep at our feet and the smouldering West Coast coal guarded us against the chill of an autumn evening. Our caving adventure was already becoming a cherished memory, a tale to be told on nights like this, when the passage of time had erased the misery and dirt, leaving only the splendour and the beauty.

Then the phone rang. It was Danielle Gemenis, a Hamilton doctor and an enthusiastic caver. She went prospecting for new caves near the summit of Mount Arthur, she said, and found a huge hole, a massive hole. 'We threw a rock down the shaft,' her voice grew excited, 'and it came back! The draft was that strong!' A quick topographical calculation established that the cave could be an extension to the Nettlebed system, possibly 1200–1400 metres deep. This could be the Big One. Danielle was already organising an expedition and Neil promptly had himself invited. Would I come as well?

I looked outside at the pile of our soiled caving gear, the mud so fresh it hadn't caked-up yet, and felt the cave grit still grinding between my teeth. I could see why there were only about 300 cavers in New Zealand, and only half of them active. The admission to the underworld was pricey — dirt, fear, danger and exhaustion — but for the elite of caving addicts, no effort was too great. They are at the cutting edge of exploration, an edge not wide but sharp and penetrating, and they will continue disappearing underground to emerge wide-eyed with wonder and full of strange tales.

I won't go with them to Mount Arthur. But I'd love to hear their stories.

POSTSCRIPT:

As this book was going to print, cavers have indeed found the Big One. An expedition sponsored by *New Zealand Geographic* and led by Kieran McKay connected the two existing systems, the Stormy Pot and the Nettlebed. under Mount Arthur in Kahurangi National Park. The entire system, whose existence has been anticipated since the 1960s, now totals 36 kilometres and is 1200 metres deep, which makes it the deepest cave in the southern hemisphere and the second longest in New Zealand. Neil Silverwood had again done his share of the digging.

The Odyssey of
Alphonse Barrington

'Exploring is delightful to look forward to and back upon, but it is not comfortable at the time, unless it be of such an easy nature, as not to deserve the name.'

Erewhon, Samuel Butler

When the walnut stock of his shotgun touched Captain Elchold's cheek the fate of yet another pigeon seemed decided. With the precision of a gun turret he tracked the bird across the sky and was about to pull the trigger when suddenly he stopped. The pigeon crash-landed into the mop of miro trees, but Elchold's attention was now elsewhere. He lowered his weapon, watching in disbelief.

Three famished men were crossing a branch of the river, dragging their feet against the swift current. Their hair and beards were long and unkempt, their faces scratched and streaked with caked blood. Bedraggled shirts and fustian trousers hung from their angular bodies like oversized potato sacks. A half-starved dog swam ahead of them and shook itself dry on the gravel bank. Its shaggy coat was stretched over protruding ribs like the bellow of a concertina. One of the men wore a ragged tunic made of a crudely stitched blanket. His eyes were lost in cavities of his skull. He muttered a feeble plea for tobacco.

Like both of his impoverished companions, Alphonse Barrington was a gold miner. Six months earlier he had set out to prospect in the unmapped South-Westland hinterland and his journey, full of misadventures and unspeakable hardship, was to become the most heroic episode in the history of New Zealand exploration, our version of the worst journey in the world, or Shackleton's escape from Antarctica.

On this crisp June morning the three men staggered out of the wilderness in such an emaciated state, Elchold, who skippered the whale-boat *Pearl* ferrying supplies across Lake Wakatipu, later described them as living skeletons covered with skin, so weak they were barely able to speak. Another witness depicted them as 'wrecks of humanity'.

It was the year 1864. Some twelve months earlier in America, President Abraham Lincoln had signed the Emancipation Act freeing all slaves in the Confederated States. On long sleepless nights French engineer Alphonse Beau de Bochas was perfecting the theory of the four-stroke combustion engine and in Paris Édouard Manet outraged the crowds at Salon des Refusés with a nude scene in his 'Le déjeuner sur l'herbe'.

The population of Australia had just reached one million and John King was the first man to cross the continent south to north and live to tell his story. Rescued from certain death by people of the Yuntruwunta tribe, he was the sole survivor of the ill-managed expedition which reached the Gulf of Carpentaria in February 1861. His nutritional depletion was so severe he never fully recovered and died six years later at the age of 33.

In New Zealand's North Island racial tempers ran sour and exploded into war when the punitive expedition of General Duncan Cameron crossed the Mangatawhiri River and entered the King Country. In the highlands of Otago, men in their thousands scarred the mountains and diverted the flow of rivers in a hurried search for gold.

The first great gold rush in Gabriel's Gully in Tuapeka, near Lawrence in Central Otago, was almost a year old when one March Sunday in 1862, a shepherd named Thomas Arthur wandered off to the Overshot (later Shotover) Creek and with a milking bucket and a knife gave it the reputation of being one of the richest gold-bearing rivers in the world at that time. In the Upper Shotover, where the river twists and foams through a steep gorge, two Maori men, Dan Ellison and Hakaria Haeroa, rushed to rescue their drowning dog and found a beach paved with gold. On their first day they gathered over eleven kilograms.

Five months later, on 14 August 1862, two Californian prospectors, Horatio Hartley and Christopher Reilly, rode into Dunedin, New Zealand's biggest city at the time, and tied their horses outside the office of the Gold Receiver, Mr J.B. Borton. They were weary and dirty with road dust after a long ride across the highlands. They came from the Dunstan Mountains, near where the Upper Clutha joins the Kawarau River and where no had one ever suspected the existence of gold. The leather saddle bag they dumped on Borton's counter contained 40 kilograms of the precious metal.

Suddenly the entire district seemed to be criss-crossed by the gold-bearing reefs and almost every day brought news and rumours of new discoveries. The gold fever in its most contagious form shuddered New Zealand and diggers flocked to Otago from the overworked Australian fields of Ballarat and Bendigo, and from California and the drying Colorado rush.

A digger was of a tough and resilient breed and lived a hard, solitary life, following new gold rushes the way nomads follow changing seasons. He travelled carrying all his possessions stashed in a calico swag or more often wrapped lengthways in a blanket, its ends tied together in a ring-like sausage and slung over a shoulder. A pick, bantam shovel, gold pan, a billy, sometimes a rifle, all strapped around or carried in a hand, gave him the appearance of a tinker.

The success of Hartley and Reilly had become every digger's dream. The fact that they had 'chased the weight' so far from the existing fields proved gold could be almost anywhere. The existing gold fields, parcelled into a mosaic of claims, were under increasing pressure. In Gabriel's Gully an average claim measured about seven by seven metres, barely enough to support a gang of miners. In the not-so-long-ago unknown gorges of Arrow and Shotover, tin dishes clattered against the river gravel and the thumping of picks echoed among the rock faces. Diggers toiled from sunrise to sundown, but the returns, tempered by the extremely high cost of living and fickle weather, were often disappointing.

Nine months of back-breaking work at Arthur's Point, near Queenstown, yielded little reward for Alphonse Barrington, a veteran of New South Wales gold rushes. The Shotover River flooded frequently, damaging cradles and sluice boxes, and the little gold that he dished out was spent on repairs. Around the beginning of November 1863 he was finally forced to leave in search of better-paying claims.

On a December afternoon, in company of Edward Dunmore and William Bayliss he landed at the head of Lake Wakatipu — today's Glenorchy where the braiding Dart River runs milky-grey with glacial silt. They walked some three kilometres and camped by the river. And so the epic journey began.

The Dart River is born among the glaciers on the south side of the Barrier Range and arches southward through a wide grassland valley scooped out by Pleistocene ice. Over the years it has built an extensive alluvial plain where pied oystercatchers and banded dotterels dawdle in the shallows and the ever-shifting gravel islands are streamlined by the swift current. It was here that Barrington and his companions had a foretaste of things to come.

After a pre-dawn start they walked up the valley, heavily laden with mining tools and provisions. They were crossing one of the branching river channels when Bayliss, having strayed from the ford, was swept off his feet and carried downstream. He desperately fought to rid himself of the heavy swag, but the leather straps held tight and the weight dragged him underwater. Barrington dumped his load in the river and swam to the rescue. They made it to the shore after Bayliss finally managed to ditch the swag, now bobbing along in the mercurial water and fast disappearing from sight.

Barrington ran some 400 metres along the bank and waited waist-deep in the river until the swag came whirling by. They lost two of their tin dishes, a long-handled shovel, and most of the tea, sugar and baking soda. Oatmeal, flour and blankets were soaked with water. It was only the second day of their journey.

The sunny Christmas Day found them camped at the junction of Stony and Wild Dog creeks (today the main and north branches of the Routeburn). The dog they had borrowed from the storekeeper at the head of the lake caught four Maori hens (weka) and they boiled a pot of plum duff. The tea they sipped by the fire tasted of wood smoke and the long-savoured bottle of brandy helped create an atmosphere of celebration and new beginnings.

From there on their route was to get progressively rougher. The valley of Wild Dog Creek, chiselled deeply between the broken wall of the Humboldt Mountains and the tussocked slopes of the Serpentine Range, was overgrown with thick scrub, which camouflaged a treacherous jumble of loosely stacked boulders. Swags and protruding tools snagged in the tangle of silver-leafed tree daisies, coprosmas and alpine Veronicas and feet punched deep holes through the densely woven undergrowth. It was on days like this, another explorer commented, that the most vigorous additions to Shakespeare's tongue were made.

The country ahead was by no means unknown. Scores of secretive prospectors had constantly combed the ranges and Barrington's party would often come across abandoned tools, remains of camp fires and makeshift shelters.

One of the more mysterious characters in this area was a man named McGuirk, better known as Maori Hen, who had the reputation of being a knowledgeable bushman. Every few months he would appear in town to sell a bagful of gold of a kind unknown in the district. Then he would buy his provisions, some gunpowder and lead shot and plenty of tobacco, and disappear again into the mountains where he lived the life of a hermit.

His gold puzzled the diggers and slyly they would try to follow him but he always managed to shake them off. So when Maori Hen unexpectedly stumbled across Barrington's party camped at the head of Wild Dog Creek, they took it for a good omen. Perhaps they were approaching his secret lode.

Together they travelled up the creek and over the North Col, a wide u-shaped dent in the skyline which, even at the height of summer, often remains under snow. A violent storm delayed them for a day and the fresh snowdrift was so deep, at times their trail resembled a trench.

They descended towards Hidden Falls Creek through the tussock fields banded with crumbling bluffs, which sent melt-water streams cascading down in a series of waterfalls. After a few hair-raising moments, his fists clenched white on bunches of short slippery snow grass, Barrington solemnly promised never to go this way again. Little did he suspect that in the following months he would cross the North Col seven times, often alone, at times in much more treacherous circumstances.

They followed Hidden Falls Creek and crossed the meadows of

Cow Saddle into the headwaters of the Olivine River. It was raining heavily on New Year's Day as they sidled along the Bryneira Range and began a steep descent from the Alabaster Pass. The next day they reached Lake Alabaster.

The lake, five kilometres long and a kilometre wide, is formed where the meandering Pyke River spills into an elongated depression between the Skippers and Bryneira ranges before joining the mighty Hollyford.

Christopher Columbus was still a scampish corsair roaming the Mediterranean in the services of René d'Anjou when Lake Alabaster was already a well-established stopover point along the old greenstone trail from Te Wahipounamu (the West Coast) to Wakatipu and Southland. The Maori inhabitants of the coastal settlements of Kotuku (today's Martin's Bay) and Awarua named it Wawahi-waka (to split wood for canoes), for to avoid an arduous traverse along the bluffed and thickly forested shores they built their single-hulled waka here and paddled the length of the lake in leisurely fashion.

After several days of rain Pyke River was running high and, unable to cross it on foot, Barrington's party also resolved to build a canoe. They felled a large kahikatea tree and with only one axe among them shaped it into a crude dug-out. They called her the *Maori Hen* and to reach a smoother stretch of the river one-and-a-half kilometres upstream, they towed the unwieldy craft through the rapids, up to their waists in the water. At night, lightning split the sky and a thunderstorm unrolled across the lake.

• • •

Barrington returned to Queenstown three times to replenish supplies while his mates prospected the country around Lake Alabaster. The first time he was delayed for a month by snowstorms, gale-force winds and an attack of dysentery. Back in the camp he found Edward Dunmore near death from starvation. He hadn't eaten for twelve days and for the previous seven he had rationed the last half kilogram of oatmeal. When all the food was gone, his fellow-sufferer, Maori Hen, tried to reach Arrowtown, but was said to have perished on the way.

• • •

On 9 March 1864 Barrington was again at the Lake Alabaster camp, this time accompanied by Welshman James Farrell and a French vagabond, Antoine Simonin. In the shanties of Wakatipu, William Bayliss had drunk himself out of the partnership and after one narrow escape, Edward Dunmore seriously decided he had had enough of the country. For several days the party camped by the lake resting, hunting and mending their clothes. Then, in the early morning of 15 March they shouldered their heavy swags and struck north along the Pyke River, weaving their way through a thicket of beech saplings. Over the next three months the newly-formed coterie was to be most severely tested.

Before entering Lake Alabaster, the Pyke River winds through a wide, steep-sided valley of dense bush and scrub patched with pale-green clearings and black, oily swamps. Cabbage trees, like feather dusters, dot the river flats and three-metre-tall tufts of flax sprout woody stalks of scarlet flowers. No longer did Barrington's party come across any vestiges of earlier visitors. Every day the country grew wilder and more remote.

It was a hard land to live off and as their supplies of flour and oatmeal were dwindling fast, in desperation they ate almost anything they could catch, shoot or gather. Weka, a robust flightless rail the size of a chicken, with rich brown-black plumage, strong legs and the neck of a heavy-weight boxer, was their staple diet. Kakapo were an easy prey for their dog and they shot eels, kaka, robins, wrens, an occasional white heron, even a hawk, which Barrington described as 'fearfully tough eating'.

In the mid-1800s, shooting was still something of a ritual requiring a great deal of patience on behalf of both the hunter and the hunted. Into the muzzle of a shotgun black powder was measured out from a powder flask and wadded with a rammer. An ounce of lead shot was then poured in, followed by another greased wad to prevent the lead from spilling out. The hammer was pulled back and a percussion cap placed on a nipple. The shotgun was thus ready to fire as long as the powder and the percussion cap were dry, a tough proposition in the West Coast rainforest.

To keep away moisture, the caps were carried in a waterproof tin and mixed with sawdust, which also cushioned them against excessive shocks and accidental detonation. Only after spotting a potential quarry would the hunter arm the shotgun with a dry percussion cap fished out of the tin (where he would also keep a small feather for cleaning the nipple). With such an elaborate procedure it is a mystery how they managed to shoot anything at all.

To supplement the erratic meat diet they also gathered anise (a plant of the carrot family), spear-grass, fern roots and wineberry (makomako), but on the whole — à la Christopher McCandless of 'Into the Wild' infamy — their knowledge of edible plants was poor.

On one occasion Simonin picked a handkerchief full of purple tutu berries, mashed them and squeezed out a pint of sweet juice, which they all enjoyed immensely. The leftover pulp with the seeds was thrown away on the beach and eaten by the ever-hungry dog. An hour later the poor beast, toughened to eat almost anything even remotely digestible, collapsed in a paroxysm of violent convulsions and to save his life the men poured billyfuls of salted water down his throat. Luckily for them all the dog survived, but they learnt just how toxic the seeds of the tutu berries can be.

The dog's primary role was to hunt and fetch flightless birds. At a time of food crisis, however, he would turn traitor, devour a bird in the bush and return to the camp with splotches of fresh blood and telltale feathers around his muzzle. Then he would not hunt any more and for the lack of anything to shoot they would go hungry for days.

After a week of rough, wet travel cutting their way through the forest barbed with thorny bush lawyer and tangled with the black, wiry vines of supplejack they reached the shore of Lake Wilmot, where a flock of white herons was feeding at the mouth of the river.

They continued north, prospecting as they went along and crossing the Pyke where it veers off eastwards towards the Main Divide. Sidling north-east, then following Gorge River to its headwaters, they climbed over a high saddle and dropped sharply down into the Cascade Valley. Here at last, on the fine-gravel beaches, littered with quartz boulders and sequined with mica crystals, there was enough gold to justify a week-long trial. They set up a camp and planned a roster of hunting and prospecting duties. These plans, however, were soon to be drastically altered.

The weather was getting progressively worse and the rivers, rising rapidly after days of rain, made prospecting impossible. Recalling yet another swift evacuation of the tent threatened by flooding, Barrington wrote: 'A creek, where last night there was only a few inches of water trickling through the boulders, this morning was a large foaming river running at twenty knots and with enough water to launch a good-sized schooner.'

The calendar was well into April now and when it didn't rain, mornings saw the river flats whitened with hoarfrost. With the perpetual dampness, their clothes and blankets were also beginning to rot. The daylight waned and the snow which fell on the mountains did not melt any more. The air smelled of winter.

The previous winter of 1863 had been particularly severe, one of the harshest in recorded history. Many of the diggers living in makeshift shelters and tents died of cold and hunger or perished in blizzards. One survivor related: '... boots and clothes were frozen like boards in the night-time and in the morning they had to be taken under the blankets and thawed.' Firewood was so scarce that after a billy was boiled, the charred sticks were put out and saved.

Spending a similar winter in the remote mountains was a frightening prospect. Almost all of Barrington's provisions were gone now, the game was sparser than ever and floods soon rendered any further prospecting impossible. Sitting under the dripping tent, the party finally made a decision to turn back, but the choice of the route almost split them into two factions. Barrington suggested going east towards Lake Hawea, a distance, he thought, of only 50 kilometres. The others opted for a beeline route back to Lake Wakatipu.

'I should go alone then,' said Barrington and later he would be sorry that he hadn't. Confining his sullenness to pages of his diary, he wrote: 'If I had a dog nothing should have prevented me from going alone, as I know it cannot be a worse road than we have had coming here.' On 29 April they cached their mining tools and headed south.

Since leaving Lake Alabaster over a month earlier and following the Pyke and Gorge rivers, they had travelled along the arch of an imaginary longbow. Now, out of hunger and despair, they cut along its string. From every saddle and mountaintop they longed to see an easy passage to Lake Wakatipu, but all they found were more mountains and glaciers barring their way. Their shortcut route would take them through some of the roughest and most remote alpine terrain in New Zealand.

• • •

On the third day of hard travelling through the gorged terraces of the Cascade River they climbed the 50-metre-high Durwards Falls and reached the slopes of Red Hills, a 60-kilometre range of barren rock, which in the delicate evening light often wears the fleeting blush of an Australian desert. Dominated by the bulk of Red Mountain (1704 metres high), the Red Hills are almost devoid of vegetation, for the ultramafic soils contain so much iron and magnesium they are poisonous to the majority of plants. Only a few species of *Dracophyllum*, stunted rata and kamahi have adapted to living in this sterile environment, their branches forming an intertwined thicket known as 'serpentine scrub'.

Here, in heavy rain, Barrington was separated from his companions. Thinking they had got ahead, he hurried up the river cooeeing and firing his gun, but there was no reply. He spent a cold and hungry night, walked all the following day and set up a lonely camp just below the bush line at the head of Pyke River. More clouds crept in from the west and the sky burst open. Torrential rain turned into wet snow, which froze as it fell. It rained and snowed continuously for nine days.

Wrapped in a half-frozen blanket, his teeth chattering, his limbs stiffened by cramps, Barrington thought of Edward Dunmore, Maori Hen and of his own strength dwindling from inactivity and lack of food. Days of torpor, freezing and sleepless nights blurred as the rain and snow persisted. Rats had stolen a little duck he'd shot on the way up. He had not eaten for six days, but now no longer felt the hunger. The pall of snow which silenced his tent was three-quarters of a metre thick.

At last the sun burnt through the clouds and in the early morning of 14 May, ten days after he had lost Farrell and Simonin, Barrington set off towards Stag Pass, a broad high-alpine saddle leading into the watershed of the Barrier River. He staggered through the deepening snow, collapsing every twenty steps, crawling, resting then getting up again. By noon he was only two kilometres above his camp. Through the overwhelming weakness he felt approaching death.

In desperation he threw away all his waterlogged belongings keeping only a blanket, gun, some powder and lead shot. A small leather pouch, where he kept a few specs of gold, fell at his feet, but he did not pick it up. After a few more hours of wading through the soft, blinding snow he finally reached the pass and looked down into the Barrier valley. He saw a grassy flat and a wispy ribbon of smoke. He had found his companions.

Barrington stayed by the fire while Farrell and Simonin, who also hadn't eaten for a day or two, went hunting and shot a pair of wekas. Two wet and hungry days later, walking up the South Branch of Barrier River they shot two magpies and ate them raw.

Climbing towards Intervention Saddle they were now on the fringe of the Olivine Ice Plateau, a large and isolated pocket of ice from which numerous glaciers ooze through the palisade of shark-tooth mountains. Today it is unthinkable to venture there without a full array of mountaineering equipment: ropes, crampons and ice axes. Barrington and his compadres had nothing but their guns, knives and a tomahawk.

That night, camped on the flats of the Forgotten River, he recalled the events of the day on the glacier: 'What a sight met our eyes. Nothing but mountains of snow and ice as far as we could see, in all directions but west. At one time Simonin was behind me; I heard him sing 'Look out'; I turned round and he was coming down the snow at a fearful rate, head first, on his back. He held the gun in one hand but had to let it go, when both he and the gun passed me at the rate of a swallow, and did not stop till they reached a little flat about two miles down, with a fall of 1000 feet. I thought he was killed, but he was all right, only a little frightened. Such a day I hope never to see again.'

Stinging sleet whipped them in the days that followed and on long fireless nights the snow around the camp lay half a metre deep. On 21 May they entered the Olivine River Gorge.

The descent through the gorge was slow and perilous. At one time Farrell volunteered to be lowered down on a rocky ledge to pass the swags across. He was about halfway down when the flax rope broke and he plummeted into a whirlpool of white water, narrowly missing a 60-metre drop. The rapids engulfed him for over a minute; Barrington and Simonin could do nothing but watch. Gasping for air, Farrell seized a handhold and clambered onto a boulder. At night they camped on bare rocks beside the river. Four days later they reached the old camp at Lake Alabaster.

Torrential rain set in and once again they were trapped in the tent. The lake level began to rise and they found themselves camped on a rapidly shrinking island. Barrington wrote: 'This is the most miserable day of my existence. We had to turn out last night at 10 o'clock, the water rose so fast we could not get anything away but our blankets. The night was very dark and before we reached the hill, a quarter of a mile distant, I got up to my arms in the water. Had to walk up and down all night, rain still pouring. If this night does not kill us we shall never die.'

When the rain stopped they managed to light a fire. Farrell shot a duck and a kaka and they boiled them with some fern roots; it was the first meal they had had for four days. The following morning Barrington found a dead rat and cooked it whole. After a breakfast of 'the sweetest meat we ever ate', they set out for the final push over the North Col.

On 7 June, they were crossing the Main Divide, plodding in deep, soft snow, changing the lead every ten metres. A day later in swirling blizzard they reached the bush line on the eastern side, where Farrell shot seven kaka and thus saved the life of the dog, who was to have featured on that night's menu. Two days later they heard the swish of kereru (native wood pigeon) wings and the echoing gaboong of a shotgun.

• • •

Captain Elchold reached for his tobacco pouch and the men lit their pipes, but the smoke they had longed for so much made them sick. Their stomachs would not accept any food. 'No one would believe the human frame could be so reduced,' lamented a witness at William Rees's station. 'Their cheek bones and noses, besides the elbows, hips and other bony parts of the body, were protruding through the skin.' Their feet were chafed and frostbitten, covered with running sores and 'all the flesh was eaten from the tops of Barrington's toes'.

Lake Wakatipu was smooth like a sheet of glass when the steamer *Alexandra* reached Queenstown after a four-hour crossing. Barrington and his companions were led ashore and taken to the newly built Frankton Public Hospital, where during the following weeks Dr James Douglas nurtured them back to health. From the hospital windows they could see the bustling town, which only two years earlier had not even existed.

In early 1863, the cluster of wooden and calico buildings which had mushroomed after the discovery of gold in the Shotover River and were known as The Camp, took on the name Queenstown. In June that year a gale flattened every canvas structure in town and a month later, when after a sudden flood the Shotover rose some ten metres through the gorge, an unknown number of miners were drowned and hundreds of tents floated downstream. But although lives were easily lost here, promises of quick fortunes outweighed the dangers. Before 1864 was over, the district had a population of 20,000.

At 8 p.m. on 20 July 1864, a large crowd gathered at Bracken's Commercial Hall on Ballarat Street. The hall was lit with kerosene lanterns and the air was thick with pipe smoke. Outside a winter breeze corrugated the lake and beyond it the stark wall of the Remarkables glittered under snow.

A year earlier Barrington would have been in a similar crowd cheering James Hector and his idea for the Hollyford valley road to the West Coast. Now the limelight was all on him and the rowdy audience was eager to hear first-hand the account of his journey. The rumours of gold in the Cascade River had spread like bushfire.

He wore a digger's Sunday's best: a grey Crimean shirt, white or cream moleskin trousers, knee-high Wellington boots and perhaps a crimson sash tied at the side. His diary, which miraculously survived in the folds of a blanket, had just been printed in the Lake Wakatipu Mail and he enjoyed a moderate popularity. There were, however, many questions surrounding the discovery of the new goldfields. There were also allegations suggesting the entire story had been fabricated in a drinking establishment at the head of the lake.

The main problem was Barrington had nothing to prove the existence of gold. He recalled his struggle for life on the snow slopes of Stag Pass, how the pouch containing all the gold specimen slipped out when he was emptying his swag and how he was too exhausted to pick it up. In the groggy cosiness of the hotel, such a scenario stirred up a wave of sarcastic smiles and malicious comments.

Then to everybody's surprise Antoine Simonin produced a coarse speck of gold, which, he explained, he had only recently found in his shot-belt. The specimen came from the Cascade River.

'Hear, hear,' the diggers cheered. A piece of 'real' dispersed all doubt. With the fervour of men in the grip of the gold fever they were ready to follow Barrington into the Cascade. He would be only too pleased to lead them.

But for all the gold in New Zealand he would not go back overland. His plan was to charter a ship and with twelve months' provisions sail to the mouth of the Arawata River. From there they would travel on foot to the river where their mining tools had been cached. Miners applauded with cheers and the preparations began at once. About a month later a flotilla of two cutters, a brig and a schooner left Port Chalmers near Dunedin and sailed south.

A sea journey along a storm-battered coastline is not a safer way to travel at the best of times. In fact, within five months of Barrington's voyage to the promised Cascade gold fields in August 1864, three of the four ships would have foundered. In early February the following year, the brig *Thames*, sailing from Marlborough and down the North Canterbury coast was totally wrecked near Saltwater Creek. A few weeks later, one of the cutters, *Nuggett*, dragged her anchor on the incoming tide and drifted over the Grey River sandbar; her seams opened and she sank fast. And a month later, the other cutter, *Petrel*, was on her way from Raglan to Manukau when she sprang a leak, forcing her captain to run her ashore.

For now though the sea was kind and the weather fair. Barrington's flotilla crossed Foveaux Strait, rounded Puysegur Point at the entrance to Preservation Inlet, skimmed past the narrow openings of the fiords and landed at the mouth of the Arawata River. From here, bending under heavy loads of provisions and mining tools, a snaking procession of prospectors headed south-west towards where the Cascade River cuts between the Red Hills and the northern Olivine Range. There, as Barrington had assured them, was the finest gold-bearing country he had seen in New Zealand.

• • •

Three days before Christmas 1864, both the *Nugget* and the *Petrel* groped their way through the shifting sandbar of the Hokitika harbour and landed a party of 38 embittered miners. The Cascade gold was a myth, 'a duffer rush', they said. For three months they had prospected up to 60 kilometres inland from Jacksons Bay and had not even seen the colour of gold. In their opinion it was not at all likely any weight was ever to be found there, they were led astray and Barrington was a liar. The *Thames* was still in Jacksons Bay, but nearly the whole prospecting party had left.

The man who had caused all this hubbub was also aboard the *Nugget*, but he said little. One time a famed prospector and explorer, now a hoaxer and outcast, he stepped ashore and vanished. This is the last time we hear of Alphonse Barrington.

Failing to fulfil the promise of opening the Cascade gold fields, Barrington and his companions lost all their credibility and their story was largely disbelieved. Did they really find payable deposits of gold or was it just a bluff to attract short-lived attention and perhaps rewards? We'll never know. Towards the turning point of the journey, when they claimed to have found gold, Barrington seemed severely disorientated and his topographical references are not reliable.

No one has ever found enough gold in the Cascade to justify an expensive mining operation in such remote and austere country. Many came looking, clawing the land with picks and shovels, upturning river boulders, sifting and panning through the mountains of glacial gravel. Among them were Andy Williamson, a Martins Bay pioneer and the legendary Arawata Bill. However, the stories of the Shotover or Dunstan rushes were not to be repeated here. So far Barrington's gold has remained a myth.

The Olivines and the neighbouring ranges of 'Barrington country' resisted any form of human conquest and development. No road cuts through it, no settlement has ever been permanent. It has become the epitome of the New Zealand wilderness — inaccessible, desolate, stark and self-contained.

More than just a record of another failed prospecting venture, the odyssey of Alphonse Barrington has, however, become an extraordinary account of human determination and survival against all odds. His journey, reckless and ill-prepared as it was, has inspired generations of mountain explorers and evoked a lasting respect for South Westland.

'I do not like to set any bounds to the limit of human endurance,' wrote Ernest Shackleton, whose epic open-boat journey across the 1500 miles of the Southern Ocean and the traverse of the unknown, glaciated interior of South Georgia has earned him the status of one of the most heroic explorers of our times.

Barrington and his companions were neither die-hard explorers nor experienced bushmen but, rather, ordinary diggers who unexpectedly found themselves in a wilderness that took them to the extremes of physical and mental endurance. That they lived to tell their story is mostly due to the remarkable powers of survival we all have within us, the powers sometimes dormant, sometimes subdued, but always ours when in need.

As Denis Glover wrote in his famous poem:

'You should have been told
Only in you was the gold.'

A fitting epitaph for an accidental hero, Alphonse Barrington.

Flower of the Sky

'The sandstorm hit over the Syrian desert . . . tossing the biplane about as if it was a feather. Suddenly it rolled her upwards and the machine stalled. Then it plunged down in a dizzying spin.'

In her heyday she was a star of the highest magnitude, more celebrated than the latter-day astronauts who walked on the moon. For her pioneering transcontinental solo flights, she was fêted, desired and worshipped; she was the Garbo of the Skies. Then, as suddenly as she appeared, she vanished; her meteoric rise to fame leaving almost no afterimage. Today, in the pantheon of New Zealand's national heroes, Jean Batten remains the most brilliant, mysterious and tragic figure.

● ● ●

The first sandstorm hit over the Syrian desert, catching and wrenching the wings of the tiny pale-blue Gipsy Moth, tossing the biplane about as if it was a feather. In the open cockpit, the young woman braced and cringed as the sand blasted into her face, chafing and stinging her skin. Brass-frame goggles protected her eyes but once she hit the wall of swirling sand she was flying blind, her simple compass and the even more basic altimeter her only guidance. She wrestled with the stick and the pedals to maintain control but the wind was too strong. Suddenly it rolled her upwards and the machine stalled. Then it plunged down in a dizzying spin.

With remarkable presence of mind, she recovered from the stall with only moments to spare. But this was neither the time nor place for aerobatics, she would have thought. Far too much was at stake. Her whole life, her future, everything. When the wind lulled briefly, she rough-landed the Moth in the desert sand, just in time. Moments later, another wave of the storm hit with full force and, with a coat over her head, she hung on for dear life to the Moth's struts and wires.

When the storm passed she took off again, only to realise that the day — the third one of her marathon flight — was already gone. It was too late and too dangerous to press on to the Baghdad aerodrome, she decided. With the engine switched off to minimise the risk of fire, she rough-landed again this time in the moonlight, her runway a camel caravan trail in the sand. She pegged the Moth out, anchoring the wings against the wind, covered the cockpit and plugged up the exhaust pipes. She pulled out a spanner from her toolbox, and with it she bashed open a tin of pineapple. She ate the fruit with some chocolate biscuits then, despite the frost, fell into an uneasy sleep next to the fuselage.

She woke up in broad daylight, surrounded by a group of desert Arabs. They seemed to be looking for the pilot. Allahu akbar, God is great, but surely He would not make a woman fly this thing ... They were in for a shock. Having distracted them with biscuits and cigarettes, the young woman woke the engine to life with a hefty swing on the propeller, and within moments the Moth was airborne and heading for Baghdad. An hour later she was devouring bacon and eggs in the RAF officers' mess. Then she was in the air again, pushing on, heading east: time was precious.

This flight was beginning to capture the headlines, though so far largely because of its eerie timing. It was April 1933. Only three years earlier a Yorkshire clerk, Amy Johnson, had flown solo from England to Darwin, northern Australia, in nineteen and a half days, and when she returned home, one million people turned up to welcome her at Croydon. This was the era of the great solo flights when a new record could get you a £10,000 reward and a knighthood. Little wonder that there were usually several stunt pilots attempting to break new records at any one time.

As the young woman sped east, she was just a day behind Italian captain Leonida Robbiano, who was also attempting to fly from England to Australia. But within hours of taking off Robbiano was dead, having plunged into the Bay of Bengal. At the same time, Bill Lancaster, a RAF pilot attempting a flight to South Africa, was lost over the Sahara, and the body of Australian aviation legend Bert Hinkler still lay undiscovered in the Apennine Mountains in Italy, where he had crashed his Puss Moth three months earlier, en route from Australia to England. Suddenly, 23-year-old New Zealander Jean Batten, pretty and immaculate in her white flying suit and perfect makeup, like an actress who had just stepped off the set of an aviation adventure movie, was the only one still flying. She was the newcomer outlasting all the pros, unwavering on her course to break the England-to-Australia record.

But it was not to be. Just short of Karachi, she was overtaken by another storm; a wall of sand engulfed and carried her along at terrifying speed, like 'a scrap of paper in the wind'. She knew she had to force-land or she would die. She turned into the wind and plopped the Moth down, in a manoeuvre known as a pancake landing. The ground, alas, was more sodden than it looked, and the aircraft sank into it heavily.

With the help of villagers who had gathered around at the sight of an aircraft falling from the sky, Jean managed to extract the Moth and put it on dry ground, only to realise that her propeller had fractured. In a despair-fuelled, two-day-long spurt of travelling by horse, camel and truck, she brought a spare propeller from Karachi back to the plane, fitted it by torchlight and took off in the first light of the following day. Her spirits rose again, but not for long.

She was just approaching the Karachi aerodrome when fate dealt her the final blow. 'There suddenly came from the engine a noise that seemed to freeze my blood,' she later wrote. 'A sharp report like a clap of thunder, followed by the sound of tearing, rending, splintering metal.' A con-rod had snapped in half and shot through the crankcase. The engine in Jean's old Moth was finished.

She crash-landed short of the aerodrome, somersaulting the Moth. Though she escaped unharmed, the aircraft was a complete write-off. Her dream, her life, her future lay there in a tangled heap. All she had owned had gone into this flight, and now she was broke. It was enough to make anyone give up. But not Jean; she was well accustomed, and somewhat immune, to such hardships and setbacks. The press were soon to nickname her the 'Try Again Girl'.

• • •

Jean Batten was born on 15 September 1909 in Rotorua, to the sound of her father Fred's musical trio rehearsing their pieces in the room next door. As the labour began, Fred enquired if they should stop playing, but Ellen — Jean's mother — found the music soothing. And so the band played on.

Fred was a dentist, and Ellen, who had already given birth to three boys (one of whom died in infancy), filled the role of the housewife, and although she filled it well, she also found it a little stifling. An art teacher and actress, with a strong domineering personality, Ellen played piano and a guitar, studied nutrition, ran roller-skating competitions, won flower shows and captained the rowing club. She was a geyser of vitality and the world around her — the provincial town of Rotorua — seemed too frustratingly small to express it. With the bright light of hindsight we can now see that she must have longed for a bigger world and higher society. And Jean would be her ticket into it.

Despite her parents' robustness — Ellen was a veritable iron lady, Fred a noted amateur boxer and rugby player — Jean was a frail child, overprotected by the family. Ellen, who had an old-wives' remedy for every occasion — hot potato for earache, mustard footbaths for colds — instilled in her daughter beliefs that 'a clean healthy mind meant a clean healthy body' and that 'there were few ailments that could not be cured or avoided by adequate fresh air, fresh food and fresh water, coupled with exercise'. Indeed, following this maxim, with the ritual of daily swims and long walks, both women were to live in untroubled health into old age.

The first four years of Jean's life seemed happy but the idyll came to an abrupt end. They moved to Auckland, and then came the war. Fred volunteered to join the army and sailed away for Europe. In the Battens' family life this was the beginning of a rift that would grow ever wider. Soon, with three kids to bring up on her own, Ellen was in financial trouble. The family moved from one rented house to another, establishing a nomadic pattern that would characterise the rest of Jean's life. But Ellen was a resourceful woman and survive they did, the hardships only strengthening the inseparable bond that was forming between Ellen and Jean in the absence of her father.

It was about that time that Jean first saw an aeroplane, at the flying school at Kohimarama in the Auckland harbour. 'The little seaplane would skim across the water throwing up a curtain of spray and rise like a seabird up into the blue sky,' she later wrote in her characteristically ornamented prose. 'At such moments as I watched spellbound and the plane turned to fly back and circle the bay with the sunlight glistening on its silver wings, I experienced such a surge of exhilaration that I felt quite sick with longing to be up there in it.'

Shortly after Fred's return from the war, the family fell apart, though appearances were kept up as if nothing had ever happened. Meanwhile, Ellen's domination of Jean's life was almost complete. From now on, she would live her own unfulfilled dreams through her daughter: it was Ellen who had taken her to see the seaplanes, and Ellen who had reportedly pinned the newspaper cutting of Blériot and his Model X monoplane above baby Jean's cot. (On 25 July 1909, six weeks before Jean's birth, Louis Blériot was the first person to fly across the English Channel.)

Slowly, during Jean's teenage years in Auckland, while she attended ballet and piano lessons, and the exclusive Ladies' College in Remuera, a plan was hatched by the mother-daughter team.

The plan turned into a conspiracy because Fred, who paid for their maintenance, when probed by Jean, categorically refused to support it. Officially, the plan was that Jean would sell her piano and, accompanied by Ellen, sail to London where she would continue to study music. In reality, once in London in early 1930, the two conspirators headed not for the Royal College of Music but the Stag Lane aerodrome, a paddock at the end of Edgware Road, next to the factory where British aircraft designer and amateur entomologist Geoffrey de Havilland was perfecting his line of Moths. The music that an unsuspecting Fred was to pay for was not Chopin's sonatas but the wind-in-the-wires song of an open-cockpit Gipsy Moth.

It was a cunning plan. Like a best-selling book or a movie deal today, in the 1930s flying was a laissez-passer to the world of the rich and famous, a shortcut out of poverty and into the echelons of the glitterati. In May 1927, it took Charles Lindbergh 33½ hours to fly from New York to Paris and into instant fame and wealth. A year later, Charles Kingsford-Smith, with a crew, flew across the Pacific to a similarly happy landing. Flying was the in thing, the pastime of the wealthy, the dream of the masses. For Ellen and Jean the only hurdle was that while they could live on £3 a week, one flying lesson cost £2. But again, as in the war years, they scraped through. On 5 December 1930, Jean Batten qualified as a private pilot.

Contrary to her own touched-up recollections, she was a slow learner and not a natural flier. Fellow students recalled how once she overshot her landing, flopping the Moth over after hitting a wire fence, and how devastated and depressed she was after the incident. But her perseverance made an impact. Her instructor, Major Herbert Travers, the same man who trained Amy Johnson, was later quoted as saying, 'She's got the dream of the century. She'll open up the air routes.'

By then, Jean was totally obsessed with flying and their secret was out. When she and Ellen visited New Zealand in 1931, Fred — ever concerned for the safety of his now-unstoppable daughter — financed her navigation course at the Auckland Aero Club. Back in London, she went on to study for her professional pilot's licence, which she thought would increase her chances of attracting sponsors for the long-distance flights she had already planned. Apart from working with the mechanics on aircraft and engine maintenance, and furthering her navigation and cross-country skills, she needed a total of 100 hours of flying time, which for someone with no real income would have been a gruelling financial ordeal. But Jean still had an unused trump card and now she brought it into play.

By all accounts, she was a knock-out girl, but so unresponsive to all overtures that the men at Stag Lane thought she was a lesbian. She was not. As it soon bcame clear, her single-minded obsessive drive for success in aviation left no room for romance ... unless the latter served to further the former. Soon, she was to be breaking not only flight records but the hearts of pilots as well.

In Jean's private life there followed a series of calculated romantic engagements. First, there was New Zealander Fred Truman, at the time a RAF pilot in India, who was so head-over-heels in love with Jean he gave his £500 gratuity — his entire life savings — to finance her flying. They studied together (he for his civilian licence) and Fred passed many of his RAF tricks-of-the-trade on to Jean. She got her professional licence in December 1932.

Then it was Victor Dorée, son of a wealthy linen merchant who, when Jean could no longer afford the aero-club subscription, generously paid for that, then promptly gave her his own Gipsy Moth to use in training, fuel and all. It was also Victor Dorée's money — borrowed from his mother — which bought the Gipsy Moth DH60 M (registration G-AALG) that Jean used on her first attempt to fly to Australia. Dorée sponsored the flight, and they were to share the profits: publicity, royalties, grants and endorsements. But, as Jean wrote the Moth off near Karachi, there were no proceeds, only debt, and so the deal turned sour, and so, as Jean saw it, did the relationship.

For a while Jean was down and out, broke and in debt, living with Ellen in a tiny Stag Lane room through a miserable London winter in which, as she wrote, 'there had been times when we had to call a cup of tea a dinner and ... unable to buy coal, would go for a sharp walk and retire to bed early to keep warm'. These were tough and seemingly hopeless times, but she never gave up her dreams of a record flight to Australia. 'Once my mind was set on something,' she wrote, 'it was quite useless to attempt to swerve me from my purpose.' It took her a year to get back her wings, to gather herself for another attempt.

Through her friendship with de Havilland, she secured a partial sponsorship from Lord Wakefield, the owner of Castrol Oil, who could see a potential rising star and the advertising opportunities she offered. Thus Jean was able to buy a fifth-hand Moth for £260 (a new one cost £700) and set about organising her second attempt. By this time, another knight-saviour appeared, a London stockbroker, Edward Walter. They were engaged within weeks.

Jean had the Moth fitted with long-range fuel tanks and a secret built-in trap-door toilet, designed by de Havilland himself. Her route was plotted out meticulously and to the last detail: 25 legs, thirteen countries, 10,800 miles to Darwin, another 2000 to Sydney, as well as daylight hours for each day, a schedule of routine engine checks, fuel usage, distances between refuellings, and each airstrip's surface type. It was a masterpiece of planning. There was only one thing she did not allow for: human error — the error of her own judgement.

The 'Try Again Girl' took off on 21 April 1934 without press fanfares. When she landed in Marseilles to refuel it was raining heavily and the airport authorities warned her that the worst of the weather was still to come. But she ignored them — she was a girl on a mission. The French officials were so adamant they refused to help her start the engine (the Moth did not have a starter, it was customary for an assistant to swing the propeller on the pilot's command of 'Contact'), then they formally forbade her to take off unless she signed an indemnity that she accepted full responsibility for the consequences. She signed it. Then she climbed back into the cockpit and took off into a storm of biblical proportions.

To fully appreciate her decision, you need to know something about flying a Moth. 'It's more akin to sailing,' Nancy Bird Walton, the first lady of Australian aviation and Jean's contemporary and acquaintance described it. 'The aircraft can cruise at 80 mph. With a strong tailwind, you can fly at a 100, but if the same wind is against you, your ground speed can drop to 15 mph. You can just about run faster than that.' (Modern-day enthusiasts joke that, watched from the ground while flying into a strong headwind, the Moth gives the impression of slowly moving backwards.)

The Moth — first the Gipsy and later the Tiger — was the most popular trainer aircraft of its era, because it was difficult to fly and seemed to magnify any piloting errors. 'The Moth is extremely rudimentary, it's a stick and rudder active kind of flying all the way,' Bird Walton told me. 'You can't take your hands off the stick or the aircraft will spin, roll or dive. It keeps you sharp and honest. The idea behind using it as a trainer was that if you could fly a Moth, you could fly just about anything else.'

Nowadays most flying takes place at altitudes from where the world is but a map, Bird Walton said, but in the days of the Moths, aviation was an adventure, a 3D out-there experience with all its associated sounds, smells, sights and uncertainties. There was never a dull moment with these aircraft, she added, which is why, for the times when things would get out of control, her instructor Kingsford-Smith taught her some practical skills. 'In emergency landings, we were to always head for the trees, and aim the plane between the trunks,' she said. 'The impact of breaking the wings off would make you slow down.'

When Jean took off into the storm, at 3 p.m., her fuel tanks were not full. She had filled them up for a seven-hour flight only — enough to get her to Rome, five and a half hours away — calculating that the fully-laden Moth might be too heavy to lift from the waterlogged Marseilles airstrip. Soon after takeoff she realised she was in trouble: thick clouds rolled in and lowered, and she lost visual contact with the ground. Soon she was flying over the Mediterranean, with no visibility and into a stiff headwind which was slowing the Moth down to about 40 mph.

She lost more time navigating her way around Corsica and by now it was getting late in the day. Then it grew dark and, not having found anywhere to land on the mountainous island (which in 1941 was to claim the life of pilot and writer Antoine de Saint-Exupéry), Jean pressed on.

She was now over the sea again, flying in heavy rain, no visibility and into a headwind, aiming for the distant coast she knew she no longer had enough fuel to reach. Her biographer called this flight 'suicidal'. Before long, she was flying on empty tanks and a prayer, and the Italian coast was still not in sight. Then she was undoing her shoelaces and helmet strap, readying for a crash-landing in the sea, pondering her own folly. 'I had made my bed and now must lie in it,' she commented. 'A watery grave was what I deserved.'

Miraculously, the lights of Rome appeared out of the gloom. Against all odds, her navigation had been impeccable. It was almost midnight — nine hours into the flight — when the engine, which had been spluttering for some time, gave out its final cough and died. Coasting now, Jean dodged one high mast, then another. She was over a communication facility of the Italian Navy. On the ground, there were trees and buildings and high-tension wires but, among all that, she crashed with such skill and precision, it was as if she had landed a helicopter.

Jean walked away with only bruises and shock, but the Moth was a mess. The Italians eyed the wreckage, and then, in a gesture of admiration for her verve and courage, proceeded to rebuild it. All Jean had to do was to pay for the parts, and by another stroke of good fortune, in a dusty corner of one of the hangars, she found what she needed most: a pair of lower wings (hers had crumpled on impact). Ten days after the crash she flew back to London in her reconditioned Moth. Take 3 of her attempt was about to begin.

At 5.30 a.m. on 8 May 1934, she took off again from Brooklands aerodrome, back on her original schedule. The weather was fair and by evening she had reached Rome. The days which followed were a blur of places: Athens, Cyprus, Damascus, Baghdad, Karachi, Calcutta, all smooth sailing until she reached Rangoon, ten days into the flight.

Her earlier interlude in Rome, and the resultant delay, was now to prove critical.

She was two weeks late, just in time for a rendezvous she so wished to avoid — a head-on encounter with the monsoon. She wrote: 'I felt uneasy, and looking out of the cockpit saw ahead of the machine a great black mass. It looked like a range of mountains — too wide to go around, too high to fly over and rolling northwards towards me like a great smokescreen obscuring everything in its path. . . . I was strongly tempted to turn back but the thought of failing a third time was too terrible.'

She flew into the storm and it was like going under a waterfall. 'I had . . . flown from day into night,' she wrote. 'Very soon I was drenched to the skin and the cockpit floor was completely flooded.' For 45 minutes she flew by instruments, illuminating them with the light from her small torch; eventually she made it through both this and several more storm cells. Day twelve saw her in Singapore and past the worst of the weather. By then the London newspapers were swarming in on Ellen. The Try Again Girl was only a Timor Sea away from her goal: 500 miles over open water, in a temperamental single-engine plane, with no life jacket or radio.

But then she was there, descending towards the red heat-haze of Australia, spiralling to land in Darwin, just past midday on 23 May. Her time was 14 days 22 hours 30 minutes, the women's solo record, bettering by four days the time of Amy Johnson. Immediately she was off to send a telegram to Ellen: 'Darling, we've done it. The aeroplane, you, me.' The newspapers simply said: JEANIUS. Jean Batten was on top of the world.

• • •

Instantly, it was adieu cold bedsitters and bon jour Ritz, as gifts, endorsements, grants and invitations began to pour in. The wave of adulation and glamour must have surprised even Jean herself. She flew on to Sydney for what turned out to be a four-week-long maelstrom of festivities, then, shipping the Moth with her, went on to New Zealand for another riotous welcome and sell-out lecture tour of the country where she gave over 150 speeches. She was compared to Joan of Arc and Florence Nightingale, she was Britannia herself, Heroine of the Empire. Jean was gutsy, and beautiful, and she arrived on the public scene at precisely the right time — the pits of the

Depression, the eve of the Second World War. The masses needed an escape, a dream, and she lived that dream for them. And so her arrival was as popular as a royal visit.

Jean, for her part, did not take long to adjust to this regal treatment. Then, like a true star, she began to demand it. Suddenly hooked on fame, intoxicated by glamour, she fell into an almost drug-like dependency on the limelight. Those close to her during the publicity tour reported that she was often arrogant and bossy, brusque and uncompromising, a prima donna who forever demanded attention and 'never pulled back her punches'.

In her life, as in her flying, she showed no give, whether to circumstances, obstacles or people. The three men who loved her and who helped her to get in the air, she barely mentioned. Ellen was her only friend, her PR, her chaperone, the only person she needed. The two formed a tight and emotionally self-sufficient unit and they cloaked their private life with impenetrable, almost obsessive secrecy. But then they went back to Australia, where suddenly and for the first time in her life — truly, madly, deeply — Jean fell in love.

His name was Beverley Shepherd, the 23-year-old son of a wealthy Sydney doctor, a handsome and likeable socialite training to be a commercial pilot. In an eye-blink, he melted the ice around Jean's heart and from then on they were constantly together. They sailed the family yacht on Darling Harbour, picnicked in the Blue Mountains, went flying about in their Moths (Beverley had a Puss Moth). There was no doubt they'd marry but, first things first, Jean had a few more ambitions to fulfil. Fame, she quickly realised, was like fireworks — it burned brightly and luxuriantly, but it needed constant reigniting. On 8 April 1935, she reloaded for another salvo. She took off from Sydney, and with Beverley escorting her all the way to Bourke, she began her return flight to England.

She nearly lost her life over the Timor Sea when, halfway between Darwin and Kupang, the Moth's engine conked out and no matter what she did it refused to restart. Jean was at 6000 feet when she began the agonising glide down towards the sea. 'I experienced a feeling of complete detachment,' she wrote later, 'as if I were an onlooker, not the central figure in the drama.' Again, as in her Rome misadventure, prayer was her last solution.

'The last few minutes were a torture,' she continued. 'In a final desperate effort, just before attempting to land, I opened and closed the throttle lever once more — but nothing immediately happened.

(Then) . . . a sudden roar broke the silence like a clap of thunder . . . Like a great sob the engine burst into life again.' For a while she was skimming the surface of the sea and then began to climb.

With the engine stuttering she made it safely to Timor where she cleaned up her fuel filters and the carburettor (putting her trouble down to dust in the fuel system). Then she pressed on, but all the way to England the engine continued to misfire, several times cutting out completely. Seventeen days and sixteen hours after leaving Australia, Jean and the Moth made it to Lympne but only just. Her return flight was acknowledged but the reception was modest. Jean knew that if she were to break any future records, she needed a new plane. Now, however, she was a woman of means and fame, the darling of the press and the aristocracy. She fronted RAF recruiting films and the BBC Empire broadcasts. On her twenty-sixth birthday, she took delivery of her dream machine: a Percival Gull Six cabin monoplane, with a six-cylinder 200-hp engine.

The Gull was sleek, fast and, at £2000, very expensive, but it had twice the speed and the range of a Moth, and more than twice its comfort. It allowed flying at 14,000 feet, thus avoiding much of the low-altitude weather, so perilous in a biplane. If a Moth was a Clydesdale, the Gull was a racehorse, and Jean was about to test its endurance limits. Between 11 and 13 November 1935, she blitzed from England to Brazil, crossing the South Atlantic and setting an absolute world record (for a pilot of either sex and any type of aircraft), becoming the first woman to fly from England to South America.

The transatlantic leg of the flight, 1900 miles of open ocean from Thies in Senegal to Natal in Brazil, was also an absolute record (thirteen hours, fifteen minutes) and a display of Jean's supernatural navigation skills. With only a tiny fuel margin, flying by dead-reckoning, without seeing a single landmark, she made a landfall with the precision of a modern 747 with all its computer navigation systems, even though she had to pass through a magnetic aberration near the Equator which had her primitive compass spin around in circles. And, she was the girl who had beaten all the boys — even the French in their four-engine mail plane.

For a while she luxuriated in the hospitality and the adoration of Latino nobility, touring Brazil, Argentina and Uruguay; then she was back in Europe for more of the same, collecting trophies and medals and honorary memberships. But soon Jean grew restless again. The Gull, with its 2000-mile range, made it possible to contemplate her ultimate dream: flying from England to New Zealand, including crossing the Tasman. On 5 October 1936, with a full media farewell, she took off from England for what was to become her signature flight.

She flew like a demon possessed, pushing on day and night. In five days she was to sleep only seven hours. The flight was exhausting but fortuitously uneventful until, over Burma, while battling through a tropical deluge and keeping low to maintain the visuals, she nearly flew straight into a mountainside. At the last moment she executed a stall turn — an acrobatic manoeuvre involving looping the Gull vertically up until it completely runs out of speed, then turning it nose-down and recovering along the same flight path and away from the obstacle.

It took her five days and twenty-one hours to reach Darwin, 24 hours faster than the fastest man. Another two days saw her in Sydney where the media proclaimed her the Empress of the Air. The Australians, it appeared, wanted it all to end there. First, the Civil Aviation authorities tried to stop Jean's trans-Tasman attempt, claiming that the weight of the fuel she needed for the crossing would cause the Gull to exceed its certificate of airworthiness. But Jean produced a special overload permit she had for the Gull and bypassed the red tape. Prominent members of the community appealed to her not to continue, and then, much more bluntly, an Australian media bigfoot, Frank Packer, offered her £5000 *not* to fly the Tasman. In 1936, £5000 would have been and-she-lived-happily-ever-after kind of money. But Jean declined. At 4.30 a.m., on 16 October, she took off along the flare path from the air force base at Richmond, climbed over Sydney, and headed out to sea. The world held its breath and waited.

Nine and a half hours later she sighted land. Though she was plagued by rain storms and doubts — she feared she had missed New Zealand altogether and was heading into the Pacific — her navigation was again like that of a homing pigeon. Over a 1200-mile journey she was barely 100 metres off course. She passed New Plymouth and flew on to the Mangere aerodrome where welcoming crowds swarmed and the traffic was backed up all the way to Auckland's city centre. Today, you'd need to fly to Mars to get such a reception.

This was the crowning moment for Jean Batten, the zenith in the trajectory of her life. She was 27 and, as she herself admitted, she had it all: health, beauty, wealth and fame, and love awaiting her in Australia. A trifle pompously perhaps — but this was Jean through and through — she was soon to plunge into writing an autobiography she called *My Life*. It was sadly prophetic for it was as if, at this still-budding age, her life did suddenly end.

First, she suffered a heart-splitting blow: just as she got to Sydney she received news that the Stinson airliner on which Beverley Shepherd was arriving to meet her had been reported missing. All ensuing search-and-rescue efforts were called off after five days but, in the Gull, Jean kept combing the New South Wales outback for another four. Then the burnt-out wreckage of the Stinson was found by a bushman. Miraculously, there were two survivors, but Beverley wasn't one of them.

Struck with grief, Jean fell into an emotional black hole, but then reached for the only remedy she knew might save her: another flight, another record. Between 19 and 24 October 1937, back in her Gull, she rocketed off to England, flying almost non-stop, taking only five days eighteen hours and fifteen minutes to get there. When she arrived at Croydon, her legs were so cramped up she couldn't walk and had to be carried. Again, she was the girl who had beaten all the men, but it was to be for the last time. Airlines were already flying the transcontinental routes. It was getting harder to make a news-breaking flight, to stay in the headlines. The era of pioneering aviators was over.

Then came the war. Jean offered her piloting skills and the Gull to the RAF, but apparently she failed her medicals due to short-sightedness. The Gull was requisitioned and Jean was wingless. Having clocked some 2600 air-hours to date, she was never to fly again. For a while she worked in an armament factory, then for the war-time propaganda machine. Briefly, she was a star again — lecturing, fund-raising, inspiring — but her flame had gone out and she could no longer rekindle it.

In the decades that followed, she would occasionally resurface in aviation circles, lobbying for the Concorde, visiting New Zealand and Australia on several aviation junkets — but life had lost its meaning for her. There were no more goals, no challenges, no way to stand in the limelight again. She seemed to live only for her past, the past that in the postwar years no one remembered any more. The once supreme navigator had now totally lost her direction.

She still had Ellen, and the bond between them was now stronger than ever. They lazed together in the world's warm climes, living in Jamaica for six years, gypsying around Europe, settling at Costa del

Sol (the Sun Coast) in southern Spain, then moving to the Canary Islands. It was there, on the island of Tenerife, that Ellen passed away, just short of her ninetieth birthday.

For Jean, it was as if a larger part of herself had died. She stayed on in Tenerife for sixteen of perhaps the emptiest and numbest years of her life. Then, searching for a quieter place (the island was becoming a tourist hotspot), she decided to move to the Spanish Mediterranean island of Majorca. There, in 1982, she vanished.

It was only through the detective work of her biographer Ian Mackersey that we know what happened. Mackersey's investigation revealed that Jean had gone to Majorca to buy an apartment in which to live out her years. She was staying in a small hotel and during one of her customary walks she was bitten by a dog. The wound caused an infection which spread into her lungs, causing a pulmonary abscess. But for whatever reason, Jean did not seek medical help.

The hotel maid found her dead in her room on 22 November 1982. As no one knew who she was, her body lay in the morgue unclaimed by neither relatives nor friends for two months before it was buried in a communal grave.

Thus, unwittingly, Jean set another precedent: her falling from the heights of glory to the darkest obscurity must surely rank as something of a world record. Her reprinted memoir is titled *Alone in the Sky*, but it's clear that she also must have been even more alone on the earth.

For the nation that prides itself on understatement, that favours the 'We knocked the bastard off' over 'That's one small step for man . . .', Jean Batten is an uncomfortable heroine to accept, much less to admire. New Zealanders like their folk heroes to pull off the world's firsts but never to brag about it, to quietly build schools or remove eye cataracts in less privileged countries.

Jean Batten is a contradiction to all that, a ruthless femme fatale who would walk over everything and everyone to achieve her goals. But she travelled a hard road, and she paid her dues. For all the glitz and glory, she did not find happiness, and her life was tragic and ultimately unfulfilled. She was the Flower of the Sky that never fully blossomed. Sometimes, a pioneer can show us not only which road to travel, but also which way not to follow.

Spare her a thought next time you are passing through the departure lounge at the Jean Batten International Terminal at Auckland Airport where, under the ceiling of the duty-free shopping centre, her Gull still hangs, like a squat arrow pointing at the waiting 747s. Outside the terminal building, a bronze statue of her greets travellers and visitors as they come and go from the arrival and departure halls. Let your mind wander to the times when flying was an adventure, not a grinding, jet-lag-inducing journey. And, who knows, you may also feel the pangs that made her 'sick with longing to be up there in it'.

FOOTNOTE:

Much of this story is based on material unearthed by film-maker, biographer and pilot Ian Mackersey, author of the definitive work *Jean Batten, the Garbo of the Skies* and a television documentary of the same title. Without Mackersey's painstaking research we would have known little about the fate of the secretive aviatrix.

The Night Belongs to the Kiwi

'There are few things in this world as beautiful as this,' McLennan whispered cradling the kiwi chick in his large hands. 'This is why I walk the forest for months. It is as though you were touching the soul of this land.'

On the edge of a mountain forest, two days' walk from the end of a gravel road, I stood still like a statue, peering into the darkness through a pair of night-vision binoculars. Without them I was blind — even my companion, ecologist John McLennan, seemed just another piece of shrubbery — and my eyes were glued to this electronic peephole and the green fluorescent view it afforded: a shimmering stage set of phantom trees and moths zapping around like kites in a high wind.

Apart from this expensive gadget, McLennan had also brought along something much less high-tech: a plastic shepherd's whistle which he carried around his neck, together with a small compass. Now I watched him fish it out from under his jacket, take a deep breath and put the whistle to his lips. The first couple of calls were misshapen and off-key, but soon he found the tune.

Crrweeee! Crrweeee! Crrweeee! He repeated the call a dozen times.

There was a moment of deep silence, then came an angry reply and the sound of rustling through the undergrowth. Something was rushing towards us, seeking confrontation.

Into my field of view ran the oddest of creatures, a shaggy pear-shaped fur-ball propelled by large T-rex feet, sniffing and snorting like an agitated hound, surprisingly small considering the amount of noise it was trying to make. It stopped to let out another battle cry — a penetrating shrill that made you want to plug up your ears — and froze to listen intently for any intruder.

We held our breaths, desperate to avoid detection and soon, reassured of its dominance, the fur-ball relaxed and resumed feeding. Its beak tapped the way ahead like a blind person's cane, and every few steps it bored in excitedly right up to the hilt in pursuit of a wriggling morsel. Now and then it paused to blow the dirt out of its nostrils, a sharp angry sneeze that further inflated its aura of territorial stroppiness and short-fuse temper. Then, with no more than a rustle of ferns, the bird vanished, though for a brief moment we could still hear it. Tap! Tap! Jab! Snort! went the kiwi, the ghost of the forest.

Here, on this extensive mountain plateau that rises like an island above the coastal forest near the mid-point of the Heaphy Track, in the heart of Kahurangi National Park, the night still belongs to the kiwi. You can hear them calling across the glades: the ululating Crrweeee! of the male and the guttural yodel of his larger partner, both ready to attack anything that blunders into their territory.

'They fight like devils,' McLennan told me. 'Put two estranged kiwi together and soon you may have only one, and a pile of feathers.' Their combat is a furious kick-and-tear kind of karate, with high jumps and lightning-fast blows with their sickle claws, but once their little kingdoms are established the birds usually resolve most territorial disputes through a duel of calls, avoiding border scraps altogether. This leaves more time for feeding, for sniffing out moth larvae from underneath the clumps of tussock, or wrestling with earthworms.

'Some of these worms can resemble a short length of a garden hose, with a diameter to match,' McLennan said. 'They are powerful and reluctant victims and usually escape after a brief struggle. But once the kiwi gets a good grip on one of them, the tug-of-war can last for several minutes. The bird applies a steady strain and waits for the opponent to yield, because yanking it would tear the worm in two and shorten the meal. Some worms phosphoresce brightly as they are withdrawn from the soil and this eerie light can illuminate the kiwi's bill and face.'

Though McLennan had been studying the lives of these nocturnal hunters for the past fifteen years, the most significant revelation of his pioneering work had not been how they fight, eat or sleep, but the simple fact that kiwi are becoming increasingly thin on the ground, trapped in the paradox of their gonzo fame. 'We revere and adore them as emblematic figures in so many everyday guises, while at the same time in the forest, the real birds are experiencing not just a decline but an all-out population collapse,' McLennan said. 'Kiwi have come to suffer from a chronic name and image overuse syndrome, becoming too much of an icon and not enough of a bird. If we don't wake up to this fact soon, within a few decades the icon will be all that's left.'

The kiwi, McLennan fears, the sobriquet for New Zealanders and a loveable forest imp, was about to perform another one of its vanishing tricks, this time never to reappear again.

• • •

Among the ratites, the family of the world's largest birds which includes emu, rhea, ostrich and cassowary, as well as the extinct elephant bird of Madagascar and the giraffe-like moa, the rooster-size kiwi is the smallest and most cryptic. The name ratitae derives from ratis, Latin for a raft, because the bird's sternum is flat and raft-like, lacking a keel to which flight muscles could be attached. And so, like all of its relatives, the kiwi is permanently grounded; its wings are atrophied into vestigial stumplets and culminate in tiny cat-claws, which inspired the bird's scientific name apteryx, meaning wingless. But here the neat Linnean taxonomy ends because the kiwi — an anomaly not just among the ratites but all other birds as well — stands alone in the eccentricities of its anatomy and behaviour.

While all other ratites thump the earth with their large dinosaur-like feet, the kiwi can walk almost silently, its loping trot muffled by fleshy foot pads, as soft as the hand of a child. It digs burrows like a badger, has a face bristled with feline whiskers, and its feathers, which lack aftershafts, resemble more the fur coat of a rodent than the plumage of a bird. According to one nineteenth-century ornithologist, in the half-light of dusk or dawn, the apteryx seems not a ratite but rather a rat-like creature.

It emerges just after sunset and, like a dog, literally follows its nose searching for food. Its long and flexible beak has a pair of extremely sensitive nostrils at its very tip, and stabbed repeatedly into the soggy world of earthworms, it serves as an olfactory underground periscope. And while, for aerodynamic reasons, the bones of birds are usually light and hollow, those of the kiwi are heavy and filled with marrow. Its skin is tough enough to be made into shoe-leather, and its body temperature, at 38°C, is closer to our own than to that of other birds. In fact, the kiwi is a remarkably un-bird-like bird. Consequently, zoologists bestowed it with the status of an honorary mammal.

So extraordinary is this bird that when the first specimen skin arrived in England around 1811, it was considered a hoax on a par with the outlandish Australian platypus, an unlikely anatomical hotchpotch skilfully stitched together by a clowning taxidermist. But then the early nineteenth century was also a time when, in the way of biological discoveries, almost anything was possible. Then, some 28 years later, a single fist-size bone fragment from the same island would convince renowned comparative anatomist Sir Richard Owen to proclaim the existence of a larger bird, which he called Dinornis, from Greek deinos, meaning huge and terrible. Commonly it would become known as the moa, the tallest bird that ever lived; a flightless, wingless browser, and, in the light of later evidence, a close relative and neighbour of the kiwi.

In 1813, the assistant keeper of zoology at the British Museum, George Shaw, described as best he could the bird that would become known as the moa's smallest sib, and gave it a name, *Apteryx australis.* The artist's impression which accompanied the description showed a penguin-like creature with a Pinocchio nose . . . but remember, both men had the dry boneless skin as the only source of information. Only later, as more specimens arrived, did it become apparent that the kiwi was neither a bird collector's jest nor an evolutionary whim, and its posture and shape were corrected.

In their folklore, the Maori called it Te Manuhuna a Tane, the Hidden Bird of Tane, the god of the forest, and while the corpulent moa provided staple meat for whole families, among some tribes the kiwi was considered food only for chiefs. The meat was roasted or steamed in underground ovens, but it was the shaggy, hair-like feathers of the kiwi that were the most sought after. These were made into kahu kiwi, exquisitely crafted cloaks worn by the chiefs during ceremonies. Like leopard-skin coats on the streets of Paris or Saint Moritz, they were the insignia of tribal status, an emblem of affluence. But by the time the first Europeans arrived in New Zealand, full-length kahu kiwi were already rare.

The Europeans themselves, hungry for the unknown riches of the new land, were less fastidious about the food it provided. Native birds, plentiful and fearless, were often the only choice, but kiwi was rarely a favourite plat du jour. Charlie Douglas, explorer and a keen ornithologist, wrote how once, crossing a large swamp, he sprained his ankle and had to crawl home for several days. Along the way he cornered two kiwi in their burrow. 'Being pushed with hunger, I ate the pair of them, under the circumstances I would have eaten the last of the Dodos,' he related. They had an earthy flavour, he added, 'like a piece of pork boiled in an old coffin'.

The apteryx, however, must have been tasty or exotic enough to be served in country inns. Rudyard Kipling had one in Tokaanu, near Taupo, and pronounced it quite acceptable, and today you can still buy a kiwi burger though it is no longer the contents but the name and the image that sell. In fact, everywhere you look you can see those nosy amiable hands-in-the-pocket bipeds advertising, enticing, welcoming. The only place you won't see them is in the wild.

One reason for this is that kiwi are masters of camouflage and stealth. Their mottled plumage blends perfectly with the forest understorey, they often use a different shelter every night and they dig their nesting burrows so long in advance that moss and ferns re-establish themselves around the entrance obliterating all signs of excavation. Leaving such a burrow for a few hours of feeding, a kiwi would mask the opening with deftly placed twigs, a cunning manoeuvre which fooled even the bush-wise Maori. As anthropologist Elsdon Best wrote: 'I have repeatedly been told that the eggs of this bird remain so long in the nest that roots grow over them.'

The only sure way to see a kiwi is to take a visit to a nocturnal house specially designed for the purpose because in the wild, the odds of seeing one are infinitesimal. For the first five months of his study into the North Island browns, John McLennan did not see a single bird. His tracking dog spent most of its time trying to get rid of the muzzle while McLennan crawled through the bush, night after night, seeing nothing but fresh kiwi footprints. Finally he managed to catch a young male in a pitfall trap. It seemed a surprise for them both.

Yet this mastery of disguise also has its drawbacks. If all or almost all kiwi suddenly disappeared, no one but a handful of field biologists would ever notice. And this was exactly what was happening. The kiwi had virtually camouflaged its own extinction.

• • •

When Tane Mahuta, the largest remaining kauri tree that towers in the Northland panhandle, was still a seedling, about 1200 years ago, there were an estimated twelve million kiwi widely spread throughout New Zealand, living in densities of up to a hundred birds per square kilometre. Because of the scantiness of fossil evidence the scientists are still unsure whether their ancestors were already here when the supercontinent of Gondwana broke up and New Zealand was cast adrift, or whether they flew in later, and then became flightless. What remains certain is that they have been here for a long time, 60–90 million years being a common estimate.

But in the mid-1990s, the biologists made a startling discovery. Suddenly there were only about 70,000 kiwi left. One species — the little spotted — the smallest and once the most common, was already gone and the populations of the others were melting away at a rate of six per cent per year, edging towards extinction.

Last century the settlers complained that you could not sleep for the noise the kiwi made. Now, again, people are losing sleep over kiwi, this time trying to figure out just why the night has gone so silent. One of them, existing for years in a state of perpetual sleep deprivation, was John McLennan.

A keen outdoorsman, more at home in the forest or mountains than in the lecture halls of academia, he paid his way through university by diving for paua and hunting white-tailed deer around the coast of Stewart Island. After completing his PhD in Aberdeen (on the flocking behaviour of wading birds), McLennan turned his attention to the lonesome kiwi, partly because the nature of the bird struck a resonant chord with his own, but also because the kiwi — unstudied, unknown, unseen — presented a formidable fieldwork challenge.

He fell in love with these snuffling fur-balls and over the years had become to them what Jane Goodall was to the chimpanzees, a tireless advocate and passionate campaigner for their cause. But even more important than McLennan's 'pulpit' work had been his investigation into what's been killing the kiwi and how their sure extinction can be averted.

His study area was on the 750-hectare Puketukutuku Peninsula which juts into Lake Waikaremoana, a misty, many-armed waterway lost among the green rolling hills of Te Urewera National Park, which in turn, is a part of the largest remaining tract of native beech forest in the North Island. It is an unaltered and relatively remote place, sprinkled with story-telling Maori names like Te Upokookahungunu, Te Taraoamohanga and Whanganuioparua, and to get there you follow one of the country's longest unsealed roads, a windy, juddering two-hour-drive.

McLennan picked me up in his battered boat which, on this none-too-large a lake, had clocked a mileage equivalent of the length of the equator, and we planed across the corrugated water to the ranger's hut which had become his second home. Late in the evening we motored to the study area; some of the eggs were due to hatch any time now and McLennan wanted to check on their progress. We walked for an hour along a thin trail marked with tiny cat-eye reflectors, then settled for a long wait in the nook of a mossy stump.

The forest was so silent and still you could hear the leaves falling, but just after midnight, there came that unmistakeable outburst of noise as if some brat had begun torturing a whistle with such force and vigour that the effort made him run out of breath. This was the sound of a male kiwi stating its territorial presence, announcing its departure for the night's hunt.

For us it was a signal that the burrow was now vacated by the incubating adult. McLennan led the way down a steep shallow gully, and in its bank found an immaculately hidden burrow. An arm's-length inside, there was one fist-sized egg, and next to it something brown, round, and spiky like a rolled-up hedgehog: a four-day-old kiwi chick.

Its beak was as long and as pink as a child's finger, its furry feathers soft and moist and smelling of a rotten log. 'There are few things in this world as beautiful as this,' McLennan whispered cradling the chick in his large hands. 'This is why I walk the forest for months. It is as though you were touching the soul of this land.'

The soul, presently drowsy to the point of nodding off, was the result of extremely unorthodox parenting. Relative to its size, the kiwi has the largest and richest egg of any bird, four times bigger than it would theoretically be expected. The egg, which grows to constitute up to 25 per cent of the bird's mass, fills up the female's body leaving no room for food, causing her to sometimes soak her belly in puddles of cold water to relieve the inflammation and to rest the weight.

Following 75 to 84 days of incubation, and the ordeal of kicking its way out of the shell, the chick — an exact miniature of the adults — emerges into the world, and what a cruel world it is!

After this level of investment of energy and effort, the parents consider their job done and move on to produce another egg, another offspring. They may do some perfunctory baby-sitting, but will neither feed, nor later even tolerate the chick on their territory. They leave it well stocked with provisions though: its tummy, taut like a balloon, is distended with nearly half of the remaining egg yolk, which will nourish it for the first week of its life.

Within a few days the chick begins to venture outside the burrow, and by day ten it's out for most of the night. Somehow it knows all about the business of being a kiwi, of finding the right food and shelter. Somehow it also knows that its only chance of survival is eating lots and growing fast. What it probably doesn't know is that almost inevitably it will fail. McLennan and his colleagues at the National Kiwi Recovery Group — a kind of war council formed to combat the species' extinction — revealed that 95 per cent of kiwi chicks die within the first few weeks of their life. They found that only one per cent survive into adulthood. They also found the killer.

• • •

New Zealand was once an Eden for birds, an ark that broke off Gondwana and never quite arrived anywhere, but stayed afloat in the South Pacific, becoming a world unto itself. Except for two species of small bats, it had no mammals and, indeed, the kiwi has filled an ecological niche elsewhere occupied by anteaters, hedgehogs or echidnas.

There are several such arks anchored around the planet — Mauritius, Hawaii, Galapagos — which though distant and distinct from each other, all have one thing in common. Life on them evolved in isolation, from a pool of original stowaways, and subsequent immigrants are few and usually of the avian kind. According to Edward O. Wilson, an eminent American naturalist, such islands are the key to our understanding of how nature works, because the links between species are simpler and more clear than in equivalent mainland ecosystems, because the ecological tapestry of islands is woven more coarsely and with fewer threads.

In 1967, Wilson and Robert MacArthur, a mathematician, published their findings in *The Theory of Island Biogeography*, which instantly became a canon of evolutionary biology. Each island, they proposed, could hold just so many species, so if a new species arrived and colonised the island, an older resident had to become extinct. There was a dynamic equilibrium between the two, a natural balance between immigration and extinction. And the key word is natural, because the arrival of human settlers to these islands, and more so the entourage of vermin that accompanied them, shredded the delicate tapestry, destroying the pattern and obliterating the design.

In New Zealand, no other creatures have been more devastating to the flightless and naïve avian fauna than the mustelids. Their mass liberation from the early 1880s in order to control the plague of rabbits was an unprecedented bungled-up effort of bio-control, the equivalent of throwing a brick on one side of a carefully counterpoised scales of ecological balance.

Among these mustelids the chief villain is the stoat. Not only is it a nimble climber, a long-distance swimmer and a far-ranging and efficient hunter, it also — uniquely among predators — has a tendency to kill more than it needs and to hoard the food for the lean times. That's why a stoat breaking into a hen-house carries the kiss of death, killing every single bird. Its genetic programming compels it to cache food for heavy winters which, in New Zealand, invariably never arrive.

At the time when the mustelids were introduced here, in the United Kingdom — a country of similar size — there were some 23,000 gamekeepers employed to do just the opposite. Since the times of Henry VIII, the English have been trying to exterminate them, but still the mustelids endured, mainly due to their dispersal abilities combined with certain paedophile tendencies. A male stoat will mate not only with a female that's just given birth, but also with all the female baby stoats in the den, even if they are still tiny and blind. This impregnation is like a pill with a delayed effect, so leaving the den they already carry within them the next generation of their kind. And because stoats are aggressively territorial, the young have to seek out their own place, fanning out far and wide, emissaries of menace — agile, tenacious, fearless.

'When a stoat looks you over head to toes, you know it's calculating, sizing you up,' a possum hunter once told me. 'If they were this big,' he pointed at his dog, 'there wouldn't be many people around. We, not the kiwi, would be becoming extinct.'

Indeed, the stoat is cunning enough not to attack prey that it cannot handle. An adult kiwi could kick it to shreds, but a gawky chick makes for a fast meal. The predator knows its match precisely, and for a kiwi, this is about 800 grams. Reaching this weight usually assures the bird's survival but it takes seventeen long and perilous weeks to get there.

This was one of McLennan's crucial findings. He experimented by creating a stoat-proof enclave, and he chose Puketukutuku because, like a fortress, it could be easily defended. Across the narrow neck of the peninsula he ran a double trap line and then, with the help of a professional hunter, eradicated all stoats inside the enclosure. He thus effectively turned the peninsula into a predator-free island, a kiwi haven. That year all of his chicks survived.

• • •

The concept of island sanctuaries is not new. In 1894, Richard Henry masterminded a transfer of kiwi and kakapo to Resolution Island at the entrance to Dusky Sound. But he underestimated the enemy. The stoats swam across from the mainland and over 750 birds, and the man's fourteen years of work, had gone to waste.

Despite such setbacks many of New Zealand's offshore islands have since become refuges for species that elsewhere are either extinct or extremely rare. Some of the islands were preserved naturally, often through their sheer inaccessibility; others, in the fashion of McLennan's peninsula, had to be restored through painstaking trapping of predatory animals and subsequent vigilance against a re-invasion. Whatever their past, these islands now serve as insular aviaries, genetic safety caches for endangered species, allowing them a second evolutionary chance, the opportunity of an assisted comeback. And for kiwi, none is a more telling example than Kapiti Island, a sliver of mountainous rain-drenched land just off the west coast north of Wellington.

Once the site of a whaling station, then a ne'er-do-well sheep farm ridden with feral animals and rodents, in 1897 the island was turned into a native flora and fauna sanctuary. The cleared forest slowly grew back and the resident caretakers methodically eradicated the vermin. Between 1980 and 1986 they removed 22,500 possums from this 2000-hectare island, and a week before my visit the reserve was officially declared free of rats.

Kapiti, now aflutter with birds unseen in most parts of the country, also hides another secret. No one quite knows how, but soemhow the last small population of little spotted kiwi held out here and, in the absence of predators and other threats, has boomed and filled the island to its full carrying capacity. There are now over 1000 individuals and a number of pairs have been shipped to other offshore islands like the Hen and Chickens, Tiritiri Matangi and Red Mercury, where they have founded healthy and self-sustaining populations.

Such restored reserves have an unparalleled educative role, Peter Daniel, a ranger who had just retired after 26 years of Kapiti custodianship told me. 'In our relationship with the natural world, there is an odd phenomenon which I call a law of diminishing expectations,' he said. 'As consumers, we insist on sleeker cars, faster computers and better medicines, but when it comes to nature, with each generation we expect to see less and less. And our children will expect less, and their children won't even know what to expect. That's why we need places like Kapiti. They remind us how rich our native fauna once was, and how rich it once again can be.'

You can glimpse these riches in a truly cathedral setting in Trounson Kauri Park, north of Dargaville. Here, the concept of island refuges had been transplanted back to the mainland, encompassing one of the last remaining stands of kauri. Alan Saunders, a man of irrepressible enthusiasm, and the head of the 'mainland islands' project explained: 'Until recently, we've been an extinction hotspot of the world, on par with Hawaii and Mauritius. But the tide is slowly turning. We are now moving from protection of single species into restoration of entire ecosystems, because as the offshore island experience shows, if you look after the habitat, if you remove some of the alien predators, the birds and other endemics will well take care of themselves.'

'Kiwi are the indicator of our progress,' ranger Tom Herbert told me in Trounson. 'Since we've began our trapping programme, their numbers have reached over 200, which is a five-fold increase.'

Ten kiwi per square kilometre may seem a lot but you could walk here for days without ever seeing one. In the kiwi's sensory world we are the blind, blunt-nosed pachyderms, and that's why, more than on his radio signals, Herbert relies on the cold, wet schnozzle of his closest adjutant, a Labrador guide-dog named Gemma.

He admits that his work may be repetitive at times, frustrating at others, but it is not without its droll moments. 'Once we found a male trying to hatch an egg-shaped rock,' he told me. 'Quite a Zen way to go about it, huh? Another one was found sitting on a beer bottle!'

'And what happened there?' I asked.

'Didn't hatch. It was a Waikato.'

Herbert is Maori, from Murupara, on the edge of the Ureweras, and he walks through the forest with natural ease, hopping from one mossy log to another, hands in pockets, endlessly conversing with the dog in a language only they two can understand. He has long greying hair gathered in a pony-tail and a proud bearing you see in Goldie's paintings of Maori warriors, an apt similitude considering that here, in this most ancient of our forests, he is indeed fighting a bloody war.

Though to a casual visitor Trounson Park is a paradise restored, a time-warp idyll with a wide boardwalk snaking among the kauri like an elevated bush railway, a place where you can unfailingly hear and sometimes see kiwi at night, behind the scenes it is a killing field. A 100-metre-square grid of trails has been imposed on the entire forest and every junction is armed with a trap. Rats, mustelids and feral cats die there by the dozen and the possums are gone already. The maintenance of the grid is a full-time job, Herbert said, but the results are worth the effort. Such is the price of ecosystem restoration, the price of saving the kiwi.

'My dream is to extend the same regime to the Waipoua,' Herbert said, referring to the 9105-hectare forest north of Trounson, where giant kauri Tane Mahuta stands. 'I'm sure this can be done. There is a strong interest in the community. People are keen because plenty of jobs could be created in the process. The problem is: what the dole department spends in a week has to last us all year. If we could only get the money to fund such projects, the kiwi there could be as thick as the kangaroos in Oz.'

• • •

If Alan Saunders had his way, there would be only three 'mainland islands' in New Zealand: North, South and Stewart. As it is, the laboriously restored fragments of native habitats, though splendid, exemplary and loud with forgotten bird song, are only micro-scale experiments, 9400 hectares in all, carefully gardened atolls in a sea of weeds. Kiwi may thrive in such enclaves but the islands are still only a form of aviary, reservations for increasingly homeless species. Yet in large parts of Northland, south of Ninety Mile Beach and north of the Dargaville-Whangarei highway, in pockets of forests, pine plantations and farmland, even on the outskirts of towns, wild kiwi are still common, resolutely surviving alongside their larger namesakes.

It is a troubled kind of neighbourhood, one in which the two sides almost never meet. When they do, the encounters are invariably confrontational: a runaway dog brings home a kiwi carcass, a possum trap catches not what it was meant to, a farmer sets fire to a useless piece of shrubbery and finds it alive with birds, a lawn-mowing contractor hits a roadside stump unearthing a two-egg burrow, sending the male kiwi bolting for cover.

The initial reaction is often one of astonishment at the very existence of kiwi in such close proximity to home. This may give way to remorse and perhaps a pang of compassion. With any kind of luck, the survivors — the injured, the lame, the traumatised — are spirited off to a bird rescue centre. In Whangarei, they are more than likely to end up on the operating table of Robert Webb.

For over 30 years this former truck driver and part-time policeman has been running a Dr Doolittle kind of surgery, incubating abandoned eggs, receiving and nursing back to health up to 750 native birds each year. It had always been a shoestring effort, run on donations and community sponsorship. Accordingly, the holding pens are made of salvaged plywood, with old oven grill trays for doors, the birds' bedding is of shredded paper donated by a local document destruction company, and the operating table itself is a converted architect's drawing board. But you can still lay a harrier hawk on it and fix its broken wing, you can even perform a Caesarean. It's Kiwi ingenuity at its best.

'When a kiwi chick hatches — and remember, they don't have

an egg-tooth to help themselves out — they often become exhausted partway through the ordeal and fall asleep.' Webb told me in his Native Bird Recovery Centre, built with the help of volunteers in the grounds of the Whangarei Museum. 'But once the shell is punctured, the bird has to get out within about eight hours. Otherwise, the air can dry the egg's internal membranes leather-hard. On occasions I've had to cut the eggs open to let the little fellows out. Some were immobilised as if by shrink wrap.'

More than just a self-trained avian paramedic, Webb is also an ardent advocate of hands-on kiwi experience, a nonconformist PR attitude that has put him at loggerheads with many conservation officials. He dismissed nocturnal houses as contrived and unnatural. The birds in them behave so differently from their usual selves, he said, you may as well be looking at a stuffed museum exhibit.

'If people can't see the real thing why the hell should they care about it?' Webb heated up to his argument. 'You can easily train a kiwi so it feeds in the daytime. On Stewart Island, for example, they are naturally diurnal. There are enough injured or unreleasable birds around, so why not make them the ambassadors for their kin? Because when you spend some intimate time with the kiwi, when you watch them up close, when you're able to touch them, they in turn touch something inside your heart. Make you want to do something about their fate. Now come, I'll show you something.'

Out of a box curtained with a towel he pulled out a brown kiwi and let it out on the lawn. Initially, like any wild kiwi I'd seen, Snoopy looked dazed, squinting into sunlight, apparently grumpy at being so rudely woken up. But in an instant his confusion turned to excitement, then to greed, then to outright gluttony. The lawn around him, freshened by the morning dew, was alive with earthworms, fat as milkshake straws, as long as shoelaces.

Lost sleep long forgotten, Snoopy was soon breakfasting frantically, plucking the worms out of the ground with swift and deadly accuracy . . . a tweezering nip of the beak; a slow withdrawing pull so as not to break the worm off; a backward flick of the head. Gulp! A quick nose-clearing snort, and a deep stab. Puuuuuuul. Gulp!

What McLennan only glimpsed during his decade and a half of intensive research, what Peter Daniel saw once in 26 years on Kapiti, Snoopy was performing on cue, no more than a couple of metres from my face. 'See, no animal will feed if it's stressed,' Webb told me. 'Look at 'im. If he was any more relaxed he'd fall over.'

Which for Snoopy was a constant possibility considering that he only had one leg. Eight years ago a gin trap near Kaitaia took his other limb and that's how he found himself in Webb's care. A local orthopaedic surgeon designed a prosthesis but the stump festered from chafing and Snoopy had to learn to go without it. His toes turned inwards, his balance realigned, and now he hops about like a tail-less kangaroo, only occasionally using his beak for a crutch.

This endearing disability turned Snoopy into a Northland celebrity with a thick file of front-page newspaper clippings to his credit. He was a regular visitor to schools, rest homes and public meetings, with Webb spreading the word about the plight of the kiwi, campaigning against gin traps. 'Once I took him to the conference of the Royal Foundation for the Blind, to people who not only have never seen a kiwi, but most likely never will,' Webb told me. 'They could touch him, and smell him, and feel the shape of his body. Their faces spoke more than a million words.'

His attention drifted back to Snoopy, who was still gobbling worms as if there was no tomorrow. 'He must get all his liquid out of these worms,' Webb said nodding at the bird. 'Put out a bowl of water, and he'll growl at you. In eight years I've never seen him drink.'

There is another overlooked fact about kiwi, Webb said. They are extremely unfussy birds. They don't need a pedestal standing, they don't need national parks or reserves. As long as there is food and shelter, they will live on the most marginal land, in bracken, in gorse even. Like sparrows or blackbirds, the kiwi will readily live with people. If only people would choose to live with them.

In a shaky and stuttering sort of way this has already been happening on the eastern side of Coromandel, near Whitianga. The 800-hectare Kuaotunu Reserve is a most unlikely wildlife sanctuary. There are no boardwalks or interpretation signs, no brochures and staff wearing smart khaki uniforms, and the closest its warden gets to a PR effort is to shoot a wild pig rooting the reserve and give the meat away to the volunteers, having first singed it with a gas blowtorch he carries in his tool kit. You get around the place on a quad bike, and at times you can't even get off it because the trails are so muddy you'd sink shin-deep and leave your gumboots behind.

Kuaotunu lies in the heart of a 5000-hectare finger of mainly private land pointing towards the Mercury Islands, steep sheep country of paddocks and gullies choked with scrub, rimmed with beaches, sea-cliffs and pohutukawa. The land has been repeatedly farmed, mined, burnt off, planted with pines and logged, and burnt off again, and still kiwi have survived here in numbers second only to Northland . . . until stoats made it to Coromandel and began methodically silencing their call.

In 1995 the local community called a meeting to see what could be done. They formed an incorporated society with 450 members, and elected a committee to run it. The farmers gave a nod of approval on condition that no random poison would be spread on their land, and two years later the mainly voluntary field work began on Project Kiwi, the first such initiative in the country. From the outset the committee had been divided in its goals and ideas of how to achieve them, succumbing at times to bitter personal squabbles, becoming a vortex of small-town politicking. But the project still marked the beginning of the Great Limp Forward in community conservation, mainly because of the unswerving drive of the society's only employee and the kiwi's most unlikely ally.

Forty-six-year-old Lance Dew had been a trapper and a hunter for over three decades, living in the bush for months on end, culling deer, shooting feral pigs, trapping possums. The possum business was particularly lucrative and in its heyday Lance was taking out of the forest some $70,000 worth of possum skins a year, more than any other hunter in New Zealand.

At the time he hated kiwi because they threatened his livelihood through the common misconception that it was the trappers who were responsible for their decline. 'I also thought they were the bumbling fools of the forest,' he says. 'Until I tried to catch one!'

That was in the early 1980s, when kiwi were still considered a fire hazard, he remembered. 'Kiwi feathers are tinder-dry and so when the foresters were burning off a logged patch of land they'd have a gang of batsmen lined up all along the fire break to stop any kiwi from trying to cross it. You could lose the whole block of pines over one flaming kiwi.'

How far we have come in just one generation!

When the possum business dried up, Lance Dew went freelance, a bushman for hire. It was then that John McLennan mobilised him as a tracker, and in the process enthused and converted him into one of the most ardent crusaders for the kiwi cause, which later lead to his position as the sole warden of Kuaotunu.

'They've ruined my life,' he laughed about kiwi, but he didn't seem to mind camping in the rubble. His house resembled a bush hut. On the deck garlanded with drying woollies there were several kinds of traps, soiled oilskins, camping gear and a threadbare backpack. Next to the pile, and shivering with anticipation, sat Murphy — a hyperactive bag of bones and the ugliest sheepdog you'd ever see, a farm reject turned superb kiwi hound, and true to its nature, a shepherd rather than a pointer. In Murphy's life all work is play, and today was no exception. We drove to the sanctuary, mounted two quad bikes and headed up a steep paddock towards the forest.

Lance was riding one-handed, scanning the bush with an aerial, listening out for any of the 26 radio-tagged kiwi. His bike was rigged up for farm work — no fancy outdoor gear, just a rifle under the handlebars, a shovel, toolbox, and slabs of animal fat at the back. Every few hundred metres he stopped to bait one of the 400 stoat traps, skewering a piece of fat on a rusty nail, wiping his hands on the grass. To Murphy's unbounded joy, we tracked down and caught several kiwi, and Lance measured and weighed them, and noted their condition as unceremoniously as a farmer checking up on his stock.

This was conservation at its crudest and most elemental, but the results were impressive. The previous year all possums were eradicated and stoats are now becoming rare. The chick survival rate reached 87 per cent in one year, and 33 in another, with twenty per cent being the target to maintain the current population. The Kuaotunu kiwi project would have been a grand success, an example, and inspiration for all to see and follow, were it not for — you've guessed it — the never-ending, crippling, nauseatingly frustrating lack of funds.

Though officially contracted by the society, Dew, who regularly works 80-hour weeks, had not been paid for months. Not only that, more and more he was forced to fund-raise, to seek out sponsors. Yet natural as he may be in the bush, he felt awkward and clumsy in the alien corporate world. 'The chairman is a cow cocky, and I'm a possum hunter,' he said. 'We don't have a clue about stringing deals.' Consequently, the job that filled virtually every moment of his life had become an upstream slog against the current of odds and indifference that continually threatens to swamp the Kuaotunu project.

But the bushman is learning. He has mastered the word processor, attended a business course, learnt to write cash-flow forecasting, even though not much cash was flowing at present. Still, watching him work with this silent and dogged determination you know that sooner or later it will. 'We'll put them back on their feet,' he assured me. 'Not quitting on this one.'

Then, to take his mind off the ever-present bogey he recounted how a local roller-crushing contractor, a lad big and strong but who stutters like a cold engine, once found a kiwi and caught it to be released in the sanctuary. 'He says to me: "La la la la Lance, I di . . . di . . . didn't ha . . . ve a blah . . . blah . . . blahdy ss . . . sack ss . . . so I had to... to...to pu . . . pu . . . ut the blah . . . blah . . . blahdy th . . . thing in me blah . . . blah . . . blahdy tool box."'

'The point is people want kiwi to stay,' Lance said. 'There is enough room here for all of us.'

He roared off up the hill — aerial across the handlebars, the receiver to his ear — and I followed, trailing plums of mud from under the donated tyres. It seemed like we were on an experimental kiwi farm. 'Get in ya mongrel,' I yelled out to Murphy, and he leapt up in one of those long oversized slow-motion jumps, and landed with a clunk of bones on the plywood platform at the back of my bike, his gangly legs instinctively splayed out wide for balance.

From the top of the hill we could see the islands — the Mercuries and the Aldermen — which appeared to float above the mirror sea like a mirage. But for Lance Dew nothing here was an illusion, not in the least the future of the Coromandel kiwi.

'I tell you, mate, in 50 years people will be running the kiwi over around here. We'll just count the road-kills. That will be our only form of monitoring.'

There are no reasons why it could not be so. 'Kiwi are born survivors, tough, adaptable and resilient,' John McLennan said. 'They can live almost anywhere. They are breeding machines, producing those huge eggs with the consistency of battery hens. All they need is some peace during the first few months of their life, because at the moment, the stoats just wait for the eggs to crack open so they can kill the hatchlings. But take the stoats away and seeing a kiwi picking worms out of your veggie garden at night might not seem like such an impossible dream.'

• • •

McLennan's dream invariably related to the kiwi that makes the gloomiest statistics and the loudest headlines — the North Island brown — the most common, yet the most endangered. But the survival of the kiwi is not just about helping the underdog and upping its numbers, but also the matter of retaining the biogeographical diversity of all species in their respective habitats, a complex proposition considering that there are still birds we know very little about. On the slopes of the Haast Range, in the remote corner of South Westland, there lives a kiwi as elusive as the Himalayan snow leopard.

In early spring, before the snowmelt began swelling the rivers, I travelled up the Waiatoto valley with Rogan Colbourne, chief scientist for the Kiwi Recovery Group. We jet-boated up a twisting vein of greenstone water born on the flanks of Mount Aspiring, slaloming through countless snags and sunken tree logs, to a forest camp at the foothills of the Haast Range.

For over twenty years Colbourne had worked with all kiwi species and their key populations, and as we set out on the first of our kiwi patrols he shared with me some of his hard-earned observations. Kiwi, for example, are strong but reluctant swimmers. Because they are so heavy and quickly become waterlogged, only the tops of their heads and backs show above the surface. This gives them a clumsy, sinking tea kettle kind of look, but below, those huge drumsticks are kicking hard, and so kiwi can make good headway even against a moderate current.

Pound for pound, Colbourne told me, the little spots are the most vicious and bad-tempered. They have the sharpest claws and use them liberally. All kiwi will put up a fight when cornered but the Stewart Island tokoeka — as large as the great spots — are the most notorious. 'They front you up with their back against the wall, their feet and claws coming down like hammers, and because they often burrow in the sand where the ground is soft and reverberant, you're lying there, with your hand down the hole, and the earth underneath you shakes as if there was a sub-woofer buried there. Oomp! Oomp! Oomp!'

He laughed.

'You have to synchronise with that rhythm and grab them on the off-beat.'

Kiwi were once thought to be the only bird that didn't turn its eggs during incubation, but Colbourne dispelled that myth as well. As part of Operation Nest Egg, whose aim is to boost the ailing populations by collecting eggs, hatching them in incubators, bringing up the chicks to safe size and releasing them back into the wild, he studied the nesting behaviour of the kiwi. Out of an infertile egg he constructed an electronic mock-up equipped with five temperature probes and placed it back in the burrow. The bird never noticed the difference and continued to brood, and in the process Colbourne found out that it did turn the egg diligently and that the temperature between the warm top and the cold bottom varied by as much as 10°C.

Even more revealing had been his insight into the social structures of kiwi populations. Among the North Island browns — the perpetual loners — only the male incubates and upon hatching the chick is left to its own devices and, nowadays, the predators. The great spots share their brooding duties, and Colbourne — the only field biologist to have ever seen their chicks in the wild — thinks that such parental strategy affords greater protection and increases the chances of the chick's survival. The Stewart Island tokoeka, on the other hand, live in large extended families. The juveniles stay on for several years and even help to incubate their parents' eggs. This not only keeps them safe from predators but also saves them from innocently blundering into foreign territories, because in places where predator numbers are low, it is another kiwi that is the chick's greatest enemy.

'It's not just that the resident birds kill the intruder,' Colbourne said. 'They have to tear and shred and pulp it, and stomp it into the ground until it's all mince and feathers, bloody mess, flat as a pancake.' Ah, kiwi — the cuddly and comical mascots. If they were any bigger we wouldn't wander about our forests at night. The bush would be haunted by furry psychopathic thugs.

Almost nothing is known about the Haast tokoeka. For one thing, they have huge territories. In a long day's work of needling our way among giant trees laced up with supplejack and silenced with moss, we barely crossed from one kiwi fiefdom to the next. A radio signal led us to a burrow and in it — a surprise! — one egg and two birds. Another burrow was too deep even for Colbourne's articulated peep-in mirror. The night was falling and we still hadn't seen a kiwi.

It was again a canine that saved the day — Colbourne's black Lab named Oscar. Under a log and among the ferns, it sniffed out a 2.9-kilogram female, unbanded, untagged, wild. It was unlike any kiwi you've ever seen, with white feet, short beak, and thick, downy coat the colour of a red deer.

Numbering no more than 300 birds, the Haast tokoeka, is the only alpine kiwi. Prior to coming to the Waiatoto, Colbourne was surveying the Haast Range population which spills into the neighbouring valleys and found that, at the end of the winter, the birds were fat and healthy, and nesting in rock crevices under half a metre of snow. He reasoned that this preference for the harshest of habitats was due to the profusion of invertebrate life: wetas, land snails and weevils. Even during heavy winters the sun warms the rocks creating miniature nunataks and the kiwi probe around their soft peripheries for the plentiful, drowsy insects. Life in the fridge can have its advantages — keeping the food fresh and the predators at bay — just as long as you can fight off the cold. Appropriately, the Haast tokoeka is as fluffy as a malamute husky.

Back in our camp that night, under a tarp stretched among the trees, in the pale-yellow light of the gas lantern, I asked Colbourne the inevitable question: beyond the panic and the news of eco-gloom, beyond the sound-bite statistics and the media hype — what was really happening to the kiwi?

'They are certainly in trouble, but not all and not everywhere,' he said. 'The great spots in Kahurangi, Paparoa and around the Arthur's Pass are holding their own. Just. The little spots are safe on offshore islands, we could easily crop a good hundred chicks every year and transfer them, if there was somewhere else to put them. The Stewart Island population of the southern tokoeka is the strongest and the most dynamic. The call counts there peak at 60 per hour, and we estimate there are 30,000-50,000 birds.

'The Okarito browns and the Haast tokoeka are the most vulnerable because there are so few of them. But Okarito has the most intensive recovery regime in the country and the birds are slowly starting to come back. We are now trying to set up a similar system here, in Haast.

'The North Island browns are the worst off. They're the media stars of avian apocalypse. There are 50,000 northern brown kiwi, say 25,000 pairs. Each pair may produce up to four eggs per year, but being conservative we calculate they can bring up only two chicks. That's 50,000 new birds and almost all of them die every year due to the introduced predators. At the moment, all we can do is to protect selected populations in their representative areas, until a large-scale solution for controlling mustelids is found. When the predators are dealt with, the kiwi will bounce back like rabbits. With just one year's recruitment of juveniles their population could double. But for now, we're just buying time.'

The time for solutions is not yet imminent but even when it comes, it is unlikely to bring with it a miraculous cure, a once-and-for-all ecologic cleansing. 'We will never get rid of all the mustelids, they are just too cunning and too numerous,' said Elaine Murphy, the country's leading researcher into introduced predators. 'Their control will always be a matter of continuous maintenance, like trimming back the ever-encroaching weeds. All we can do is to significantly curb their numbers, to give the birds a more even break, to rebalance the predator-prey equilibrium. Only then can the two coexist.'

And coexist they can. Already in Trounson, Tom Herbert told me how he was once radio-tracking a kiwi and the signal took him straight to a stoat den lined with bird feathers. 'My heart sank,' he said. 'I thought I'd be looking for a transmitter here, but no. The kiwi burrow was on the other side of the same patch of pampas grass, and in it the bird was fast asleep. She had bite marks all over her beak. You could see that they'd had a scrap but she wasn't about to give in. It was her burrow and she was staying.' They seemed to have fought out a kind of compromise.

• • •

From Haast I drove up to the glaciers, to the block of land between the Waiho and Okarito rivers, to walk in the coastal forest at night, to listen out for the rarest of our kiwi, the Okarito brown. There wasn't much hope of hearing them, Colbourne told me, because the night was bright, near the full moon, and that usually put a damper on kiwi vocalisation. But I continued to hope for something — a call, a glimpse, an assurance that they were still there.

They didn't call. I walked quietly among the moonlit trees hearing nothing but moreporks and the croaking of frogs, pondering the arithmetic of extinction, wondering what does it take for a species to survive. Suddenly there was a rustle in the ferns, then a dog-like snuffling, and out of the forest, across a small ditch and on to the trail, there hopped a familiar hunchbacked figure.

This was not the all-out charge I experienced in Kahurangi, but more of the stop-go approach of a pup, frightened yet also curious. It moved in with series of jolty, patting footfalls, freezing, craning its neck, sniffing, taking a few more steps.

Both its feet were banded, and they flashed with strips of

reflective tape like the heels of a night jogger. Its beak, this multi-purpose gardening tool — a drill, a prod and hoe and tweezers, all in one — was soiled, and crumbs of mud clung to its whiskers.

There it stood, at my feet, the rarest kiwi in the world, touching me with its beak, examining me as a doctor would with a stethoscope. And I melted into this magical moment, the communion with a ghost of the forest, and felt my throat knotting up, and thought of what McLennan told me about the soul of the land and how it touched his own.

And then the little rascal jumped up and kicked me.

It was a kangaroo kind of kick, with a cat-like scratch, as feeble and experimental as the bird was young, but the attitude was there already, and the message was clear: 'This is my turf now. Get out!'

I took heed. The bird, I later learnt, was of the new generation of kiwi, hatched and brought up in captivity, released back into the wild. It had obviously succeeded. It found, claimed and defended its territory — no mean feat in this tough neighbourhood; it went industriously about its business; it was curious and brave, streetwise and assertive; it stood its ground against anything and anyone.

What better totem creature could a country choose for itself?

The kiwi must survive, of that there can be little doubt. Otherwise, like the marsupial wolf that is now the emblem of Tasmania, it would be a sorry logo, a symbol of failure and short-sightedness. And without the wild kiwi the concept of Kiwiana would become just an empty catchword, a memento from another lost battle, a carapace without its eccentric soul.

In Praise of the Humble Lichen

'Lichenologists are a peculiar lot . . . dreamy-eyed and detached, they seem to inhabit a different dimension. They speak a language only they can understand and haunt places the rest of us usually avoid.'

How did I ever get myself into a trap like this: no way up and certainly no way to climb back down?

A wall of vertical granite fell away beneath my feet — anything dropped from here would not touch down for several hundred metres — and gravity, so deftly defied until now, returned with fierce omnipotence, like an earthbound wind coming in gusts. My hands were sweating, legs beginning to tremble. I was stuck, spread-eagled facing the wall, partway through a climbing move I could neither complete nor retreat from. Until now, I realised, I never really knew the meaning of panic.

We were following a classic mountaineering route which snaked gracefully up a wall of a granite spire. Or rather, we did not follow it exactly because, from down below, straightening the route and making it into a more direct and elegant line seemed like a sporting proposition. With modern climbing equipment we were doing a swift job of it too, cutting directly through most of the oxbows and meanders, delighting in our fitness and speed until, within sight of the easy ground above, I had made several irreversible moves and suddenly run out of handholds and protection.

The rock face in front of me was smooth and blank but for a stubble of velvet growth. Worse still, a slight bulge in it was pushing me out, adding to the sense of crucifixion. I had moments, perhaps seconds only, before my overtaxed muscles shook me off the rock face, sending me plummeting down towards a few bits of protection I did not fully trust, and my climbing partner, who could not yet know what was coming. Unbidden, a thought entered my mind: is this how it's all going to end? A life well-lived but sadly foreshortened.

It was then that I noticed it. A line of black-green lichen, a thickening in the growth that covered the rock. Reaching out and balancing around that awful bulge, I ran my fingers over it and found it soft and yielding, like a seam of sponge. There was something under it. A crack in the rock perhaps. A glimmer of hope?

With fingers like the claws of a garden hoe I frantically began to dig at it. A fingernail gave way and smears of bright blood blotted the lichen but I never felt the pain. There was a crack there, alright; maybe only four centimetres deep but with sharp parallel edges.

I scraped out the lichen, then, from a harness gear loop, plucked a camming device known as a flexi-friend which has spring-loaded jaws opening outwards when released. Just the friend I needed here.

I jammed it into the crack and felt the satisfying bite as the serrated alloy jaws locked against the coarse grain of granite. There was no time for testing. I barely managed to thread a wrist through the friend's webbing loop when my right foot slipped and I felt myself pendulum around the bulge. The sharp pain of a cramp filled my leg like a burn. I had just enough strength left to pull up the rope, clip it into the new anchor and yell to my partner to take up the slack. Then, totally spent and breathing like a sprinter, I sagged on to the rope, closed my eyes and leaned my head against the rock, the beak of the helmet scraping against the velvet growth. My entire universe filled with the musky smell of the lichen that had just saved my life.

When the surge of emotions had passed, when I was able to

breathe and think coherently again, I examined the lichen more closely. It transpired that in this sterile and weather-beaten place the crevice in the rock face was like a vertical irrigation ditch which the lichen had colonised and overgrown, until the crack was no longer visible.

We finished our route, even got a mention in the season's roundup of first ascents, but what stayed with me for years afterwards was my tête-à-tête with lichens and a certain quiet fondness for them. They are a world unto themselves, unseen in plain view yet omnipresent, and they are some of the most remarkable living things you could ever encounter.

• • •

After you notice one, you see them everywhere. They grow on the summit rocks of Mount Cook and on river stones, on fences, walls of old houses and the bark and leaves of trees, and on the coarseness of tarmac and pavements, even on glass, and gravestones, and old cars. They astonish with diversity of form and design. *Rhizocarpon geographicum*, for example, forms vivid map-like patches whose beauty and complexity echo satellite images of the earth. *Graphis librata* resembles hieroglyphic writing etched into tree bark, while the high-alpine *Xanthoria elegans* grows in colourful patterns which bring to mind the dot paintings of Australian Aboriginals. They are one of the planet's most successful colonisers and they add texture and colour to our world, and even hint at the mystery of how life goes about its business of evolution and survival.

Lichens are not plants but composite structures, miniature ecosystems comprising a fungus and a photosynthetic partner, usually an alga or cyanobacterium, sometimes both. Traditionally, this arrangement has been considered symbiotic but some lichenologists suggest that although the algae are not reliant on the fungi to survive (as the fungi are on them), they do thrive better with them than without. They talk of agriculture — or rather algaculture — in which the fungi capture the algae with their web-like filaments, then cultivate them as a farmer would a crop. The fungi do not pass any nutrients to the algae but in return for 'milking' them of the carbohydrates they produce, they protect the algal cells from mechanical damage, excessive sunlight, and keep them moist, which can be a matter of survival.

Whatever its definition, the fungi-algae arrangement has been so successful, life has chosen this particular evolutionary path not just once, but several times, independently. The partnership is stable and resilient and it not only allows the fungi and algae to survive together where each would surely perish on their own, but also makes it possible for lichens to live, and often flourish, in environments where most life as we know it cannot survive at all.

Lichens can be found at altitudes approaching the Himalayan death zone of 8000 metres; they are the dominant flora of the polar regions; and they thrive in deserts where the rocks are too hot to touch. By lapsing into a metabolic suspension, they are able to tolerate periods of severe desiccation, during which they can withstand extremes of temperature, even radiation.

Perhaps the most telling example of lichens' ability to survive the extremes was an experiment conducted by the European Space Agency. In May 2005, two species of lichen, the aforementioned *R. geographicum* and *X. elegans*, were sealed in a capsule and launched into space on the Russian rocket Soyuz. Once in orbit the capsules were opened and the lichens were directly exposed to the vacuum of space, its near-absolute zero temperature and the complete spectrum of solar ultra-violet light and cosmic rays. After fifteen days the lichens were brought back to earth. They were found to be in perfect health, with no discernible damage from their time in orbit.

'When it comes to lichens, the closer you look the more curious things get,' Allison Knight told me. As one of the country's most active and passionate lichenologists, and author of the *Field Guide to New Zealand Lichens*, she proved to be just the mentor I needed to enter the world of lichens. One wet and gloomy Otago day in late spring we set out to the coast to botanise among the lichens at the Orokonui Ecosanctuary high on the hill above Otago Harbour.

'I'm glad it's raining,' Allison said as we set out along the Rimu Trail. 'The rain always brings out the true colour and texture in lichens.' In strong sunlight, lichens often appear drab, matt and opaque, she went on, but that's just the fungi protecting their algal garden from excessive exposure to sunlight. When moistened by rain, dew or fog, lichen surfaces become translucent allowing the sunlight through and turning on photosynthesis of nutrients.

Simultaneous presence of water and sunlight is the key requirement of photosynthesis and because of their limited ability to store moisture, lichens evolved this peculiar survival strategy. A tree, for example, with its vast reserves of water and untold number of chlorophyll cells, can photosynthesise and therefore grow during all the hours of sunlight. But in lichens the window of opportunity for photosynthesis is greatly reduced, often to as little as an hour or two a day, mainly in the morning, before the night's moisture evaporates. For the rest of the time, the lichens shut down their metabolism, weathering the heat by making good use of their protective sunscreens.

'Because of all this, lichens exist on a timescale completely different from ours,' Allison said. 'Some New Zealand lichens can grow as much as 1–2 centimetres a year but there are others which manage only 0.02–2 millimetres of radial growth per year, and this makes them perhaps the slowest growing of all known organisms. When you consider the size of the largest known specimen, they could well be over 5000 years old, surely among the oldest living organisms on earth.'

Orokonui, only twenty minutes' drive from Dunedin, is an ecological island in time. Protected by a 2-metre high and 8.7-kilometre-long pest-proof fence, fitted with electronic surveillance and patrolled daily by volunteers, the 307-hectare reserve is a community effort to create a safe-haven habitat for native fauna and a glimpse of what New Zealand was like centuries ago, before the arrival of the first humans. A successful effort too, because Orokonui is the first and only place in mainland South Island where native birds, animals and insects can live a life safe from introduced predators.

In the regenerating bush reminiscent of Gondwana's cloud forest, native birds chirp and chatter, inquisitive and fearless, and on the trunks of miro and matai trees you can see axe-like gashes where a kaka used its beak to get at the sap. Our visit coincided with the release of the first contingent of kiwi, the endangered Haast tokoeka, into the sanctuary, and there are plans, and dreams, to bring in takahe and one day, perhaps, the kakapo as well.

The lichens are everywhere, though, as always, against the grandeur of a forest they are all but invisible. We had to change our lens of perception, get down on our knees, and look closely at the minutiae with the aid of a 10x magnifying glass, because the beauty and complexity of an entire forest is echoed in a mosaic pattern of lichen growth confined to a single rock.

Some look like peeling paint, others like rust, still others like a miniature coral reef or aerial views of a lettuce field. Together they

NOBLE VIEWPOINT

The sun still lingers on the western flanks of Mount Cook when the rest of the country is already in twilight. For generations of adventurers, this pinnacle of the Southern Alps has been an inspiration and a challenge, a place to explore both the outer and inner landscapes.

AL FRESCO

Comfortably at home in his snow bivouac, navy mountaineering instructor and Antarctic guide Ross Hickey fires up his portable barbecue.

KIWI-SAVERS

Rogan Colbourne keeps a firm grip on a wild Haast kiwi during a population survey in the Waiatoto Valley — mind those deadly claws! — while John McLennan listens out for signs of life from kiwi fitted with radio-transmitters along Lake Waikaremoana in Te Urewera National Park.

TOUGH CHILDHOOD

All on its own, as the parents have already moved on to produce another offspring, a kiwi hatchling breaks out of its egg to face the world of extreme survival against introduced predators. (PHOTO: ROD MORRIS)

REMARKABLE KIWI

Conservationist, film-maker and diving compadre of Kelly Tarlton, Wade Doak emerges from another dive at his beloved Poor Knights Islands which, since their discovery by Kelly's bunch, have become one of the top-ten scuba destinations in the world.

MOONSTRUCK

Much of the climbing around Mount Cook takes place at night when the danger of avalanches and falling ice is lessened by frost.

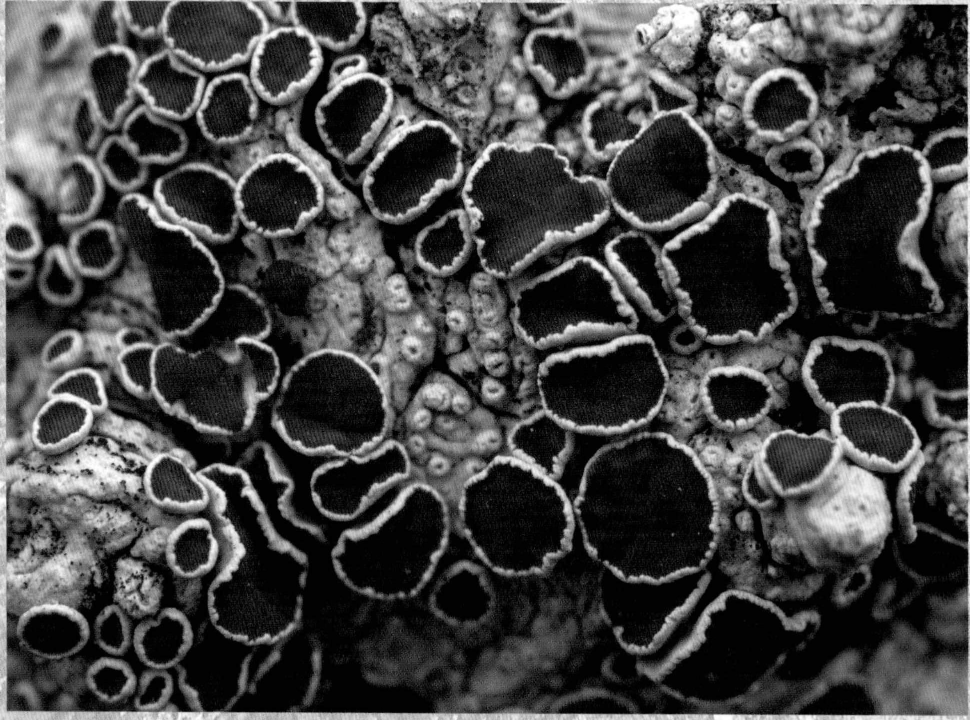

THE SKIN OF ROCKS

Often no more than a furry growth under climbers' fingers, lichens, like this stunning Haematomma alpinum, *are an extreme world unto themselves when examined up close.* (PHOTO, BOTTOM: BRYCE McQUILLAN)

ROADS LESS TRAVELLED

Kennedy Warne, founding editor of New Zealand Geographic *and companion along the roads less travelled, made many of my own departures possible, including ski touring on the West Coast glaciers (top).* (PHOTO. BOTTOM: KENNEDY WARNE COLLECTION)

POWDER HOUNDS

Training my personal avalanche dog Maya. Not much official progress but a lot of fun.

(PHOTOS: GEOFFREY BLACKLER)

form complex and varied communities though it'd be a mistake to think it's all harmony and peaceful coexistence.

'Lichens are not all that benign. When you look at them with enough magnification they are like states at war with all their neighbours,' Allison said, pointing to the distinct outlines each lichen keeps around its perimeter. 'See, these zones are called prothalli, they're like chemical walls lichens build around themselves to protect their crops of algae. They deter invasions of other lichens with specifically formulated fungicides.' Scientists have extracted and described over 700 substances produced by lichens. Many are sunscreens and healing agents with anti-cancer properties, but many more are antibiotics and antifungals, chemical weapons to inhibit the growth of competitors.

A few hours had passed and along the trail at Orokonui we had moved maybe 50 metres. Allison was taking one sample after another, her roller-blading knee-pads leaving soft imprints at the base of rocks she was examining. It seems for a lichenologist the field trip is but the beginning of the journey. A far more intriguing voyage begins back home, through the lens of a microscope.

'For every day spent outdoors there is a month of work in the lab,' Allison said later that afternoon she unpacked the samples on the table of her home microscope. I could see this was the part she preferred, becoming like a stargazer exploring the wonders of nature unseen with the naked eye.

Through a microscope, even the most unremarkable-looking lichens — the drab peeling-paint variety — can surprise with intricate beauty. Stalks become like tree trunks and boughs; hair-like rhizines, a tangle of roots (which they are); spore bodies glisten like red and yellow sequins; and pixie-cups that resemble meteoric craters. Turning the focus knob gives an impression of moving through a labyrinthine forest. The illusion is so convincing I found myself wanting to duck under a branch which had suddenly materialised in front of my eyes.

'I wish more people could see this,' Allison said, looking up from the eyepiece. 'Lichens have always been something of a "forgotten flora", even botanists tend to walk right past without seeing them. And yet New Zealand is exceptionally rich in lichens. We have some ten per cent of the world's known lichens here, and many more are not yet discovered, named or described.'

Recently more people have been looking at New Zealand

lichens, the surge in interest a direct result of the work of David Galloway, the country's pre-eminent lichenologist. For 22 years Galloway worked in the lichen section of the Natural History Museum in London where he compiled the first edition of *Flora of New Zealand Lichens*, the definitive work on all that's known about lichens in this country. Returning home in 1994, Galloway revised the hefty tome to include the newly discovered and described species. The most current edition comprises 1765 species in 366 taxonomic groups.

I got the man's two-volume lifetime work out from the library but it's not your average bedtime read. The bibliography alone is over 200 pages. But for serious lichen enthusiasts the books have become a bible to explore by and, as the doyen of the small but active lichenology community, Galloway gets to see most of the results and samples. He estimates that since the publication of the *Flora*'s first edition, the level of activity in study of New Zealand lichens has increased tenfold.

I wanted to mention this to Allison — who took up the challenge of popularising the essence of the *Flora*, and making its subjects less daunting to the general public — but in the end I thought better of it, not wanting to disturb. When I left, she was still at her microscope, eyes wide-open in quiet fascination, wandering the Lilliputian forests of the lichens.

• • •

For all their microscopic beauty, lichens have so far been considered mostly as a commodity. Some derivatives of lichens have long been established in popular culture even if their origins are no longer remembered. *Usnea longissima*, for example, also known as the long-beard lichen or Methuselah's beard, is often seen festooning spruce branches and is said to be the inspiration behind decorating Christmas trees with tinsel and angel's hair. The biblical manna is thought to be a lichen too, Lecanora esculenta, a type prone to explosive growth and being borne by the wind in such quantities it can form hummocky wind-drifts in the valleys where it settles — veritable bread raining from heaven.

Many cultures, from Egyptians, to Tartars, to Native North Americas, used lichens to make so-called 'earth bread', and a species of *Umbilicaria*, commonly known as rock tripe, saved the members of John Franklin's 1829 arctic expedition from sure starvation who, before discovering the edibility of lichens, had resorted to boiling bits of leather equipment as a bouillon of sorts.

But culinary curiosities aside, it was in the dyeing of silk and wool that lichens found their most common use. The process of extraction was not easy. The lichen's colour gives no indication of the colour of the resultant dye and it could take up to a month to coax the hues out of the hardy 'weed' by grinding it to powder, soaking, boiling, and treating it with ammonia, potash and soda. But when it all worked out, the results were so stunning a booming industry was built around the humble lichen.

Around northern Europe, and in Scotland especially, entire families went out to scrape lichens off rocks and the resultant dyes were used in many high-end garments, from robes of religious dignitaries to homespun Harris tweeds. Apparently, wool dyed with lichens is not invaded by moths, which may account for the fabric's famous durability. The industry peaked in the nineteenth century when the lichen known as the orchilla weed was listed on the international exchange of commodities, alongside spices, gold, coffee, and crude oil, fetching as much as £1000 per ton on the London market. Since then, the steady influx of synthetic dyes has replaced those obtained from lichens.

However, lichens have remained in heavy use in the perfume industry and, around the Mediterranean alone, some 8000 to 9000 tons are harvested every year. It is not that lichens have a seductive scent of their own, but the essential oil extracted from Cyprus powder, a mix of *Cladonia*, *Parmelia* and *Usnea* genera, makes an ideal 'concrete' for perfumes — a fixative which easily takes on other scents, then releases them slowly.

Closer to home, Maori traditionally used *Usnea* lichens to make baby nappies and sanitary pads, somehow innately knowing what modern science is now proving: that the usnic acid present in lichens has strong antiseptic properties and thus helps prevent skin irritations and rashes. The litmus paper you can buy in a health shop, and which is commonly used to quickly assess the body's acid-alkaline balance, is also based on a lichen dye.

In 1999, Nigel Perry, a Dunedin chemist working for the Plant Extracts Research Unit, examined 69 species of New Zealand lichens and found them rich with secondary compounds — antibiotic, antiviral, cytotoxic and protective against ultra-violet — but further research was stunted by the fact that lichens are so slow to grow. You just cannot base an industry on an ingredient which can only be harvested every 30 or 50 years. And maybe just as well because, having dismissed lichens from potential use, we are now coming to understand how huge and fundamental a role they play in everyday life on earth. In New Zealand, this is nowhere more visible than on the lava shores of Rangitoto Island in the Hauraki Gulf.

• • •

It was David Galloway who suggested I visit Rangitoto because the island is a classic study of primary succession, how life colonises new land and how it all begins with lichens. He recommended taking the best magnifying glass I could find, then cautioned me to walk slowly. 'The lichen flora is so rich on the island,' he said, 'we spent the whole day there once and we never got beyond earshot of the wharf.'

Sombrero-shaped Rangitoto, the youngest, largest and least modified crater in the Auckland volcanic field, came into being during a series of eruptions between 600 and 700 years ago. Despite appearing green from the distance, up close it is still a harsh and raw-looking place, made of sharp black basalt and lava stones called scoria. It is also exceptionally arid because there is virtually no water here and the lava fields are poor at retaining rainfall. In short, Rangitoto is an ideal habitat for lichens and no surprise some 194 species — one of the country's highest diversity rates — have been recorded there.

Walking the trails of Rangitoto is like taking in the history of plant life on fast-forward. Barely did the lava begin to cool when the first wind-borne spores of lichens arrived, anchoring into the porous new world. For many years, centuries perhaps, the rocks would not have looked much different. Just more splotches of paint-like growth, velvet or crust, here and there, green, black, white, or vividly yellow where the eye-catching *Xanthoria ligulata* had colonised.

But spreading imperceptibly, growing, dying and decomposing, the lichens built the very foundation for life, the first thin layer of soil. Into it, airborne dust and seabirds' guano was fixed, adding nutrients and depth and, with time, more complex lichens arrived, then mosses and ferns. Follow this ecological trajectory and, in the case of Rangitoto, a few hundred years later you have the largest stand of pohutukawa in the world, laced with ferns and orchids — all told, over 200 species of trees and flowers in the place that was once a barren and sterile rock.

And all thanks to the lowly lichen, *rustici pauperrimi*, the poor little peasants of nature, as Linnaeus called them in his 1753 book, *Species Plantarum*. They not only become soil and humus; they actively create it. Their hair-like rhizines, despite their tiny size, can exert enormous pressure on the rock to which they anchor and they don't just grow over rocks, they grow into them as well. In some species the rhizines can penetrate the rock to the depth of six to eight millimetres and the oxalic acid within them reacts with most metals and minerals until it is impossible to tell where the rock ends and the lichen begins. Thus they also stabilise the soil on which they grow, binding pebbles and organic matter, preventing erosion by wind and water. Just about the only place where lichens do not grow well are the scree slopes. Above all else they need stability, and the scree slopes are the antithesis of that.

I had for a guide the lichen chapter in the *Natural History of Rangitoto Island* but after a while even that proved overwhelming. The lichen growth is so lush and diverse here, often it is impossible to see the bedrock of the lava fields itself. I took transient pleasure in identifying some of the lichens: the unmistakable *X. ligulata* and old friend *R. geographicum*. The high-tide marks of *Lichina confinis* and *Verrucaria*, the white patches of *Poeltiaria turgescens* with their rusty prothalli where the inner acids were eating away at the volcanic basalt, the coral-like *Cladia* and *Cladonia* species hiding in among the boulders where a hint of moisture persisted.

But for the most part I settled for the aesthetics of these miniature forests, peering into them through my looking glass, walking not with feet but with my eyes. I even felt an uncharacteristic urge to collect some samples, to keep some of this beauty, to take it with me. It was a passing sensation and a needless one because the lichens of Rangitoto are particularly rich and well represented in the collections of many museums. Curiously enough, while almost all other natural history exhibits are taxidermised, reconstructed or pinned to display boards, the lichens are still very much alive. Given a good wetting and dose of sunshine they would most likely start growing again.

• • •

Lichenologists are a peculiar lot. They seem dreamy-eyed and detached, and like the subjects of their study, they inhabit a different dimension of time and space. They speak a language only they can understand and haunt places the rest of us usually avoid. When I finally met with David Galloway, of all the places we could go he took me for a stroll in Dunedin's Northern Cemetery.

'Cemeteries are places of great stability and lichens do not like change,' he explained as we walked along the solemn aisles where some of Dunedin's most notable pioneers, like William Larnach, Charles Speight and Thomas Bracken were laid to rest. But it was not the people, their past or achievements that interested Galloway. It was their tombstones, solid slabs of marble or concrete, with names and dates of birth and death inscribed on them. Between the dates were the dashes — the lengths of human lives — and all of it was covered with a patina of lichens, small and big, mostly circular, undisturbed in their natural radial growth.

The advantages of studying lichens in cemeteries are that you know the surface on which they grow and you have them more or less already dated, Galloway explained. Measuring the size of lichens and, knowing their growth rate, estimating how old they are is called lichenometry. The method is not infallible, since sometimes two or more lichens could grow into one another, fuse, and give a false reading. But it is still a quick and cost-effective way to date rock surfaces to determine, for example, the retreat rate of glaciers. I thought of *R. geographicum*, growing only two to twenty millimetres per century. The oldest specimen at the cemetery, nearly as old as the country, would have been the size of a fifty cent coin.

We may have not fully acknowledged it, but Linnaeus' *Rustici pauperrimi* play a critical role in life on earth. 'In effect, lichens change an inorganic environment into an organic one,' Galloway told me, 'and that, if you think about it, is a miracle of life in itself. But they don't stop there. They are also one of nature's best healing agents. Like raw honey we used to put on cuts and abrasions, the lichens appear on wounds in the earth and seal them, until the skin of life grows over them again.'

This skin of life — continually being sealed, reopened and healed again — is especially evident where the Franz Josef and Fox glaciers pour from high alpine névés, through the bottleneck constriction of their gorges, to run out of momentum and ice onto the gravel riverbeds below. The transition zone is abrupt, from permanent snowfields to evergreen forest within a few kilometres, and the earth here is scoured raw from the abrasion by ice that bulldozes all in its way.

We were coming down to Almer Hut from a day of ski-touring on the upper Franz Joseph glacier. The long climb up the Salisbury Snowfield and the endless run down the shelf-like ridge of Drummond Peak were already becoming a memory, and the day was fading fast, the sun, a long way below us, about to dip into the Tasman Sea. Within sight of the hut, perched like an eyrie above the jumble of moving ice, we stopped for one last rest to take in the vistas below, not wanting to miss the sunset.

As we sat there, Lydia Bradey, indefatigable mountain woman and a Mount Everest habitué, began telling us how, across the icefall and somewhere in the Huntington Ridge, there was a little-known hanging valley where the retreating glacier had stacked stones and boulders into the most fantastical shapes. They were like mushrooms on rocky stalks, table tops and pyramids, and from these rocks, quartz crystals of enormous sizes grew out like fairy flowers.

'The place is, like, cosmic, man,' Lydia enthused. 'Really trippy. Out of this world. Crystals everywhere, like nothing you've ever seen. And it's not that far from here.' There was more than a hint of suggestion in those last words.

Out of the skis, I sat on a flat rock and as I propped my hands behind me for balance, my fingers immediately found the crustose growth of a lichen, black and drab-olive, and dry like papier-mâché. In winter, the glacial névés are like a piece of the Antarctic transplanted on to our shores, cold and sterile, covered with metres of snow and seemingly lifeless. Yet this lichen flourished here. It grew on an island of rock amid the torrent of ice, for in the timescale of its life the glacial icefall next to it must have been gushing by like white water. It grew without any pests or competitors it could not handle, and it was easily a century old. Perhaps much more.

There were others around it, colours and patterns blending into one another. And I thought: There were over 18,000 known species, and the researchers suggest there might be as many as 24,000. Yet all we had to encompass this incredible diversity of life was one simple little word: lichen. Cosmic? Certainly. Out of this world? For sure. But what other organisms could survive travelling naked through interplanetary space? If there was ever a case of life arriving here on the back of an asteroid, lichens would be prime candidates for such a seeding. Like nothing we've ever seen? Not until we look close and with good optics.

The most wondrous things are not always in the next valley over or beyond the horizon. Some are all around us, so common we rarely notice them at all.

Kelly

'The work was tough and dirty, the seas boisterous, the water cold, the visibility nil.'

On the troubled North Sea waters between the islands of Vlieland and Terschelling, off the coast of Holland, a 54-metre tug named *Yak* stood crucified on its four-point mooring, its solid rectangular hull trembling from the onslaught of the gale and the sea currents harping at the anchor cables. On board, four divers — three New Zealanders and a Brit — waited for a break in the hellish weather; even the slightest of spells which would allow them to confirm, perhaps even to claim, their prize.

Somewhere under the hull, buried deep below the constantly shifting black sands, lay one of the greatest treasures ever lost. When the 32-gun frigate *Lutine* struck a sand bar during a similarly violent storm on the night of 9 October 1799, she perished with her entire crew of 240 and the reputed cargo of 914 gold bars, worth, at the time of this salvage attempt, an estimated $NZ25 million.

Some of the treasure had already been recovered, the four

men knew. A year after the sinking 58 gold and 38 silver bars, plus over 40,000 coins were scooped up with iron nets while the wreck was not yet smothered by the sands. More gold was salvaged in 1858, with the use of a diving bell. But the bulk of it was still there, awaiting the lucky, the prepared and the daring, and the four certainly saw themselves as such.

Their leader was Kelly Tarlton, instantly recognisable by his bald pate, wild mane of hair and beard, and the thick spectacles which framed his friendly face. It was the Northern summer of 1980 and Kelly was already a world-renowned marine archaeologist and treasure hunter.

Only two years earlier he was working with Mel Fisher in the Caribbean looking for the fabled treasures of the *Atocha* and *Santa Margarita*, Spanish galleons which sank with Inca gold on board, and there were even talks of a joint venture.

But the *Lutine* drew him away. It was his project — biggest to date, best organised and financed, with the highest stakes. He had with him his most capable and trusted veteran divers, Steve MacIntyre, Willy Bullock and Peter Oselton, the aforementioned Pom. Two years earlier, Kelly had commissioned an electronic survey of the search area which pinpointed a string of 120 possible targets scattered over some five square kilometres. To cope with the sand cover, he designed two prop-wash units — tubes redirecting the propellers' outwash — capable of moving 3000 tonnes of sand in twenty minutes. They blasted twelve metre-wide craters in the bottom which then served as prospecting shafts. All Kelly needed was some decent weather and this was proving a tall order.

The diving conditions were desperate, even by professional standards. Steve MacIntyre recalled: 'It was the only diving job I remember when your fellow divers would not take your turn for you. When we left, none of us was ever going to go back there again, except maybe Kelly. He didn't say.'

The water was only six to seven metres deep, MacIntyre said, but they were well offshore and in horrendously rough seas.

'It was like being on the bar of the Manukau Harbour,' he said. 'We worked in holes dug 20 to 30 feet deep in the sand, with the walls collapsing, and fluidised sand settling around you. It was like being in a bog, usually with no visibility at all. Kelly was the only one to prefer an aqualung — perhaps he thought it saved time. We reckoned that if you were on a hose (a hookah system where a diver trails an air hose reinforced with a rope) and the sand caved in, you'd live another ten minutes and the guys on board might be able to follow the hose down to you. If a twenty-foot wall of sand collapsed on you when you were wearing a 'lung, that would be it.' But it was equally dangerous to be tethered to the ship which pitched and rolled violently as it was buffeted by waves and wind.

And yet, despite the setbacks and dangers, under Kelly's leadership, the work of blasting holes, diving them, then moving to the next target proceeded with such professional expediency the observers concluded that finding gold was only a matter of time. Kelly was even called off to Amsterdam and asked to pay advance VAT (equivalent of GST) on soon-to-be-salvaged gold and silver. The Dutch officials estimated the tax at three to four million dollars. In his diary Kelly fumed: '... the ridiculousness of being asked to pay duty in advance, before we even found the goddamned gold, is beyond belief.'

Earlier, while the *Yak* was undergoing yet another repair caused by the unrelenting seas, using the smaller and faster Zeehond, the team had found a wreck. Kelly wrote: 'Stephen [MacIntyre] and I descended the shot-rope, and in the murk we could make out the shape of huge timbers of a sailing ship. Our excitement mounted as we could see in the beams of our torches the flat floor timbers of the hull scattered with ballast stones. Big copper bolts protruded through the timbers.'

It was ten days before they got the *Yak* over the find, and when the weather finally allowed them to dive, their spirits soared. Kelly again: '... it is a huge piece of ship ... more than 30 feet in beam and at least 100 feet in length. We exposed this whole section ... in one day's digging, which indicates that if we found a ship semi-intact we would empty it out of sand in no time at all. If we could find a section of *Lutine* with gold in it, we could have the whole job finished in twelve hours.'

But it was not the *Lutine*. More detailed finds dated the wreck at around the 1850s. They continued the search but all they found was junk from previous salvage attempts. Eventually, with the budget allowing only for 40 to 50 days of tug charter, with black liquid sand pouring back into the holes the moment they stopped blasting them, with the *Yak* retreating to port for yet another repair, Kelly had to admit defeat.

The final straw was when the *Yak* again lost two anchors and crossed the wires of the other two, and the strain on the latter was such that, as MacIntyre put it, '. . . a winch weighing tonnes was ripped right out'.

They limped to port where the boat repairs were to cost $NZ100,000. After two months of searching, they had nothing to show but a few bits of shipwreck debris. Such apparent failure would have been enough to dampen anyone's enthusiasm. But not Kelly's. He returned home and began dreaming up an even grander project. In this one he would succeed beyond anybody's expectations. It would be the project he'd be most remembered for, one that would also claim his life.

• • •

There were no early indications that Kelvin Tarlton, born near Dargaville on 31 October 1937, the only son of Ewart and Elsie, was to become a larger-than-life figure in the New Zealand maritime community, or that his future dreams and exploits were to touch and inspire so many lives. As a child, he was neither scholarly nor especially healthy, though when the family moved to Christchurch, Kelly showed a focused passion for climbing, and he joined the Canterbury Mountaineering Club, quickly progressing through its training programme.

But then fate played its trump card. In 1956 Kelly was to join a climbing expedition to Peru when that country was swept by a wave of unrest and closed its borders. The legend has it that with a few hundred pounds of hard-earned savings and nowhere to go, Kelly wandered into a cinema which was showing Jacques Cousteau's 'Silent World', one of the first underwater films ever made. It was the turning point in Kelly's life.

He wrote: 'I tore down the road and ordered an aqualung. I could not get one straight away, but then found that one of my friends living in Auckland was using one.' Kelly travelled up from Christchurch to learn how to use it and his first diving experience was, like most of his future underwater missions, an off-the-deep-end and make-it-up-as-you-go-along affair. He recalled in his diary: 'He [the friend, Robin Hall] did not tell me anything about how to use an aqualung at all. We went out on a local boat; he put the thing on my back, put a mask over my face, gave me some fins and leapt over the side. I leapt too. He grabbed me by one hand and dragged me in eighteen-inches visibility to about 30 feet down. He had not told me about clearing my ears or getting water out of my mask. I was getting this tremendous pain in one of my ears . . . and my mask was slowly filling up with water. I thought I was going to drown.'

But he survived. He was a diver. The earache, the flooding mask were just 'details' to be worked out later.

Back in Christchurch, Kelly met Wade Doak who, equally eager to dive, had already made an underwater breathing apparatus out of an ice cream tin, garden hose and a bicycle pump operated by a buddy on the surface. Together they formed the nucleus of a diving fraternity which began to explore and document the hitherto unknown silent world of New Zealand's underwater.

Scuba diving was still in its infancy and what gear Kelly and Wade could not buy, they made themselves, cannibalising parts and ideas, brainstorming for the missing links, putting it all together into workable units. This included a regulator out of aircraft parts, diving masks from tyre tubes, several versions of camera housings, and air tanks converted from industrial oxygen cylinders.

Thus Kelly found his calling, both in the ocean, and in the tinkerer-inventor's tool shed. Never bothering about patenting anything, he designed and made, or had made, whatever was required for the task at hand.

He constructed the first buoyancy compensator seen in New Zealand, from waterproof canvas and a piece of garden hose, connecting it to the snorkel mouthpiece. He played with the design and testing of manta boards — underwater wings on which, with a degree of depth control and manoeuvrability, a diver could be towed during sea floor explorations. One manta board, like something out of Jules Verne, was a shark-proof Perspex wing enclosing the diver. It used its windscreen as a down thruster and was 'flown' with the control of a joystick. (Kelly crushed it against a reef after ploughing into a school of sardines and losing all visibility.)

Again with Doak, he perfected a Venturi suction dredge for vacuuming the sand and sludge from shipwrecks (the first version used the air recycled from a diver's regulator but it was soon abandoned since it required the operator to breathe like a farrier's bellows.) Roger Grace, who later joined Kelly's bunch, commented: 'If anything was possible, Kelly would do it. If something wasn't working, Kelly would fix it. If a wreck or any other marine object was somewhere on the sea floor, Kelly would find it.'

John Dearling, a close associate and partner of Kelly's on

innumerable projects added: 'If something broke down Kelly could fix it with a broom handle and a bit of wire whereas everyone else would have to get an electrician or an engineer. He was a wizard with electronics. He could make things out of nothing.'

At 21, in Cousteau-on-a-budget style, Kelly led his first diving expedition. To attract publicity, he organised a public demonstration of ice diving under the frozen surface of Lake Ida, and set the New Zealand free-diving depth record in Queen Charlotte Sound reaching 24 metres (he later bettered it to 34.7 metres).

Originally the team of four (Kelly, Ron Crockel, Andy Lawrence and Dennis Fowler) was undecided where to go, but that was quickly settled when, as fallout from their publicity campaign, an invitation arrived from the Hermit Islands off the northern coast of New Guinea. For Kelly and his friends this was a dream come true — five months in a tropical paradise, remote and rarely dived, resplendent with coral reefs, sharks and manta rays.

Their plan was to produce a movie like 'Silent World', one that would jump-start their careers as underwater filmmakers. Unfortunately, in the tropical heat their film emulsion had melted and blotched and the colours becoming psychedelic. Most of the footage was unusable. Yet despite the film project turning into a dud, the expedition was a magical journey, casting a spell firm and lasting. After that there was no going back.

For a while Kelly's bunch kept their attention on tropical reefs, organising annual trips to New Caledonia. Then they found an equally exciting location close to home, one that would later be proclaimed among the top ten diving destinations in the world.

The underwater riches and cathedral splendour of the Poor Knights Islands were 'discovered', causing so much excitement in the diving community that both Kelly and Wade Doak promptly moved up north to be near them. They dived the Knights in every spare moment — Doak does it to this day — discovering new species, exploring underwater caves, photographing their finds. Meanwhile, Kelly had married Rosemary Hastie and was soon to quit his technician job with the Post and Telegraph Department to launch, at 29, a commercial diving venture, Underwater Construction Ltd. It was in this new capacity as a professional diver that his inventor's genius would unfold into its full potential.

Commercial diving is the antithesis of scuba as we know it. Kelly recorded his impressions from a contract job putting in a caisson wharf at Port Chalmers: 'Visibility was usually zero and the temperature often just above freezing. . . . in the winter . . . we were going under water before daylight and . . . coming out after dark.'

At the beginning the going was tough. Kelly also freelanced as a writer and photographer and they often had to rely on Rosemary's veggie garden and the beds of pipis outside their front door. Spear-fishing was not a hobby but an existential necessity.

The diving jobs varied, from looking for a lost engagement ring and raising a sunken fishing boat, to industrial contracts like burying pipes and cables under the sea floor or surveying coastal strips for sand and gravel deposits. Some of them involved major feats of engineering.

Ian Mellsop remembered one such contract. 'There was a water intake structure for the Waikato River for which we built this 350-tonne concrete structure. We built it on the bank and had to winch it out into the river where we had dug a big hole. It was a horrendous job . . . after two weeks we were using inch-and-a-half wire ropes and 300 tonne winches. We finally got this thing down the slope and it took off at about 30 miles an hour down this big, greasy slope. Kelly was standing eyes agog. It went down, hit the bottom and then stood upright in exactly the right spot . . . Kelly shook his head and said, 'Remind me, Mellsop, to never, ever, ever do another job with you.' Of course, one of their future projects was the Underwater World.

As his reputation for getting hard things done without fuss spread — he became known as No Bullshit Tarlton — Kelly was soon in demand, then before long, in too much demand. He confided in his diary: 'Everything is happening at once. They want the Mount Maunganui pipe finished urgently; I'm being asked to bury two miles of . . . water pipe across Tauranga Harbour; Fullers want the Kerikeri River deepened by three feet for half a mile; the harbour board at Whangarei wants to talk to me about burying power cables to the harbour beacons; and I want to work on wrecks.'

Shipwrecks, their research, exploration and salvage, had become a major part of Kelly's life, his favourite pursuit. He worked on many wrecks at the same time, returning again and again with more knowledge, improved tools, new ideas.

His first major wreck was the *Elingamite* which sank in heavy fog off the Three Kings Islands on 9 November 1902. She disappeared in twenty minutes, first coming to rest on a rock ledge at sixteen metres, then sliding down deeper, stopping only when her nose planted into the bottom at 40 below. She took with her a consignment of 4000 gold half-sovereigns and one and a half tonnes of silver coins, a treasure which, because of the bends-inducing depth at which it rested, would claim the lives of several future salvors.

Kelly first visited the Three Kings on a spear-fishing expedition in 1963. He returned two years later and located the wreck. It was not long before he started finding gold and silver coins and the treasure fever was upon him.

Wade Doak, Dave Moran and John Pettit were his salvage partners. Wade wrote: 'With picks, crowbars, screwdrivers and knives we levered out silver coins. Some, neatly stacked in vertical seams, could be chipped out one by one. Others came out in great black chunks of tumbled half-crowns, florins and shillings. The immense pressure of the collapsing wreck had flattened some coins to wafer thinness, or doubled them . . . Some coins were found adhering by their edges to the roof of the cave.'

But underwater treasure hunting is rarely as simple as picking gold coins off the bottom, for the sea guards its secrets, shifting and burying them under sand, encrusting them with marine growth. Finding them required a technical and pragmatic mind, like Kelly's. 'We'll need a three-inch air lift driven by a piston-type compressor,' he planned. 'We lift off all the heavy rubble, loosen the whole area with explosives, airlift it to the boat and sort it out through chicken-net screens.'

Kelly became known for his trigger-happy approach to using underwater explosives like gelignite to clear the obstacles to artefacts and treasures. This propensity earned him an insider nickname: Jelly Kelly.

During another *Elingamite* expedition he wrote: 'As master-blaster, my diving time had consisted mainly of digging holes and cramming in charges which grow progressively bigger as we try desperately to uncover the mother lode. The site now looks like a battlefield, with bomb craters gaping at regular intervals among the wreckage.'

Still, despite several expeditions with more and more complex equipment, much of the gold had eluded them. This was partly due to the extremely limited bottom time which the depth allowed (about five minutes according to the recreational diving tables). To overcome this problem and to make the diving safer, in 1979 Kelly designed a two-person recompression chamber.

John Pettit recalled: 'Our divers always worked in pairs and, after about 70 minutes' bottom time ... would come slowly back to the surface. The helpers on deck would literally tear their equipment off them so that within two minutes, the two divers would be inside the air lock ... [they] would take seats in the main chamber ... and breathe pure oxygen through mouthpieces for twenty to twenty-five minutes at two atmospheres' pressure. It was the quickest and most efficient method of defeating the bends.'

Though their pickings, spread over a decade of diving, were impressive they never found the mother-lode of gold half-sovereigns. Kelly saw it as a failure. 'If I ever go back it would be with a good system for moving boulders,' he wrote after his last dive on the *Elingamite* in March 1981. '... the coins must be there somewhere, unless there was extensive salvage in 1908–1915 that we do not know about, and that is unlikely.'

The other of Kelly's signature projects was the wreck of the *Tasmania*. The 86-metre passenger steamer foundered in gale conditions while rounding Mahia Peninsula on the night of 29 July 1897. The diving on the *Tasmania* was just as hard but the rewards would be much greater due to one Isadore Rothschild, who had travelled aboard the ship with a case of jewellery he intended to sell in New Zealand. Rothschild survived the ordeal, including the capsizing of his lifeboat, but the jewellery was left in his cabin. In 1973, Kelly found the wreck, 30 metres down and buried under sand.

A year later he returned with a home-made suction dredge and salvage rights acquired from the Rothschild family. He wrote: 'When we measured the ship, we found that where the [Rothschild's] cabin should be was covered with four metres of sand. We sucked at this sand with venturi dredges and cleared it off; but the cabin wasn't there. It had completely broken up. So we started searching to the side of the ship, sucking up more sand. Then we found the floor of the cabin. It was in one piece.' On the floor were five pieces of gold jewellery.

Better gear was needed to remove the mud which smothered the wreck and after a stint in his workshop Kelly came back with a blower made by harnessing the outlet of his jet boat motor. The jet stream, redirected with a fire hose to a nozzle operated by the diver, created an underwater mud storm which was then swept clear by the current, revealing the wreck.

The work was tough and dirty, the seas boisterous, the water cold, the visibility nil. Kelly referred to it as his most difficult dive but the venturi dredge kept picking up pieces of treasure one after another.

Kelly catalogued 103 items recovered between October and December 1976: rings, brooches, studs and cuff-links. It was his best find ever and it kept him coming back until February 1983. By that time, he estimated the divers recovered about one third of the jewellery.

The wrecks were now Kelly's driving passion and he was looking for the most attractive way of displaying his finds to the public. That is how his Museum of Shipwrecks at Waitangi came to be. First he found the *Tui*, a 100-foot sugar-lighter with a kauri hull. Then he salvaged the rigging from a wrecked Canadian barque, the *Endeavour II* and had local kauri milled to make up the broken and missing spars. Then, as if by providence, a master boat builder and an expert on square-rigged ships, Ian Barrett, came sailing into the Bay of Islands and in no time threw himself into the work (typical Kelly — he could enthuse anyone over his projects). On 12 January 1970 the first visitor walked over the gangplank into the museum. The collection included artefacts from the *Wairarapa*, *Wahine*, *Elingamite*, *Tararua* and the *Tasmania*.

The museum gave Kelly all the more impetus to pursue other wrecks. He dived on more of them than any other New Zealander. In one of his road trips, from Paihia to Stewart Island, Kelly and John Dearling explored over 30 shipwrecks. By 1971, Kelly had chartered and researched some 1200 wrecks around New Zealand, assessing their potential, making a 'to do' list of some 300. He compiled files on all major wrecks and acquired salvage rights to some of them.

He took on challenges that defeated many who had tried before him. For example, through sheer detective power he located the enormous anchors lost by French explorer de Surville who visited our coast in 1769. Though the Frenchman left precise records and coordinates of his tribulations, all previous searches for the anchors failed. It was Kelly who deduced that the reason for failure was that the searchers did not allow for magnetic variation, which in 1769 was 12 degrees and 40 minutes. With the new coordinates — which pointed to near Whatuwhiwhi on Cape Karikari — Kelly found the first anchor after only a twelve-minute underwater ride on his manta board. It still counts as the oldest authenticated relic of European contact with Aotearoa.

Far more perilous in its execution was Kelly's quest for the remains of another French ship, the frigate *Alcmène* which in 1851 came to grief in the pounding surf off the coast of Dargaville. She was easy to spot from a light aircraft flying low over the breakers, but nothing was easy after that. 'Diving in the surf is a completely new experience,' Kelly wrote. 'The lack of visibility and turbulence mean that often you do not even know if you are right way up. The sea is not water but liquid sand. If you turn side on, it will knock off your mask; if you turn into it, your face is plastered with sand. There is a strong rip. Lifelines become a must; two of our divers lost theirs, one was swept away and was lucky to be carried ashore again down the beach.'

With winches and tow-trucks they dragged their prizes ashore: anchors and cannons which Kelly rushed off to preserve. He was now more of a marine archaeologist than a treasure hunter; in a Perth museum he had undergone intensive training in the treatment of underwater artefacts. There were more wrecks, more adventures: two unsuccessful attempts to locate the remains of the *General Grant* along the treacherous west coast of the Auckland Islands, then the memorable search for the *Lutine*. And all the while Kelly was doodling plans for what would become his greatest undertaking, his legacy to the nation.

His dream was to give the public an opportunity to experience the undersea wonders from the diver's point of view, and the result todays is Kelly Tarlton's Underwater World. The project began on 2 April 1984, with the backing of a finance company and mucky sewage tanks on Auckland's waterfront. These were important, but again the key components of success would prove to be Kelly's preternatural 'don't worry, it'll be all right' enthusiasm, and his ability to, as his biographer E.V. Sale phrased it, 'persuade people that the impossible was really nothing unusual'.

It was a homespun project beginning to end, realised on a shoe-string budget of $2.2 million. (Jean-Paul Cousteau was later to say that he could have not built anything similar for less than fourteen or twenty million.)

The greatest challenge was the 120-metre acrylic tunnel from the inside of which the visitors were to view the sampling of marine creatures. The acrylic was seven centimetres thick and had to be bent and joined with precision. Its failure could jeopardise the entire project.

The technological details for working with acrylic — the correct temperatures and timing — were perfected in Mrs Tarlton's oven. Then Kelly and his team built a 60-kilowatt furnace the size of a small house. The sheets of acrylic were heated for eight hours, bent in the mould, then left to cool for another twelve hours. Kelly's tunnel was curved — the first such feat anywhere — and even before his aquarium was finished he received how-to enquires from several marine parks overseas. Rob Davy, who perfected this technology for Kelly, went on to install similar tunnels around the world.

For nine months they toiled, working fifteen to eighteen-hour days. The finance company put a crippling pressure on Kelly. As he was heard to say, every hour the place wasn't opened cost them $1000. The Tarltons sold their Paihia house and put the money into the project. Failure was not an option.

They made it, though just exactly how remains in the domain of the supernatural. Ian Mellsop remembered that '... the guys were painting walls and putting the carpet down ... at six o'clock in the morning and we were opening at eight.'

And open they did, on 25 January 1985. In the first hour, 200 people came through the door. The place was an instant success.

Kelly's main attraction was the big sharks and already, during the construction, he had an outside billboard which proclaimed: THE SHARKS ARE COMING. Now, with the benefit of hindsight, we can see this as an almost prophetic warning. The sharks did come, but they wore suits and ties. The fast money the aquarium generated was like blood in the water to them.

Sharks of the marine variety proved to be much more nervous and fragile creatures. Kelly had to 'walk' them for hours through the aquarium (sharks have to swim to breathe) and even then, several died from stress. But Kelly knew he was on the home stretch and he gave it his all. He spent 24 hours at sea, catching three grey nurse sharks around White Island, then kept them alive on the back of a truck all the way from Whakatane to Auckland. His legs were raw from rubbing against the sharks' sandpaper skin, but in the end, those sharks swam just outside the acrylic tunnel and the thousands of visitors gaped in wonder.

The success of the aquarium was so overwhelming even Kelly found it hard to believe it. In just one day the cashiers took in $27,000. For the first time ever he was in the clear financially. It would take no time at all to pay off the loan. With the steady profits he could finance any expedition that took his fancy, cast his eyes towards far-ranging targets — the treasures of the Spanish Armada perhaps, the secret riches of the Indian Ocean pirates. Within eighteen months the millionth visitor would pass through the doors. But sadly Kelly was not be there to greet them.

On 17 March 1985, after he'd welcomed the 100,000th visitor to his underwater world, Kelly looked even more tired than usual. He went to bed early. Sometime during the night his heart gave up. He was 47.

• • •

If there is any blame to be allotted, both his friends and family agreed that it was all Kelly's for even though he knew he had a heart problem — a dicky ticker, as his mates called it — he continued to be his own worst pace-maker. Dave Moran, now the publisher of widely-read *Dive New Zealand* magazine, who was the aquarium's electrician and later its manager, said that Kelly always had time for everyone. Everyone, it seems, except himself.

The aftermath of his death left an enormous vacuum among his friends and fans. No one could ever replace him, no one would come even close. Rosemary Tarlton found herself the majority shareholder of the Underwater World but later, in the murky waters of high-end corporate machinations, the sharks closed in, and trusting as she was, she was misled and she lost the lot. Today Kelly's aquarium continues to rate as the country's top tourist attraction.

But what of Kelly, what of the legend? His ashes were scattered at the Poor Knights, which seems telling for he himself was something of a poor knight, chivalrous and kind, always crusading, forever unconcerned with things material. His friend and diving buddy Quentin Bennett said: 'I don't think he ever looked at the economics of things. That was one of the great things: even when the *Tui* was going really well and Kelly could have just stood by the door and taken the shekels . . . he kept on and on and on finding more stuff and doing more wrecks.'

For him it was the hunt itself not the treasure that counted most and even through his time of fame and high achievements he remained the quintessential Kiwi bloke with a shed full of tools and inventions, and a sketch book filled with dreams. A man who, as E.V. Sale put it, 'took the whole world for his friend'.

'He had the mana,' John Pettit said, noting that doors that were closed to others would miraculously open for Kelly. 'He seemed to be able to walk up to people and they would want to help him,' he said. Dave Moran added: 'His charisma could gather people around him and because people believed in him — because Kelly was going to do it, we all just went in and made it happen for him.'

Peter Pettigrew, who dived with Kelly regularly if infrequently, said: 'He led from the middle of the pack and took everybody with him. The reason he achieved what he did was that he was just not frightened at all about taking on a project. He wasn't technologically, mechanically or scientifically frightened by anything, even though to begin with he might not know everything about how he was going to do it, he'd just go out and teach himself.' And this is perhaps the closest we can now get to defining the phenomenon that was Kelly Tarlton.

For a long time after his death, when faced with a problem or a challenge, his friends would find themselves thinking, What would Kelly do? Unconsciously perhaps some of them already knew the answer: he'd doodle something in his notepad, scratch his bald head, doodle some more. Then he would nod, smile and say: 'Don't worry, it'll be all right.'

AVALANCHE!

'Under the snow, deep in the avalanche debris, it is silent, dark and surprisingly warm, perfectly still but for the raging torrent of thoughts and emotions ... the gagging fear of being buried alive and never found, the ultimate claustrophobia.'

They were skiing together all morning, on this most special of days. A slow-moving weather system had deposited over 60 centimetres of eiderdown snow on the mountains around Wanaka and all of it fell without wind, a rare thing in the New Zealand alps. On such occasions ski towns like Queenstown, Ohakune, Methven or Wanaka become gripped by 'powder fever'. Shops are closed — 'Powder day! Back in the afternoon' — and tradesmen down their tools and race up the mountain; road rage is not uncommon. Even the classrooms are empty, and this despite stern memos from principals that parents are not allowed to take their kids out of school on 'powder days'. The towns are likewise deserted as most of the able-bodied populace is up the mountain, indulging one of the greatest joys known to humankind: skiing or boarding the fresh deep snow, pure and pristine and sparkling as if it was made of microscopic diamonds.

That Sunday it was *the* powder day of the season, the biggest in years. As he did most mornings during winter, Dave Harmer (who you may remember for his caving exploration in Megamania) drove the ski shuttle bus up the mountain, gave his passengers an orientation talk in the Treble Cone car park and ensured they all knew the departure time. He did his talk on the double, eager to hit the slopes himself. Like most seasoned ski bums — and this was his twelfth winter here — Harmer didn't work for the money, which was marginal, but for the opportunity to ski. Driving a mountain shuttle wasn't much of a job but it paid for his skiing and allowed him to be up here every day, and this was a pay-off beyond measure.

That memorable day, Harmer teamed up with an old friend Geoffrey Blackler, another winter local for whom skiing has become something of a spiritual pursuit. They made a good team — quick, competent, intimately familiar with the mountain — and thus they were finding plenty of fresh lines. But as the day unfolded and powder-fever raged like a pandemic, even the most secret runs were getting 'tracked out' and so the two expert skiers ventured further and further outside the boundaries of the ski area, always looping back to the lifts for another run.

Each run was a plunge into ecstasy, a dance with gravity to the rhythm of hearts pounding with *joie de vivre*.

At the top of another lift ride they had a moment of indecision.

'C'mmon Geoff! One more run!' Harmer enthused.

'Mate, I'm starvin',' Blackler replied in his Cockney lilt. ''aven't got anuva run in me. Go'a go down to the caf and eat somethin'.'

Harmer hesitated but only briefly. The pull of the snow was just too strong. During a lift ride he'd already chomped on a muesli bar. That'd have to do till the day's end. And so, having promised to meet up two laps hence, the pair split, skiing off in opposite directions. They would never see each other again.

Blackler headed down the easy trail while Harmer began a long traverse above the entire ski field, south, towards more untracked snow. An unknown snowboarder joined him and perhaps Harmer felt safer knowing he was not alone.

Beyond the southern end of Treble Cone there is an area called Hollywood Bowl, a wide open slope which steepens as it funnels into several experts-only couloirs known as the Motatapu Chutes. The snow in the Bowl was the most delicious yet, sheltered and untouched either by a skier or a breath of wind. Harmer would have been smiling as he plunged down the Bowl, his ski tracks etching a calligraphic squiggle onto the mountain, high on adrenalin like a surfer catching the wave of a lifetime.

Then, somewhere above, there was a muffled whoomph!

A fracture line opened in the snow and raced along the rim of the Bowl. At the same time, the white surface below shattered into blocks and, instantly, the entire layer of new snow — tons and tons of it — sheared off the hard icy base and began to slide down the mountain, liquefying and gathering speed, funnelling towards the chutes.

'AVALANCHE!'

If the snowboarder above had shouted, Harmer may not have heard it. He was still moving and now the entire slope was moving with him, but faster than he was. He fell, his skis came off, and the torrent of snow overwhelmed and engulfed him, pulling him down and under its turbulent surface. The walls of the Bowl closed in and the avalanche poured into the narrowing and down into one of the couloirs, the way an ocean breaker pounds through a gap between rocks. Moments later the torrent of snow stopped at the bottom of the chute and all went deathly still.

Statistically, most avalanche survivors are dug out within the first fifteen minutes. The chances of surviving a full burial are down to 30 per cent after 20 to 30 minutes under snow, and they drop off exponentially beyond that. Though they both wore avalanche transceivers — small electronic devices which can be radio-located when buried under snow — the snowboarder could not find Harmer in time, and when the ski-patrollers arrived on the scene and located the buried man it was already too late.

'We did all we could,' said Gordon Smith, the ski-patroller who led the search, 'but the avalanche realities are if you are not found by the members of your own team your chances of surviving a full burial are near zero. The first fifteen minutes are the most critical.'

The snow around Harmer's body had compacted so hard it immobilised him like a full body cast. There was a 'death mask' around his face, an imprint of his facial features in the frozen snow.

'He was about a metre down, his body badly twisted, his

backpack on his chest,' Gordon Smith told me. 'He may have been alive for some time after the avalanche had stopped. The snow is just water and air but when you breathe out into it, the warmth of your breath melts the crystals immediately near your face and the water quickly refreezes creating a layer of ice. This effectively cuts you off from any air within the snow and makes you re-breathe your own out-breath, which is mainly carbon dioxide. And so you die of asphyxia.'

It was 19 August 2001. Dave Harmer was 40 years old.

• • •

There are few spectacles in nature which inspire such a heady mix of fear and awe as avalanches plummeting down the mountainside, creating their own blizzard, boiling and billowing, unstoppable in their path. Commonly, they have been portrayed as white death, lurking in the silent stillness of the mountains only to explode upon unwary and innocent passers-by, baring their fangs and hell-bent on swallowing the intruders whole. But avalanches are not taniwha, unpredictable and cruel towards those who trespass into their domain. There is a science to the ways snow accumulates and moves, and even more importantly, to how we interpret these ways. In all this, there are distinctions to be made, and these can save lives.

Dale Atkins, a leading snow rescue expert and researcher, writes that nine out of ten of all victims trigger their own avalanches, and that most such accidents could be prevented if the same mistakes were not being repeated over and over again. The problem, Atkins says, is not a lack of information but what we do with the information we have and how we make decisions based upon it.

By definition, an avalanche is any sudden and often explosive flow of quantities of snow seeking new equilibrium at lower elevations. As such, they are not unlike flash floods in rivers and, indeed, the most traditional advice offered to people caught in avalanches has been to 'swim' their way out, as if they were swept by a torrent of white water. The vast majority of avalanches are natural. They are the mountains' way of shaking off the excess snow and after a big snowfall in places like Mount Cook National Park, you can see them everywhere, their paths etched down the vertical landscape like dried-up waterfalls. This common geoclimatic phenomenon only attracts our attention when the paths of avalanches and people cross, with fatal timing.

Snow professionals like Penny Goddard — who authored *Avalanche Awareness in the New Zealand Backcountry*, the New Zealand Alpine Club's definitive book on the subject — distinguish between loose snow avalanches, which start from a single release point and fan down the mountain, and slabs, which are caused by linear fractures in the snowpack. Of the two, the slabs are more destructive and harder to predict.

Snow falls in cycles — storm, clearing, another storm — and most avalanches occur within the 24-hour period following a snowstorm, explains Goddard, who also worked on the snow safety of the Milford Road. The snow that stays on accumulates in layers of differing thickness and characteristics, depending on its density and the amount of sunshine, wind and other variables. If you dig a test pit into it you can see these layers, like chapters in a book of the winter's weather.

The connoisseurs have so many words to describe the quality of snow they would leave the proverbial Eskimos at a loss. One source lists 165 terms, from Champagne powder and cold smoke, through butter, whipped cream, sugar, corn and chalk, to less desirable types like crud, mash, crust and the self-descriptive elephant snot. But what the avalanche forecasters are most interested in is how these different types of snow bond and interact together.

Often the layers stick as if glued and this makes the snow safe, Goddard says. But if you get an incoherent layer like hoarfrost or graupel crystals buried under more snow, this may create a weakness which can persist for days, weeks or even months.

Hoarfrost, for example, grows on the surface of snow during cold and clear below-zero nights. To a naked eye it looks sort of like ice mould, sparkling and beautiful, but under a magnifying glass (which every snow professional carries) it resembles a glassy cityscape, each crystal a miniature high-rise, fragile like a snowflake. If new snow falls on top of hoarfrost, it buries the crystals but does not break their structure. They become like brittle houses of cards supporting the weight above them in a precarious balance. Often all it takes is the weight of a skier, a ski line, sometimes even a noise, to trigger their collapse.

They collapse, Goddard explains, like thousands of tiny domino pieces, and all the snow accumulated on top of them goes down the mountain in one big slide. And don't think you can outrun it. An avalanche can travel down at speeds reaching 200 kilometres an hour.

Something like that happened in Dave Harmer's case. The 60 centimetres of powder fell on a hard base, shiny like the surface of an ice rink. I distinctly remember turning back from the Motatapu Chutes the day before that epic snowfall; the steep surface was too icy to get the ski edges into it and I traversed out after a couple of scratchy turns. But powder-fever, like a euphoria-inducing psychedelic, has a way of clouding even the best of judgements, while megatons of new snow poised to slide need but a feather trigger to set them off.

Dave Harmer was such a trigger.

• • •

Avalanches are endemic to all mountain regions where there is enough snowfall and steepness of terrain — most commonly between 30 and 45 degrees — from Mount Ruapehu and Mount Taranaki, down the entire length of the Southern Alps. Like all of our weather, New Zealand snow too has a maritime quality to it — it's wetter, denser and heavier than in more continental climates. Strong winds transport and accumulate this snow on to lee slopes, and the lack of trees above the snow line to anchor and stabilise it creates a set of conditions in which even small avalanches are heavy enough to be potentially lethal.

A phenomenon peculiar to New Zealand are the tree avalanches you can see in Milford Sound and other steep fiords. Here, all but the most overhanging rock walls are covered with densely-woven trees and bushes, a kind of vertical forest. As there is almost no soil the trees cling precariously to the rock and to each other. When they become saturated with rain, strips of forest tear down and peel off like wet wallpaper, tumbling into the sea, disappearing in its depths, and the avalanche paths you see left behind are the size of small airport runways.

At times, snow too can add weight to these hanging forests and trigger a tree avalanche, but in Fiordland most of the danger comes from vast quantities of wet snow accumulating on the less steep summit slopes, the roofs and eaves of the mountains above their near-vertical walls. This is why the Milford Road has its own avalanche programme, with helicopter crews monitoring the accumulation of snow and bombing it to trigger controlled avalanches when necessary. The size of avalanches is expressed on a logarithmic scale of 1–5, with Size/Class 1 being harmless to humans and anything over Class 3 being increasingly more cataclysmic. Fiordland is the only region in New Zealand where Class 5 avalanches occur with regularity. This means they are as big and potentially as destructive as anywhere in the world.

Since records have been kept, beginning in 1860, some 140 people have died in avalanches in New Zealand, though these figures are severely skewed by one extreme event. On 14 August 1863, the year of the great snows, a huge avalanche buried an entire camp of gold miners in Otago's Serpentine Gully near Dunstan. Fifty men were caught and only nine survived. Since then, snow slides of varying magnitudes have claimed the lives of musterers, trampers and a hunter, soldiers in survival training, road and ski field workers, heli-skiers and guides. But most of the fatalities occurred during climbing and, surprisingly enough, not in winter or after snowstorms.

We tend to think of avalanches as winter phenomena and forget that in high mountains the snow persists until late summer, sometimes year-round, and that by then it is saturated with water, extremely heavy and just waiting to slide.

'I was nearly caught out myself once, rock climbing in the Darran Mountains [in Fiordland],' Penny Goddard says. 'We were wearing shorts and carrying no avalanche rescue gear. It was summer. We crossed a gully and were wandering among the alpine herbs and flowers, carefree and soaking up the sunshine, when there came this tremendous roar from above, a free-falling cascade of snow, and within moments the gully where we had been only minutes earlier was gone, choked to the brim with blocks of snow as big as cars. I still felt sick the next day.'

It seems you cannot know enough about avalanches and what you do know, even at a professional level, is no guarantee of safety. Included in the above statistics is the death of Dave 'Snowman' McNulty, a heli-skiing guide and the country's foremost avalanche expert of his era.

In July 1989, McNulty was guiding a ski trip in the Ben Ohau Range. There were some 30 centimetres of new light dry snow on the ranges, providing fabulous skiing, but going into the second run of the day, one called Whispering Silk, McNulty was concerned about hard slab conditions below the helicopter landing zone on the ridge. As it is customary in uncertain conditions, he suggested skiing 'one at a time,' then led off down the hill.

He was 40 metres below when the snow fractured between him and his group and a moderate avalanche started to slide towards him. Hearing a warning shouted from above McNulty managed to ski off the avalanche, seeking refuge under a band of cliffs to his left. The ruse would have worked if not for the fact that the crack which caused the first avalanche propagated further left and across the slope triggering a second and much larger slide. This second avalanche poured over the cliffs under which McNulty was sheltering and took him out and down, and when he was dug out by his fellow guides no amount of CPR would revive him.

• • •

Under the snow, deep in the avalanche debris, it is silent, dark and surprisingly warm, perfectly still but for the torrent of thoughts and emotions raging in my head and body. The strongest of these is the gagging fear of being buried alive — fully conscious yet unable to move — and never found, the ultimate claustrophobia. I have camped in snow caves many times, comfortable if snug, but the space around me now feels nothing like it, the snow not the heavenly eiderdown we so passionately seek but more like quicksand, oppressing and immobilising, inexorably sapping life out of the body. A snow cave you can shape and carve to your tastes and preferences; a snow grave like this shapes itself to you, filling in all the empty spaces, and congealing so hard if you get caught on an out-breath the concrete corset of snow around your chest won't let you breathe in again.

My ski-touring backpack has built-in spine protection and I'm lying on it now, knees drawn up halfway into a foetal position. Before being buried I thankfully remembered to grab with one hand the opposite shoulder strap of the pack and, holding my face in the crook of my elbow, create a half-decent air pocket. Other than that, I cannot move much. Minutes pass and the cold starts creeping in. I poke at the snow around me with my free hand but it's no use, like digging a hole in the rocky ground with your fingernails. The only sound is the thumping of my heart. I think of Dave Harmer. So this is what it's like to be dying under the snow.

Suddenly, there is a crunching noise above, a staccato of light and hasty footsteps. Something punches through the snow above me and in the fist-sized opening a black shiny muzzle appears, then a pair of dog feet digging so furiously fast they are a blur. I snap out of the morbid reveries and remember my role just as, true to his name, Rocket the avalanche rescue dog explodes into the confines of the snow hole into which his handlers have entombed me only minutes earlier.

'Good dog, Rocket! Good dog! GOOD DOG!' I greet him but Rocket totally ignores me. He's not finished yet. 'Where is it?' he casts about the hole, bouncing off its walls and me, stirring up a flurry of snow. Where is it? More snow blizzard. Then I show it to him — his favourite, his only ever toy — a thick piece of knotted rope, and he clamps his teeth on one end and for a long while we play rough-and-tumble tug of war with much encouragement, praises and swirling snow. I let my end go and he rockets out of the hole to play with his prize, and I crawl after him, into the sunlight and fresh air. The dog is beside himself with happiness at having his toy again. This is what he dug in here to find. That he found me is but a by-product of searching for his toy. Standing amid the debris blocks of an avalanche that was triggered a day earlier during routine ski-field control work, dog-handler Matt Gunn grins with satisfaction.

'It took him under ten seconds to find you,' he says, then turns to his dog again, to praise him some more, to reinforce the positive association, magically converting simple dog play with a toy rope into saving human lives.

In 1991, Gunn was working at the Ohau ski field when, on a Closed Day, a large avalanche buried a ski lift and three of his friends who were working on it. Two were not wearing transceivers and one of them was found too late. For Gunn, the incident was an inspiration to train avalanche rescue dogs, and it had a flow-on effect on restarting and revamping similar programmes around the country.

'In New Zealand people started using dogs in avalanche searches from about the mid-1980s,' he tells me. 'Dave McNulty had a dog named Radar, and there were others, but the efforts were largely unstructured and they kind of ran out of momentum and collapsed.' Gunn, who from early age spent holidays on his uncle's farm, with plenty of working dogs around him, reasoned that if there were trained avalanche dog-and-handler teams stationed on ski fields, deployable at a moment's notice, lives could be saved, tragedies averted.

In 2000, he started training his first avalanche dog, named Blizzid, and by 2009, with fellow ski-patrollers, established Aspiring Avalanche Dogs, a non-profit charity based at Treble Cone in Wanaka, creating what he hopes to be a template for other ski fields to use. Currently, there are twelve avalanche dog-and-handler teams around the country and six more are in training.

'Where the dogs can really save lives is in what we call the side-country, immediately out of bounds of a ski field,' Gunn says. 'This is not an avalanche-controlled area but not the full backcountry either, which you'd treat with due respect and caution. People go charging into this side-country, often with little or no mountain experience but hyped-up on YouTube clips and looking for fresh snow, being totally under an illusion that just because they're within cooee of the field it must be safe. It may not be. If they get caught in an avalanche there, and if they can't be saved by the members of their own group, the dogs may be their only chance of survival.'

Being rescued by avalanche dogs, or watching them work, you cannot help but wonder at the animal's sense of smell. Last year, coming back from a ski tour in the Treble Cone backcountry, we watched the dogs being trained on the summit slopes above the field. I remembered my companion, a local vet, joking about it. 'If you want to be found quickly,' he said, 'always carry an avalanche transceiver and, in your pocket, a big piece of salami as well.'

'Dried pigs ears are even better,' Gunn laughs when I tell him the story. 'But you don't need them. Dogs have found people buried under up to seven metres of snow. They can pick up your scent from 300–500 metres away and beeline for you without hesitation. Cast them over an avalanche debris and within minutes you'll know for sure whether or not people are buried under it. When every second counts this can mean the difference between someone's life and death.'

• • •

Every mountain winter, as the layers of new snow fall, morph and metamorphose, the ever-growing numbers of backcountry enthusiasts — the sensible ones at least — daily turn their attention to the national oracle of snow safety and danger rating, the avalanche forecasting website www.avalanche.net.nz run by the New Zealand Mountain Safety Council (MSC). What began as the snow industry information exchange, where mountain guides, snow-patrollers and ski-field staff could compare their observations, has evolved into a public forum and a portal with the most up-to-date information from all regions of the country where avalanches occur. All this in the name of preventing snow-related mishaps.

Gordon Smith, now the Assistant Avalanche Programme Manager at the MSC, has been at the forefront of the effort. 'We want more people going into the hills and enjoying all the fresh snow out there, but we want them to come back as well,' he told me. 'We found that all the professional snow jargon of facets, aspects, angles, profiles and layers, crystalline forms and temperature gradients goes right over most of the recreational users' heads — too much data and not enough conclusions — and so we've simplified the avalanche forecasting, translating it into lay speak and making it more visual. For all the wonderful and fascinating snow science, when you're standing on top of a hill about to ski down you only really need to answer one question: 'Is it a Go or a No-go?' This is not unlike standing at the traffic lights. But these are only in your head so you have to obey them in a much more disciplined way.'

Since 1993, like many others for whom the science of snow has become both a vocation and a lifestyle, Smith has followed the winters from one hemisphere to another. He has had his share of mishaps, once being buried right up to his neck, and these have given him a first-hand no-nonsense approach to the realities of avalanche danger.

'What most people don't understand about avalanches is that it all happens so fast,' he told me. 'You're cruising in fresh powder, feeling euphoric and invincible, having the time of your life, and in the next instant the slope around you shatters like a pane of glass. It feels like the earth has been pulled out from under your feet. The snow swallows you up, drags you down like a riptide, and all the while you're tumbling as if down a waterfall. That's why most of the advice about what to do when caught in an avalanche is purely theoretical. Try to ski off it? Swim backstroke up the hill? I'm sorry, if the avalanche is big enough it's just not going to happen.'

When caught in an avalanche, Smith said, the critical points are trying to stay on the surface if at all possible and, before the snow comes to a stop, to secure an air pocket around your face, like I did during the dog rescue exercise. 'When certain types of snow are moving, as individual grains rather than in stiff slabs, the surface of each grain melts a little due to friction. When such an avalanche suddenly stops, the grains of snow compress on impact and their liquefied surfaces freeze together. That's why the snow can set so hard and why it's absolutely critical to protect your air passages from it.'

As for staying on the surface, Smith added, using airbags like Snowpulse or ABS, is possibly the best option — new technology which has already been proven to save lives. A large airbag, like those used in modern cars but shaped into a flotation device, is stored in the frame or collar of the backpack and is deployed with a parachute-style rip cord. It can not only keep the avalanche victim on the surface but also protects the head and neck from impact trauma.

However, the best way of surviving an avalanche is not getting caught in it in the first place. 'With rare exceptions, in any avalanche terrain YOU and your team are the greatest danger to yourselves, but this is good news because it's something you can control,' said Smith, and this favouring of prevention over cure is the central message of his work. 'Like pilots and stock exchange traders, people venturing into backcountry snow need to have a fail-safe checklist to get the emotions out of their decision-making. They need a system, a plan, and the discipline to stick to it no matter what.'

For example, on powder days there is an enormous pressure on snow patrol staff to open the ski fields as quickly as possible. The field managers are eager for business, there are traffic snarl-ups a long way down the access roads, people queue in hour-long lines to get their few minutes of powder magic.

'And yet, all this pressure has nothing to do with the stability of the snow,' Smith said. 'You have to separate the two, the emotions and the facts, whether you are a professional or a weekend snow warrior. The snow is either safe or not and how badly you want to ski it, or how you want to impress the people you're with, should not cloud your judgement of the facts. Intuition is good but I'd only trust it if it's telling me not to go. One test I often use is to ask myself: 'Would I ski this if I was alone? If the answer is NO then I probably should not ski it at all.'

The traffic-lights snow assessment works like this: you ask yourself questions and answer them honestly, without bending your own rules. Am I in avalanche terrain? Yes or no. Is the snow stable? Yes or no. What are the consequences if I trigger an avalanche? Is it really worth the risk? Are there safer alternatives? The red lights are obvious and so are the green. Invariably, most of the accidents occur in the great wide amber-light zone of indecision. This is where the highest awareness and caution are needed because the most desirable snow — deepest, steepest, most exhilarating — is also the most dangerous and the ski tracks in it often trace a fine line between euphoria and deathly peril.

• • •

Beyond the Hollywood Bowl in the Treble Cone backcountry there is a mountain we locals call Gottlieb. Like many peaks in this part of the Alps, Gottlieb has distinct profiles, some ridged and fluted with gullies, one — like the 'Matterhorn' aspect of the nearby Mount Aspiring — a perfect white pyramid. One late spring day I stood on its elegant summit with Geoffrey Blackler, peeling off the climbing skins from our skis. It was an awkward climb to get here, against the grain of the mountain, but we had made the effort and now the reward was at our feet: a steep thrilling descent down the centre of the face, pristine and achingly beautiful, untouched by another skier.

'Do this one for Dave?' I asked.

'Yeah. He'd 'ave loved to be 'ere with us,' Geoff said.

But he was with us always, I thought, in the way we now skied, in how much more we've come to respect even the lesser mountains; his death in our playground had struck so close to home and heart. We could talk snow science with the pros now, we fed and cultivated our individual feeling for snow. As one avalanche expert wrote: 'Good judgment comes from experience and experience comes from bad judgment.' We have learnt that the bad judgements did not have to be our own, that there is wisdom in learning from all those before us in the hope of not repeating their errors.

Looking down the seductive slope of the mountain I went through the avalanche checklist in my head and got a mix of traffic-light colours, though none of them were red. I knew Geoff was doing the same.

He poked at the cornice with his ski pole.

'It'll be all right. Shall we go?' he asked and I nodded.

'One at a time though.'

'Always.'

He pushed off the cornice and I watched him find his rhythm, and the graceful effortless ski line that traced his descent and whose shape I knew so well. When you ski with someone long enough you learn to recognise the shape and style of their ski lines as you would their hand-writing.

Several hundred metres below, now but a tiny red-and-black speck at the end of his deeply-carved squiggle in the snow, Geoff pulled out on to a high knoll which rose from the slope like an island, a safe spot should any avalanche come down the face. He waved his arms, a signal that he was now watching me, belaying with his eyes. The mountain snow sparkled in the sun, still and silent, magical. A place to play hard but never gamble.

It was my turn to ski.

Run For Your Life

'. . . running was mankind's first fine art, our original act of inspired creation. Way before we were scratching pictures on caves or beating rhythms on hollow trees, we were perfecting the art of combining our breath and mind and muscles into fluid self-propulsion over wild terrain.'

Born to Run, Christopher McDougall

Maybe it was the lengthy book project or the endless music rehearsals, both of which entailed untold sedentary hours, with the heart rate elevated only by coffee and mental athletics. Or perhaps it was just normal ageing, proceeding on schedule but unacknowledged, if not outright denied. The worst thing was, in my mind, I could still do it. In my mind, I could still run up mountains where others had to walk. No matter how temporarily slothful I became, I always had enough residual fitness to be up for any adventure with anyone. Alas, my self-image was seriously out of date, and the strength of the delusion only made for a greater shock at what followed.

There is a hill called Mount Iron on the outskirts of our town, shaped like a sphinx and clearly the work of Ice Age glaciers. In other places you'd call it a mountain, but in Wanaka, on the edge of the Southern Alps, it's merely a hill, its zigzagging trails a jogging loop for the town's folk of all ages. Anytime in the past I could easily run up and down this hill, twice in a session, then jog back home as if I had just been for a stroll and a chat with a friend.

But this time it was different. As soon as I reached the bottom hairpin bend of the climb I knew something was wrong. My heartbeat had a subwoofer quality to it and the speed of a runaway metronome. Despite all the wheezing and gasping I wasn't getting enough air and my legs felt like they weren't my own. By the time I had climbed to the third bend my body refused to go on. I stopped, bent double, hands on knees, feeling I might faint, sucking air like a man drowning.

'You okay dear?' through the techno thumping of my heart I heard a woman's voice, tinged with concern. 'There, sit down and have a spell.' I felt her guiding me to the track's embankment. 'It's quite steep through here, isn't it?'

She was twenty years my senior, maybe more: permed platinum hair under a visor cap, jogging shorts, ruddy face and a friendly smile but not a hint of overexertion. She had been jogging right behind me but in my tunnel-vision uphill grind I never noticed. She regarded me closely and must have concluded the crisis was not life-threatening after all.

'I'll check on you again on my way down,' grandma said, 'you take it easy now, won't you?' Then she was off, trotting lightly up the hill which here had the gradient of a staircase, not racing, but looking comfortably at ease, as if she could go on forever.

I buried my face in my hands. This was tragic! I wasn't just out of shape. I was an amorphous mess — heart attack material.

I walked the rest of the uphill while joggers and runners passed me in both directions, grandma among them, hot-footing down the track like someone half her age. Down from the summit I too broke into a cautious trot, and soon found an easy gravity-assisted pace. Suddenly, it felt good to be alive, to just run with next to no effort. I had forgotten the feeling but I would never forget it again, I vowed. I would get fit, and stay fit, and keep improving so that from now on I'd always be the fittest I've ever been. During the downhill I was buoyed by the idea and the sensations of the run: the cooling breeze against the skin, the views, the whiffs of sun-dried wild thyme, the mesmeric rhythm of my footfalls. The runner's high.

But as soon as I stopped, the doubts swarmed in. Getting fit was clearly a must but was running really the best tool for the job?

• • •

It was a postural specialist — an osteologist — who had planted the seed of doubt. More than a decade earlier, I had gone through a short sharp bout of back problems resulting from a moment of tomfoolery on skis. It led to X-rays, consultations and, after the healing, the inevitable 'where to from here'. Running would have been my first choice of rehab, and physio, but the good doctor had a different idea.

'I wouldn't bother with running if I were you,' he said, 'in fact, I'd avoid it at all costs. There are better ways of rehabilitation and keeping fit. Get a bike or take up swimming. It'll be better for you long-term.'

Running, he went on, was stressful on the human body, its repetitive jarring on ankles, knees and lower back causing slow but cumulative damage, not obvious at any one time but compounding over the years into wear and tear that was potentially beyond repair. 'If you feel you have to do it, half an hour three times a week is about the maximum I'd recommend,' he concluded. 'Any more and you'll be doing yourself more damage than good.'

And yet, how could this be, I questioned. Wasn't running the most natural thing to do, the first play children indulged in after they had learnt to walk? Wasn't it the activity of choice we turned to when 'getting into shape', losing weight, or just clearing our minds? Every day, millions of people put on their shoes and go for a run as if responding to some deep inner compulsion. Running was by far the world's most popular participation sport and, barring the disabled, almost all of us would have at some point at least tried it. And wasn't running the very reason our anatomy evolved the way it has?

Evolutionary biologist and champion runner Bernd Heinrich certainly thought so. 'Our speciality as bipedal runners spans a history of at least six million years,' he wrote in *Why We Run, A*

Natural History. Humans have evolved as 'endurance predators', Heinrich argued, not catching our quarry during an explosive do-or-die sprint as most predators do, but by running the hunted animal into exhaustion. A deer or a gazelle can easily out-sprint us over a short distance but they have little sense of speed and pacing. Keep at them for a length of time, Heinrich said, and they eventually 'blow out' like a sprinter who has unwittingly entered a marathon. He cited many indigenous people — the Kalahari Bushmen, the Tarahumara of Mexico, the Navajos and the Australian Aborigines — who've used this strategy.

But it was not all about hunting either. In *Born to Run*, the best-selling book which acquired something of a cult status among the sport's enthusiasts, Christopher McDougall took in a larger view of our evolutionary adaptation as runners. 'Distance running was revered because it was indispensable,' he writes. 'It was the way we survived and thrived and spread across the planet. You ran to eat and to avoid being eaten; you ran to find a mate and to impress her, and with her you ran off to start a new life together. You had to love running, or you wouldn't live to love anything else.' Running, McDougall reasons, is not a passion or sport. It is a genetically encoded ancestral necessity.

Why then such polarised views? If we were born to run how could running be bad for us? And if it wasn't bad, why were running-related injuries so prevalent? Chondromalacia (runner's knee) and ankle sprains, snapping hips and stress fractures, shin splints, plantar fasciitis and Achilles tendonitis — if you ran regularly, you were almost guaranteed to suffer from these at one point or another. Grandma, for one, seemed in fine shape but were her knees and hips medical time-bombs she was not aware of? Was it the running itself or the way we did it? I was confused. Clearly, there was more to know here.

• • •

Fortunately for the world of modern running, one New Zealander did not suffer from such doubts or confusion though his own wake-up call from the slumber of poor fitness was not dissimilar to my own. As the Second World War was coming to an end, Arthur Lydiard was only 27 and, being a swimmer, a rugby player and a well-rounded athlete, considered himself in decent physical shape . . . until a friend invited him for a ten-kilometre run. 'My pulse rate rose rapidly,' Lydiard recalled. 'I blew hard and gasped for air, my lungs and throat felt as if they'd been scorched, my legs were like rubber.'

There had to be a lot more to fitness than splashing in a warm sea or chasing after a ball, Lydiard realised. He set out to investigate, using himself as the subject of his experiments, running daily, building up mileage and varying intensities, at one point clocking as much as 400 kilometres a week. It took him nearly twenty years to perfect his system, to understand the nature of human endurance, how it can be built most efficiently, and what enormous benefits it brings into our daily lives. Almost as a by-product of this, Lydiard became the country's top long-distance runner, at the time when marathons were still considered potentially harmful to a human body. Soon several young track athletes — Murray Halberg, Peter Snell and Barry Magee — began gravitating around him, following the controversial 'Lydiard method' of running far in order to run fast.

The result of this collaboration was the Golden Era of New Zealand running in the early 1960s. Halberg became the first New Zealander to run a sub-four-minute mile, and at the 1960 Olympic Games in Rome he won gold in the 5000 metres. Peter Snell, winning gold and a record in the 800 metres and, four years later, double gold in Tokyo in the 800 and 1500 metres, had been hailed as the country's sportsman of the century. Also at the Rome Olympics, Barry Magee came third in the marathon, only two minutes behind the barefoot sensation Abebe Bikila, becoming the world's fastest non-African marathoner of the time.

However, Lydiard's vision for running was far greater than the arena of elite sports. Though it was fascinating to watch the super-athletes chase each other and shave seconds off the world records, for Lydiard, running wasn't really a spectator sport. It was about participation. And so, about the time Snell and Co. were stomping out their mark in the history of athletics, Lydiard entered into another collaboration, with a PR specialist and running convert Garth Gilmour.

Both men set out on the crusade to save and prolong ordinary lives, appalled by the general state of health and fitness among the populace in the so-called developed countries. 'New Zealand shares with the US, Canada and Australia the dubious privilege of having one of the highest rates of heart disease in the world,' they wrote. More New Zealanders over 50 died from a dicky ticker than from all other causes combined, cancers and car accidents included. Yet there was an easy and practical solution to that, a preventive and a panacea for the ills brought about by increasingly stressful and sedentary lifestyles.

In their 1965 manifesto *Run For Your Life*, Lydiard and Gilmour wrote: 'It's almost exclusively in your hands whether you enjoy a healthy vigorous life to a ripe old age or whether you succumb to the slovenly, non-energetic existence and probable premature breakdown of health which happens to most people in countries with a high standard of living.'

By then, they had the proof to such a claim, solid results in turning around lives on the brink of collapse. In 1961, a small group of men gathered around Lydiard, most of them overweight middle-aged businessmen with a history of coronary problems. Lydiard took them to the Auckland waterfront, and had them 'walk from one telegraph pole to the next, jog to the one after that', walk and jog, walk and jog, until they covered a mile. 'It took quite a while at first but gradually they got fitter and fitter until they were running the whole distance,' Lydiard recalled. The transformation in the men was such that their associates began asking what was it they did to get into such good shape.

Soon another gathering took place in Cornwall Park, within One Tree Hill Domain in Auckland. About twenty people turned up after a general invitation to the public, Garth Gilmour remembered, average age 47 and in all stages of unfitness, big stomachs and double chins everywhere. There was a talk from a cardiologist, then coach Lydiard stepped in, warning all present not to turn the run into a competition. Apparently, they looked around at each other and laughed. There was never any danger of that. Most of them couldn't run more than 400 metres, and some barely staggered the distance. But in eight months of his regular 'train don't strain' regimen, Lydiard would have them lose weight, drop their cholesterol levels and heart rates to reasonable again, and seven of the men would comfortably run a marathon and clock fairly decent times.

Thus, in the early 1960s jogging was born. Until then, it would have been rare to see a person running for pleasure and fitness unless he or she was a serious athlete in training. Now, inspired in part by their Olympic heroes, hundreds, then thousands of New Zealanders took to the streets and distance running as if their lives depended on it, which, as Lydiard and Gilmour insisted, they did. Out of suburban Auckland, the phenomenon of jogging, and the idea of distance running as the best foundation for all other sports, spread around the globe in a veritable firestorm of enthusiasm and Lydiard was soon hailed as the world's best running coach of all time. But even as his gospel of jogging for health and wellbeing was finding its way into homes and offices everywhere, trouble was already afoot.

Foreign coaches began visiting Lydiard to gleam his secrets and one of them was Bill Bowerman from Oregon. For a coach of athletics, Bowerman was in terrible shape himself. He joined the Cornwall Park weekly outing, which by then was developing into the Auckland Joggers Club, and found himself unable to keep up even with the slowest group. Only Andy Stedman, 74 and a survivor of three heart attacks, waited for Bowerman, and only out of politeness.

Lydiard recalled that the incident gave Bowerman the shock of his life and plunged him into the discipline of daily jogging. Within the month he stayed in New Zealand, Bowerman trimmed fifteen centimetres off his 132-centimetre waistline and was able to keep up with Lydiard during a 32-kilomtere run around the old goldfields of Arrowtown. He was sold on the idea of jogging and in turn became its most ardent advocate. 'Arthur Lydiard is a prophet and I am his disciple,' Bowerman would be fond of saying.

In no time at all he had some 3000 people showing up regularly at his jogging class on a race track in Portland, Oregon. He produced a three-page guide to Lydiard's method which became a national model for fitness programmes in the US, and later a book titled *Jogging*. The book sold over a million copies and is largely credited as the catalyst for the worldwide explosion of jogging. But for Bowerman, this was only the beginning.

While still together in New Zealand the two men discussed running shoes, and this was a critical juncture in the evolution of jogging. Lydiard was a shoemaker by trade but Bowerman already had his own ideas how to make running and jogging an easier experience. Back home he began experimenting with different types of rubber soles, cushioning and support. He was also a sharp salesman and, as Christopher McDougall points out in *Born to Run*, Bowerman wanted people to jog and run, the more the merrier, but he wanted them to run in his shoes. In this he succeeded beyond all expectations. That first jogging shoe was called Cortez and, like the conquistador it was named after, it would take the New World by storm. Bowerman formed a company to sell it and, after the Greek goddess of victory, he named it Nike. Its current annual revenues are in excess of NZ$22.5 billion.

But it was in the workshop of Bill Bowerman, according to contemporary research in biomechanics of the human body, where things went wrong for jogging and for millions of enthused followers. The rate of heart problems may have subsided but only to be replaced by a catastrophic plague of running-related injuries.

In his enthusiasm for spreading Lydiard's gospel Bowerman went too far. He wanted to make the running experience more comfortable by cushioning the runners' feet, protecting them from the ground with layers of soft rubber and arch support. Eventually he added gel cushions under heels to soften the impact of footfalls against the asphalt.

According to Dr Daniel Lieberman, a professor of biological anthropology at Harvard University, those 'silicone implants' under heels fundamentally altered the way we run. They encourage longer, heavier, stomping strides. Instead of using the shock-absorbing ability of the foot arches, our natural suspension mechanisms, we let the gel cushion absorb the impact of the stride. But this impact is only fractionally dissipated by the gel, Lieberman pointed out. The rest of the shock force travels up the limbs and the skeletal structure, compounding wear and tear and bringing about all those dreaded injuries.

For all his best intentions and enthusiasm to spread the gospel of jogging, it appears Bowerman did not get his original teachings quite right. Thus his subsequent tinkering with running shoes, so profoundly affecting the biomechanics of running, would indeed cause more harm than good. This was further compounded by the fact that to keep up with Nike's phenomenal success, other shoe manufacturers followed suit; eventually there was hardly an alternative available.

It bears pointing out that, for all the mileage he had clocked, alone and training with athletes around the world, Arthur Lydiard never had an injury from running. When he did ruin his knee, it was by helping a contractor to lift a concrete pipe on his property in Manurewa. Heavy weight and uneven ground caused a painful knee twist and the complications that followed spelled the end of his daily jogs.

Lydiard was adamant that running shoes should not be technological marvels with their own built-in suspension, orthopaedic corrections and structures that overprotect the foot. 'We ran in canvas shoes,' he said. 'We didn't get plantar fascia, we didn't pronate or supinate, we might have lost a bit of skin from the rough canvas when we were running marathons, but, generally speaking, we didn't have foot problems.'

For coach Lydiard the matter was rather simple: 'You support an area, it gets weaker. Use it extensively, it gets stronger. Run barefoot and you don't have all those troubles.' Following this advice, I found myself tiptoeing on the grass of the postage-stamp size park in downtown Queenstown, wearing a pair of shoes that looked like frog feet.

The human foot is a work of art and a masterpiece of engineering.
Leonardo Da Vinci

There were about a dozen of us milling about the park that crisp autumn morning, all wearing those funny shoes called Vibram FiveFingers. Originally evolved from non-slippery boat shoes, the FiveFingers are like work gloves for the feet and the idea behind them is that they protect your feet and toes from harsh surfaces, stones and pebbles, while maintaining the sensation of being barefoot.

It was the day after the annual Routeburn Classic, a race which follows one of our greatest walks from the Divide to the trailhead north of Glenorchy, and the man around whom we gathered was still mildly disappointed. James Kuegler, an elite endurance athlete and coach, top-ten Coast-to-Coast competitor and winner of notable ultra-marathons, came all the way from Auckland to claim the Routeburn trophy but in the end, out of 350 runners, he only placed fourth overall. 'Just didn't have it in me when it mattered most,' he laughed, and it sounded almost apologetic.

Kuegler is a new force in New Zealand running and a standard-bearer for the revolution which is sweeping the country. The funny shoes are an accessory to that but the main thrust of the movement is towards natural running — re-learning to run the way our bodies were always meant to, without injuries and limitations of mileage and frequency. Kuegler's natural running workshop was the first such event in the South Island.

'Your feet each comprise 26 bones, 33 joints, numerous muscles and countless sensory receptors,' said Kuegler, who has also just completed a chiropractic degree. 'They are amazing suspension mechanisms, working with harmonious fluidity, constantly reading the ground, adjusting to it. If we let them, that is, and most of the running shoes we wear do not.'

An efficient runner is like a wheel rolling along the ground, Kuegler explained, with his or her centre of gravity being the hub and the feet connecting with the ground directly beneath it like L-shaped spokes. There is no bobbing up and down but a sensation of falling forwards, hinging from the ankles. The footwork, which converts this falling into forward propulsion, is light, short and fast, with the optimal cadence at around 180 steps per minute. The feet are kissing the ground, not stomping it, landing slightly forward of the mid-sole, then touching down with the heel as if in an afterthought. The gait, at least as demonstrated by Kuegler, is nearly silent.

I thought back to Daniel Lieberman's study, published in the January 2010 issue of *Nature*. Using sensitive scales, high-speed cameras and 3D motion analysis, Lieberman and his team compared running styles, and especially the foot strikes, of five groups of athletes, including US runners and natives of the Rift Valley in Kenya. 'Humans have engaged in endurance running for millions of years but the modern running shoe was not invented until the 1970s,' Lieberman wrote. Those modern shoes make us run heel-first and the impact this causes, he calculated, is the equivalent of someone hitting your heel with a hammer with up to three times your body weight. At every step.

Not even the naturally born runners are immune to this. Lieberman analysed running styles of youngsters from two Kenyan schools, one in which the kids were still barefoot, the other where they already wore shoes. The difference was startling, the conclusion obvious: put even the Kenyans into modern running shoes and soon enough they will start running badly as well. The good news was that we naturally correct our running from the moment the shoes come off. The heels pounding the dirt just hurt too much to go on. It seems modern running shoes block not the impact but pain, and pain is a coach in how to run correctly.

Back in the Queenstown park, James Kuegler was taking us through his drills to let us find that natural stride again, and also talking about pain. 'The biggest thing to remember is that it takes time to wake your feet up again, especially for the calf muscles and Achilles tendons to regain their elasticity,' he said. 'They've been locked in a state of sensory deprivation for decades. It's like people who've been deaf their whole life and after an operation they gain their hearing. At first, they perceive all sound as pain. The body needs time to readjust.'

I should have listened. Back home in Wanaka, and still wearing the FiveFingers, I ran the new Deans Bank trail above the Clutha River, my daily dog walk. It felt effortless and light, delicious like a long foot massage. And so I kept on, and on, way beyond where I should have stopped. For the next week my calves felt like they'd been tenderised with a shotgun. I had to go backwards whenever there were any stairs to descend. In runners' vernacular this was called DOMS — delayed onset of muscle fatigue. The pain was exquisite.

• • •

'There are three kinds of pain in running,' Lisa Tamati told me at the foothills of the 12,947-hectare Northburn Station near Cromwell. 'There is the superficial pain like chafing and blisters, deep throbbing pain usually caused by inflammation, and the systemic pain from torn muscles, ligaments and tendons. It's really important to differentiate between these types. The first two can be worked through. But don't be a hero and try running through the third type of pain as it's likely to cause long-term damage.'

As the country's top ultra-marathon runner, Tamati has been intimate with all three kinds of pain and the ways of overcoming, or at least surviving them. Twice she completed the 243-kilometre Marathon des Sables, which involves six days of running across the sandscape of the Moroccan Sahara, and twice she finished the 217-kilometre Badwater Marathon across Death Valley in the US. In 2009, she ran the length of New Zealand, 2200 kilometres, in 33 days. Now she had just sent 30 competitors out into the drylands of the Northburn 100, the first 100-mile race in the country, and certainly the toughest ever. The 160-kilometre trail run, a combination of farm tracks and goat paths across bare-bone Otago schist country, sunburnt and bristling with runaway briar rose, incorporates a total ascent of 8000 metres — a Himalayan climb — and the same amount of descent, which is even harder because the downhill is more punishing on the leg muscles than the climb. Tamati set the cut-off time at 48 hours.

'This may not be everyone's idea of going for a run,' she told me, 'but overall New Zealanders love "tough" and extreme race events and here we are hoping to raise the standard of "tough" to a whole new level. It also shows the wider public just what the human body and mind are capable of. You only need to look at someone like Dharbhasana Lynn to see that we are not reaching anywhere near our full potential.'

In 2010, Hamilton man Dharbhasana Lynn completed the world's longest footrace: 4990 kilometres, averaging some 96 km a day for 52 days straight. He didn't do it for the scenery because the race track was an 883-metre loop around a residential block in Queens, New York. During the race he wore out fifteen pairs of running shoes and developed a detachment from pain that to the rest of us would seem both miraculous and mystical.

Lynn is a follower of Bengali spiritual teacher Sri Chinmoy, whose philosophy proposes the use of running as a form of self-transcendence. During long-distance running, Chinmoy suggested, the mind gets exhausted long before the body does, and it drops off into silence, and what's left in its place is the mystical Zone, a space of no-mind from which artists create and elite athletes perform. As with other transcendental experiences, such states do not lend themselves to expression in words, but after completing the nearly 5000 km run, Lynn offered this morsel of wisdom: 'We tend to judge ourselves by our limitations and not by our greater potentiality,' he said. 'Set no limits (on yourself) so you'll have none.'

This was clearly advice the Northburn 100 participants would have taken to heart. Hours after the pre-dawn start I watched the first two, Martin Lukes and Matt Bixley, coming into the race checkpoint. Though they had just covered more than 50 hard cross-country kilometres they looked as fresh as if indulging in a Sunday morning jog. They chatted and bantered, refilling their hydration packs and snack pockets, and then they were gone again, into the great rocky vastness of the Northburn, out of sight and into their own mindscapes, or perhaps already beyond them. Watching this I felt a pang of desire to be out there with them. Running really isn't a spectator sport.

Where does all this leave us lunch-time joggers and accidental runners, weekend warriors and would-be competitors? In a pretty good position and with excellent prospects, according to Richard Keene.

Keene is a retired Manukau businessman, a recreational athlete and an importer of innovative running equipment. New Zealand is indeed a nation on the run, he told me. Look at the national calendar of events and not a day passes without an organised run somewhere, from after-work trots and weekend ultras to Auckland's Round the Bays, one of the world's largest fun-runs with an estimated 70,000 participants following an 8.4-kilometre section of the Waitemata Harbour coastline.

Knowledge of the proper biomechanics of running has so far been largely the domain of elite athletes, their secret weapon against other competitors, Keene went on, but now, thanks to the work of coaches like James Kuegler this is rapidly changing. However, though barefoot running is a beautifully pure idea, it needs to be considered as a method of retraining only, Keene cautioned. We no longer live in a barefoot environment, so good, even if minimal, foot protection is crucially important.

'But there is more to this natural-running revolution than just getting away from cushioned shoes and into minimal footwear,' Keene told me. 'In New Zealand, the last ten years have seen an explosion of interest in running in more natural environments, along tracks and trails so far frequented only by trampers.'

Keene became a trail-running convert while working on a contract in California, brought the new-found passion home with him and began exploring the country as if for the first time. 'It is such a joy to travel light and fast,' he told me. 'Just a hydration pack and a bite to eat, ultra-light raincoat and a good pair of shoes, and off you go, alone or with friends. There are trails everywhere, and no cars, no noise or pollution . . . a total immersion in nature. That's how, I believe, we were always meant to run, not along the verge of a motorway during rush-hour traffic. And look around New Zealand. We live in the country of trails.'

I did look, and saw a whole new layer of geography, a veritable spaghetti of unlimited trail runs. 'We are preparing a web database of trails from the point of view of runners' needs,' Keene said. 'Grading trails by difficulties, suggesting optimal direction of travel and transport arrangements. What to expect and what to avoid. Running something like the Abel Tasman track, for example, is a whole new experience from walking it over a few days.'

Indeed. And how about the other famous tracks — Heaphy and Milford, Tongariro and Croesus Crossings, Avalanche Peak and the loop around Lake Rotoiti — each suddenly an epic and a considerable personal challenge if one is willing to run it.

There are no rest days in Arthur Lydiard's training regime — even recovery is done on the run, albeit a slow one — and following it I have now become a regular on the Mount Iron track. I had run for my life there, reclaimed my old fitness and I have bettered it since. Sometimes, I see grandma there and, would you believe it, she now too sports a pair of FiveFingers, though hers are a Day-Glo pink, no doubt to go with those platinum curls. She is training for the Kepler Challenge, she told me, using Mount Iron as her Stairmaster training for the Kepler's punishing climb, the Luxmore Grunt.

Out of the myriad of New Zealand's running events, the 60-kilometre Kepler Challenge is one of the oldest, grandest and most popular, a distilled essence of all that is most appealing in trail running. It begins with a long and hellishly steep climb up Mount Luxmore, continues along a ridgeline traverse of unparalleled scenery, before descending in sharp zigzags to finish with a marathon's worth of lake and riverside forest trail silenced with beech leaves.

'It's a long way to run but if you go quietly and pace yourself it's nowhere near as far as it seems,' grandma told me as we were catching our breaths after another lap of Mount Iron. 'And after you've done it, well, you sort of feel invincible. If I can run the Kepler, with all its hard miles up and down, I feel I can do anything.'

Perhaps, fitness and good health aside, challenges like Kepler may be worth doing for this reason alone.

Heroes Who Walk Among Us

'No matter what the emergency, if you need help, just call . . . that big red truck always comes. Just being able to offer such help to the public is what makes all our time and effort worthwhile.'

Though she had been waiting for it for nearly eight months, when it finally came it still took Heather Reid by surprise. Sure, she had felt it grow, and move, and turn inside her, the new life she so eagerly awaited. She had studied the process, conferred with her midwife, attended tests and consultations with religious regularity; she thought she had planned for everything. Except that it would happen like this: six weeks before her little baby girl was due, so quickly and without any warning, just as she was home alone, with all her anxiety, with all the pain.

That unforgettable morning, as her husband kissed her goodbye and dashed off, already late, for his morning shift, Heather again decided to stay in bed just a little longer. The pregnancy had been smooth but it was wearing her down and she had developed a habit of easing herself and her bulging belly into the day, lolling in the warm comfort of daydreams and anticipation. That morning was no different, until the pain came.

It was like nothing she had ever known, not the usual Braxton-Hicks mock contractions she was used to. This was pain of such intensity it choked her breath and voice, and curled her into a foetal position, making her bite her knuckles for relief. It eased briefly but was soon followed by another wave, then another, each surge stronger and more painful than the one before, if such a thing was possible.

Heather did not need her studies to know what was happening. This was it. The baby was coming. In a flash she recollected what the midwife had said: If a baby is way early it usually wants to come out in a hurry. She felt panic rise within her. She was alone, miles from her husband, and even further from the hospital.

On her knees, hugging the precious cargo of her belly, she crawled to the living room, waiting out the moments when the contractions immobilised her. She felt something pop inside and knew her waters had broken though she only gave them enough attention to check that they were clear, without undue smells that would signal danger. Her complete focus was now on the phone receiver. She knew she should call her midwife first but that barely seemed adequate. No, things were happening far too fast. She needed more help and quickly, and so with a shaking hand, she reached out and dialled 111.

Follow the electronic signal now, as it raced down the wires, from the Reids' suburban house in Rolleston north to the St John Ambulance South Comms Centre at 174 Durham Street in Christchurch. Heather's voice was increasingly frantic and punctuated with groans and screams, but that of the operator was calm and comforting. As he extracted the information from her — the critical what and where — the operator also activated another electronic signal which shot down the comms network, pausing briefly for approval at another emergency communications centre on Hereford Street, only a few blocks away. Then, given the go ahead there, the signal rushed on, cloning itself into multiple callouts, activating pagers, switching on a siren.

All the while, the operator crooned reassurances to Heather, whose pain and distress were palpable even through the telephone wires.

'Just hang in there Ma'am,' he said as he heard her cry out in pain again. 'Just hang in there. Help is on its way.' He would have loved to stay on the line but could not. Another distress call was coming from somewhere else in the country.

Heather was still on the floor by the phone when, only two minutes later, she heard the approaching siren and saw red lights strobing through her windows. There was a firm knock at the door, then four uniformed men appeared. The promised help had arrived but it was nothing like she had imagined. She stared in amazement, her eyes wide. It wasn't an ambulance with paramedics in crisply starched scrubs, not a delivery room on wheels. The four men wore inky-blue paratroopers' overalls and through the window Heather caught a glimpse of a big red fire truck with extendable ladders and rolled-down doors that housed coils of hoses. She couldn't believe her eyes. This had to be a mistake. They sent a fire truck to a childbirth?

• • •

Nigel Lilley, the officer in charge at the Rolleston Fire Brigade's First Response Unit took one look at Heather and made his decision. It was too late to go anywhere now. It would all have to happen here.

He felt just a twinge of apprehension. They'd practised on mannequin dummies giving birth to mannequin babies but he had never delivered a real child. Still, the number one rule was never show any doubts, even if you had them.

He smiled at Heather Reid and said: 'Ma'am, the ambulance will be here shortly. Until then, we're here to help.'

And so it was that four burly firemen delivered a healthy baby girl — let's call her Jill Reid — on the living room floor of a Rolleston home. When the ambulance, which had to travel from a station 30 minutes away, finally arrived, they were mopping up the scene and Heather was cradling the newborn to her breast. Lilley took it for a sign that it was safe to recall his troops back to base. They lingered a little, soaking up the magic of the moment that the happy arrival of new life had brought about. Usually they had to deal with people at the other end of their lifespan, or those coming perilously close to it. When the moment had passed they tactfully withdrew, leaving the ambulance crew to the details.

Only minutes later, after the gear was cleaned and neatly stowed away ready for another time, before the crew dispersed to their homes and families, officer Lilley was making four cups of instant coffee back at the station, the spoon clanging the sides of the cup like the clapper of a bell signalling knock-off time. He passed the cups around, took his own and slumped his rugby-prop physique into an armchair.

'Geez, that was intense,' he sighed taking a sip of scalding hot liquid. 'Give me a good fire any day.'

Within less than twelve hours his wish would be granted.

• • •

This entire incident would seem like a nothing-out-of-the-ordinary emergency dispatch, one of thousands occurring every day on the planet. But there is one more thing you need to know about it, and about all those mentioned here. Though you'd never realise it at the scene, none of the rescuers was a professional fire-fighter. They may appear to be such, and they certainly perform like the pros, but they are all unpaid volunteers, with jobs, lives, families and hobbies of their own. Lilley, for one, is a Rolleston publican, while Gaza loads planes at the airport (in soldierly fashion, the fire-fighters delight in nicknames.) Inky drives trucks, Kaffer is an IT whiz. Among them there are builders and butchers, seamstresses and the unemployed. Yet their jobs and families and everything else become secondary the moment their pagers go off, when the station siren howls its urgent summons. Then they down their tools, drop whatever they have been doing and race to the rescue of complete strangers.

Sounds like a noble thing to do once in a while? Think again. Last year, the Rolleston volunteer fire brigade — one of the busiest in the country — responded to 444 distress calls. On a busy day there may be five or six callouts, the busiest one ever clocked in at seventeen. Their turn-up time — the interval between when their pagers ring and the moment the fire truck roars out of the station — is 90 seconds. Impressive? Apparently not, because, as Lilley smirks, at every callout they're trying to better even that.

Around the country there are thousands of men and women who live in a state of perpetual readiness. With their callouts, weekly training sessions and weekend specialised courses — which can vary from emergency driving, abseiling and containment of chemical spills to advanced first aid and, yes, assisting at a childbirth — they spend more time on their fire-fighting than you'd put into an average hobby. Their lives are ruled by their beepers to a point that when planning a 'night on the town' or a day away, they notify their stations so that another person can cover them.

In the news we watch and read they are rarely mentioned. But know that every story of a road accident, a fire or a personal tragedy has a positive side to it, for these men and women have been to the scene. They secured it, contained the damage, took care of the victims, made sure no more people were hurt. They also cleaned up the aftermath, swept the shattered glass off the road, washed away the blood and oil spills and reassured the survivors, always moving with measured confident steps, balancing the urgency with strict operational procedures.

Watching them work in their trained and efficient ways it's all too easy to assume they must be a municipal service provided by a local authority. They are not. They do it all in their own time, and often at an expense to themselves and to their employers, and the less tangible costs to their family life. But they do it nonetheless, and they love it with the passion others reserve for their favourite adventure pursuits. 'When on a job we're all pros, just some of us get paid for it and most don't,' Mike Lennard, a professional fire-fighter and the trainer of the South Island volunteers, told me. 'But we all pride ourselves that from the moment we arrive on the scene things don't get any worse.'

• • •

Up the staircase of an austere concrete building in suburban Christchurch a trio of volunteer fire-fighters are running in full battle gear — yellow Gore-Tex fire suits, balaclava-like flash hoods and helmets with visors, fireproof gloves and gumboots. Their faces are hidden behind the masks of the BAs (breathing apparatuses) and, in the darkness and the 70°C heat, their shouts are muffled, their panting laboured like that of Darth Vader running at a sprint. Only a weak flashing light reveals their figures, freeze-framing the progress they make. Despite the gloom and hellish temperature the trio works with the precision of crack troops taking over the building but, as their enemy is fire, their only weapon is a water gun. The first man carries the squat nozzle, the other two help to lay the unwieldy fire hose along the stairs and around corners.

At a landing they crouch by the closed metal door, instantly regrouping.

'Ready?'

'READY.'

'Okay. Open.'

One of the men yanks the door ajar while the nozzle carrier thrusts his weapon into the opening to fight off any flames that may lick at them from the interior. No flames come and the first man slams the door shut again.

'Okay, this time we're going in. Ready? Let's GO!'

The door swings open again and they burst in, the third man following close behind, dragging the hose, an obstinate red serpent thick as a forearm and stiff with internal pressure. Now they are in an even deeper darkness and they have to feel their way ahead blindly, sweeping the floor with their feet, each probing out with one gloved hand while the other always stays anchored on the hose. Their voices are urgent, calling out reassurances, commands, and changes in direction. Still, confusion slowly creeps in, particularly after they find what they have come here to retrieve.

'THERE IS A BODY.'

'I'VE GOT HIM.'

The two lead men are about to pick the body up to drag it out the way they came when there is a commotion off to one side, then the till then flickering light comes full on, followed by a relaxed, easy-going voice:

'Whoa! Let's pause it right there chaps,' Gary Luff, the fire-fighting trainer, cuts in. 'Have a look what's happened.'

What has happened is that somehow the hose has acquired a huge knot in it and the two fire-fighters, having rushed for the body, lost their prescribed formation and the proper contact with the hose.

Like a choreographer Luff corrects them, showing a more efficient and safer way of dealing with the situation he himself had designed: how to handle the body, how to drag it out using the fire hose as a guideline, keeping one heel on either side of it.

'Remember, the fire hose is your lifeline,' he reminds them. 'If you get in trouble tie yourself to the end of it. That way the truck won't go home without you.'

Then he turns off his light, plunging the interior into darkness once more.

'Let's pick it up again,' he calls. 'The clock is ticking. GO!'

They do, and moments later the 90-kilogram dummy is safely out of danger. After a brief pause, the trio drags it back in where they found it so that another team can train on the same scenario. Then they go outside to breathe fresh air and to strip off their fire suits. Their undergarments are saturated with sweat as if they had just emerged from a steam sauna.

This is how heroes and heroines are forged and re-forged, and, in the South Island at least, this happens at the Woolston training facility in Christchurch during a week-long recruitment course, the initiation into this brotherhood of the flames. Some 120 recruits pass through the centre every year and Gary Luff is their chief trainer, a Hephaestus of all this new talent.

After 43 years in the Fire Service and a decade as a trainer there isn't much Luff has not seen, both in fire-fighting and in human psychology.

'Amazing things happen when people are under fire together,' he says. 'Trust, bonds and lifelong friendships develop. Personal fires are put out, inner dragons slain. Those with a fear of heights climb ladders. Those with claustrophobia manage to don a BA and crawl through tunnels. Introverts become team-players. It gives me a tremendous buzz to be a part of and a witness to it all.'

More part of than witness probably because Luff is well known for designing training scenarios that are all too realistic.

'It pays to learn well because if you do it wrong, it can hurt like hell, which is why we're not into a "let's pretend" approach during exercises,' he says. 'When we do first aid or accidents, for example, we hire the local drama group. They do such a good job of it, with screams and fake blood and all, even though everyone knows it's only an exercise some of the recruits turn pale just looking at it.'

To further facilitate this reality training, the five-storey exercise building is equipped with strategically-placed eject buttons which activate a sprinkler system and turn on powerful suction fans. 'That's for when things turn to custard during a live fire practice,' Luff says though, in the same breath, he admits he does not remember the last time they did.

As if setting fire to fully-furnished rooms wasn't realistic enough, the Fire Service routinely demolishes unwanted homes and abandoned cars allowing every trainee a baptism of real fire.

'For training purposes we burn around 30 houses a year,' Luff says. 'It costs roughly $10,000 to demolish a house and we offer to do it for nothing as long as we get enough notice to design an exercise around it. We also burn and cut up cars, practising victim extraction. With most of our callouts being to road accidents you can never have enough training at that.'

When houses or cars are not available, they exercise using shipping containers dressed up as living rooms, equipped with TVs, drapes and junkyard furniture and complete with the usual culprits in fires: toasters, heaters and gas appliances. Temperatures in those metal hot-boxes are fierce, the heat like a breath of furnace air, melting all the desire to go in. But go in they must. Luff says: 'Fire-fighters are the people who rush in when everyone else is trying to get the hell out.' Which is probably why they are consistently voted the number one most trusted public service in the country, ahead of the ambulance and the police.

'These are big shoes to keep fitting into but it's also what drives us to continually improve,' Luff says, and his face beams with the expression of a man who loves what he does and knows it. 'No matter what the emergency, whether you're an elderly lady treed by a mouse, a driver that skidded into a ditch, or a farmer about to lose a hayshed to fire, if you need help, you call 111 and that big red truck always comes within minutes. Just being able to offer such help to the public is what makes all our time and effort worthwhile.'

• • •

All the 111 calls requesting Fire Service assistance are directed to one of the three communications centre in Auckland, Wellington or Christchurch; the last covers the entire South Island. Its Fire Comms takes up a small corner of one floor of the city police station on Hereford Street and has two call-takers, two dispatchers, a supervisor, and a lot of high-end computer equipment.

Andrew Norris, the supervisor of the shift during my visit explains the workings of this place, which is partly like an air-traffic control room, partly a listening-out station, continually taking the pulse of both the natural and the manmade trouble that befalls the entire island.

'Fire rescue is a bit of a misnomer because we respond to such a wide range of mishaps and accidents,' Norris says. 'We send crews to everything from cats stuck up trees and chickens that have fallen down wells to exploding barbeques, burst hot water cylinders, controlled burn-offs that got out of control and ship fires in ports, chemical spills, helicopter crashes, train and truck collisions and highway head-ons with multiple fatalities.

'Our call-takers always try to gauge the caller's lever of distress,' Norris goes on, 'because the elderly especially are often embarrassed to have to ask for help. They give you more apologies for the trouble than details of what's happening. They also frequently understate the situation and so we've learnt that it's often better to send in a crew anyway, just in case. You have to remember, as a rule of thumb, the fire can double in size and ferocity with every passing minute. A smoking toaster or a faulty electric blanket can turn into a large-scale plantation fire in no time at all.'

As if to reinforce his words, a call comes in about a small scrub fire near Mataura in Southland and with a few strokes of his keyboard, Norris alerts the nearest crew. Seven hundred kilometres away men and women drop everything and race to their fire truck. Barely two minutes later a beep on Norris's computer announces that the crew has already left the station and are heading into the hot zone. From the comms centre this seems like a computer game but in Mataura real people are fighting a real fire and the fire is winning.

Like a good strategist Norris plays his cards carefully. Soon there are three fire trucks on the scene, plus a tanker, and more reinforcements are on the way. Then another call comes in, this time it's a medical emergency near Rolleston, and I have to leave Norris to his fire-fighting game. What was a quiet day so far is rapidly heating up.

In dispatching fire crews and their machines, Norris and his colleagues around the country make little distinction between sending out paid staff (of which there are only some 1600) or volunteers, who number over 11,000. Indeed the two factions often work side by side. There seems to be plenty for everyone to do.

Together, the pros and the vollies (volunteers) staff 437 stations and operate around 800 fire trucks and tankers. For the past few years the number of emergency calls has sat steadily around 65,000 annually, some 35 per cent of which have been false alarms. Real fires make for another 35 per cent of all calls and these include some 4000 home incidents. The rest of the dispatches are to situations involving hazardous substances, natural disasters and the ubiquitous medical emergencies (MEs).

In rural areas it is not uncommon for the fire brigades to attend to all the MEs — anything from bad cuts like chainsaw accidents to cardiac arrests — because the fire crew can be on the scene much quicker than an ambulance. In cases of cardiac arrests, which call for the use of defibrillators, this can mean the difference between the patient living through the ordeal or not, as the golden window of opportunity is only about five minutes before often irreversible brain damage begins to set in. 'The defibrillator jobs are among the most satisfying to attend because just by showing up in time and performing a simple procedure you can save that person's life,' Nigel Lilley says. 'And it's funny too, because they have absolutely no recall of what's happened. They wake up and look at you totally surprised, and ask something like, "What are you doing here?" And you can just smile and say: "Nothing, just passing through."'

• • •

The call came through on Saturday, when they were attending the Wings and Wheels air show at the RNZAF base in Wigram. It was only a small fire in West Melton but the conditions were tinder-dry, and a strong southerly threatened to fan the blaze out. Lilley and a senior station officer, Mike Tasker, were manning the Rolleston brigade's yellow 5000-litre tanker and they raced to the scene as a support crew.

By the time they got there the fire had spread, forming a strong, fast-moving front. It razed fields, paddocks and windbreak hedges, then it reached a plantation of pines and, finding a more plentiful and combustive fuel supply, it accelerated, igniting the canopy into a uniform blaze, exploding individual trees, leaping the roads that were supposed to serve as firebreaks, growing into an ever-widening fan of destruction.

Lilley and Tasker found themselves racing along the left flank of the fire, attempting to head it off in what is known in the business as a pincer technique. Lilley was driving and Tasker rode the water gun, and though the speeds of the tanker and the fire were evenly matched, they were making good progress, almost succeeding in cutting the fire off to turn it back on itself. But then, unexpectedly, the wind changed, from the strong southerly to the dreaded nor'wester, hot and gusty, and creating an even stronger bellows effect.

The fire front swung around, the inferno engulfing the rest of the plantation, and Lilley and Tasker found themselves driving through a tunnel of flames. 'By then, it was getting really big,' Mike Tasker recalled. 'There were dozens of fire trucks all around the scene, and the choppers and fixed-wing planes were starting to come in too. And we were right in the middle of it all. The smoke was so thick all around us we had no idea where we were, whether we were going away from the fire or into it.'

At some point during the ordeal, Lilley, who is a man both big and strong, and tempered by experience, could not suppress a plaintive cry:

'Mikey! Let's not get ourselves killed here!'

To make things worse, the smoke starved their petrol Firemaster water pump of all air, depriving them of the only weapon they had against the fire. There was nothing left but to make a run for it.

By now, having burst into the open, they were driving cross-country through paddocks, cutting fences and ramming gates, partly to get through and out themselves, partly to open the way for the horses and sheep to flee from the fire.

Meanwhile, at the nearby Orana Park open-range zoo now imminently threatened by the blaze, the rangers did not have such luxury. With no time to truck their exotic beasts out and, since freeing Sumatran tigers, white rhinos, cheetahs and lions was not really an option, they were preparing to shoot the animals to spare them the agony of a death in the flames.

Lilley and Tasker broke out and got through to Orana where, alongside many other crews and fire trucks, they made their stand against the fire, restarting their pump, supplementing the water supply from the streams and moats of the animal enclosures. The fire took four days to put out but in the end, Orana Park and all of its wild beasts survived unscathed.

'We were in the field for 24 hours, home for a brief nap, then back out for another 24-hour stint. It took us three or four weeks to recover,' Lilley recalled, then, as an afterthought, he added fondly: 'Best fire I've ever been to.'

The smile that ruffled Mike Tasker's imperial moustache was a sure sign that he too shared the sentiment.

• • •

Like most volunteer fire brigades around the country, from Stewart Island to Kaitaia, the Rolleston station is both a community centre and a sort of dangerous sports club for it is undeniable that a great deal of fire-fighting's allure is the adventure, an opportunity for problem-solving and rising to a challenge when under fire. The community aspects and the brigade culture are equally strong however, and they go back to the time of the earliest Pakeha settlers, the days when, out of necessity, everyone was a fire-fighter and each fire was an all-hands-on-deck call to arms against the calamity.

In Rolleston these calls occurred especially frequently because the loam soils of the region are fast-draining and store little or no moisture, and the nor'wester blow-dries the land, desiccating wheat fields and pine, wattle and gum tree plantations into tinder. All that was needed to set them ablaze was a spark and these were liberally provided by steam trains stoking up for the uphill climb to Sheffield, en route to Arthur's Pass. The six o'clock express was the most notorious culprit. During dry periods, fires occurred most evenings and the locals would beat them down with shovels, wet sacks and tree branches.

With time, the techniques and equipment became more sophisticated, the organisation of fire-fighters more formalised, but the community spirit remained unchanged.

'The smaller the community the bigger their involvement with the fire brigade,' says Rolleston's chief fire officer Glenn Cockburn, who in his professional life is a St John paramedic. 'In rural areas the fire station often becomes the hub of all social activities. At Rolleston, we've had birthday celebrations, weddings and funerals. In summer we often rig up a projector and turn the station into an open-air movie theatre, having film nights for the kids.'

Indeed, the back of the Rolly station is a large, well-appointed grassy patio, with an extensive children's playground: trampoline, swings and seesaws, and a colourful McDonald's-style castle bought on Trade Me. An old concrete-block pool, once used for cleaning fire hoses, is now often filled with water for the kids to paddle around in. It's all overlooked by a shady veranda featuring three hexagonal wooden tables and a barbeque big enough to grill an entire cattle beast. There is a bar and a large kitchen, and enough space to accommodate all 30 fire-fighters and their families.

'You've got to remember that it's the families that are the unseen heroes in all this,' says fireman Aron Brown, in his other life a Mercedes-Benz dealer in town. 'We get to play with fire and save lives, but if you've promised your kids you'll take them to the beach, and you're all packed and ready to go, and the next moment your beeper goes off and you're gone — again! — it won't be long before they start resenting this whole fire-fighting business. Which is why it's so important the families are included in the life of the brigade, feel a part of it.'

Looking at the playground again I can't shake off an impression that I've seen it somewhere before. Yes, the resemblance is remarkable. With its crawl-throughs, swings and bridges, the playground is a scaled-down version of the obstacle course where the fire-fighters perform their drills during their weekly training sessions. A coincidence?

'Not at all,' Mike Tasker grins. 'You've got to get them when they're young, which is why we've created this play station for our kids. After all, they are the next generation of fire-fighters.'

• • •

Driving back home, wondering at the phenomenon of volunteer fire-fighting, I stop for a break at the old Rangitata river bridge near Arundel and see that someone else had the very same idea. A man in green-and-lime farming overalls is fussing about in the trunk of his white station wagon. It is the height of the salmon season and the man is rigging up for some after-work fishing, assembling an ancient rod with a rickety egg-beater reel, threading the line. Then, of all things, he puts on a cap with a logo that reads Fire Rescue.

His skin is tanned into cracked leather from years in the sun, and black rings of engine grease around his fingernails tell that he cannot only drive a tractor but fix one as well. Is he a fireman too? I ask.

Too right, he replies. Joined at sixteen and seen a lot of action in 37 years of service. Car crashes mainly, not so many fires, though a few good ones. Big plantation blazes. Exciting stuff. Fire-fighting is just the thing a bloke does in the country, to help others, to socialise.

'I only quit 'cause I buggered me back,' he says. 'Best team sport you could ever play, and an adventure too.'

He puts on a weight-lifter's belt, wide and made of leather, just in case he does hook into a big salmon. I watch him pace down the bank, lobbing a hefty ticer across and into the turquoise waters, and realise I have not even asked for his name.

In all likelihood he'd just give me his nickname. Not ones to brag about their deeds, or to claim any credit for them, the volunteer firemen are likely to remain our anonymous heroes.

Gaza, Beetle, Lily and Jaq, Inky, Tootle, Shrek and Kaffer — every town and community has them. They style themselves as ordinary people but their lives and service are anything but ordinary, for under the veneer of quotidian life and clothing, each seems to wear a Superman's outfit. Whenever an accident occurs, they're likely to be the first help on the scene, having dropped everything they were doing — building houses, milking cows, selling bread or petrol, being with their families — to rush off to help someone in need, answering a distress call from a stranger.

When you see them racing past in their big red truck, lights flashing, siren blaring, ready to handle any emergency they may come across, stand tall and grateful, and know that you're witnessing the highest manifestation of the human spirit, even if the fire-fighters themselves would never entertain such a preposterous thought.

You may even want to salute them. I know I will.

Selected Reading

CAVING

Caves: Delving Deeper — Half A Century of Cave Discovery in New Zealand, Moira Lipyeat. New Zealand Speleological Society, Waitomo/Hazard Press, Christchurch, 2003

Great Caves of the World, Tony Waltham. Natural History Museum, London, 2008

Underground Worlds, Donald Dale Jackson. Time-Life Books, Alexandria, Virginia, 1982

EXPLORING

Mr Explorer Douglas: John Pascoe's New Zealand Classic, John Pascoe, Graham Langton (ed.). Canterbury University Press, Christchurch, 2000

New Zealand Explorers: Great Journeys of Discovery, Philip Temple. Viking/Allen Lane, London, 1989

JEAN BATTEN

Jean Batten: The Garbo of the Skies, Ian Mackersey. David Bateman Ltd, Auckland, 2013

My Life, Jean Batten. George C. Harrap & Co. Ltd, London, 1938; reissued as *Alone in the Sky*, Airlife, Auckland, 1979

KAKAPO

Kakapo Country: The Story of the World's Most Unusual Bird, David Cemmick. Hodder & Stoughton, Auckland, 1987

Kakapo Recovery Plan, 1996–2005, M.M. Cresswell. Kakapo Management Group, Department of Conservation, Wellington, 1996

Kakapo, H.A. Best. New Zealand Wildlife Service/Wellington, McIndoe/Dunedin, 1985

Kakapo, Hoki: The Story of a Kakapo, Gideon Climo. Godwit, Auckland, 1997

Last Chance to See, Douglas Adams & Mark Carwardine. Arrow Books/ Random House, London, 2009

Quest for the Kakapo, David Butler. Heinemann Reed, Auckland 1989

Reischek's 1890 Paper on the Kakapo (Strigops Habroptilus) *in the Wild and in Captivity*, Kaj E. Westerskov. Ornithological society of New Zealand, Auckland, 1981

KELLY TARLTON

Kelly: The Adventurous Life of Kelly Tarlton, Edmund Vernon Sale. Heinemann Reed, Auckland, 1988

New Zealand Shipwrecks: Over 200 Years of Disasters at Sea, Lynton Diggle, Edith Diggle & Keith Gordon. Hodder Moa, Auckland, 2007

The Adventures of a New Zealand Treasure Hunter, John Pettit. Halcyon Press, Auckland, 2008

Throw me the Wreck Johnny: Memories of Kelly Tarlton — the Man behind the Legend, Steve Locker-Lampson. Halcyon Press, Auckland, 2000

KIWI

Kiwi (Apteryx *spp.) Recovery Plan, 1996–2006*, Hugh A. Robertson. Biodiversity Recovery Unit, Department of Conservation, Wellington, 2003

Kiwi: A Secret Life, J.N. Jolly. New Zealand Natural Heritage Foundation, Palmerston North, 1991

Kiwi: New Zealand's Remarkable Bird, Neville Peat. Godwit, Auckland, 1999

The Incredible Kiwi: A Wild South Book, Neville Peat. Random Century (in association with TVNZ), Auckland, 1990

LICHENS

Flora of New Zealand: Lichens, David J. Galloway. Government Printer Publications, Wellington, 1985

Lichens (Life), William Purvis & Jacqui Morris. The Natural History Museum, London, 2000

Lichens: Including Lichen-forming and Lichenicolous Fungi: vols. 1 & 2 (Flora of New Zealand), D. J. Galloway, Manaaki Whenua Press, Lincoln/Christchurch, 2008

Natural History of Rangitoto Island, Hauraki Gulf, Auckland, New Zealand, Mike D. Wilcox (ed.). Auckland Botanical Society Inc., Auckland, 2008

MIKHAIL LERMONTOV

Death of a Cruise Ship: The Mystery of the Mikhail Lermontov, Tom O'Connor. Cape Catley, Whatamango Bay/Marlborough Sounds, New Zealand, 1999

The Mikhail Lermontov Enigma: Facts after 12 Years of Speculation!, Michael Guerin. Chartwell Unternehmen, Blenheim, N.Z, 1998

The Wreck Book: Rediscovered New Zealand Shipwrecks, Steve Locker-Lampson. Halcyon Press, Auckland, 1994

RUNNING

Born to Run, Christopher McDougall. Profile Books Ltd, London, 2009

Run for Your Life: Jogging with Arthur Lydiard, Arthur Lydiard & Garth Gilmour. Minerva, Auckland, 1965

Why We Run, A Natural History, Bernd Heinrich. Harper Collins, New York, 2001

OTHER

Erewhon (or *Over the Range*), Samuel Butler. Jonathan Cape, London, 1921

Also by Derek Grzelewski

The Trout Bohemia
Fly-fishing travels in New Zealand

David Bateman Ltd, Auckland, 2013

'Derek Grzelewski writes like a dazzling impressionist. *The Trout Bohemia* will make you think that fly-fishing was just invented, and that every river is waiting to be explored for the first time.' Marshall Cutchin, *MidCurrent*

'If *The Trout Bohemia* is not the best book ever written on trout fishing in New Zealand, I would like to know what is.' Adrian Bell, *Rod & Rifle*

'If you liked his *Trout Diaries*, this is even better.' Rob Sloane, editor, *FlyLife*

The Trout Diaries
A year of fly-fishing in New Zealand

David Bateman Ltd, Auckland, 2011

'Rarely has a book received so much universal praise . . . The writing is engaging and compelling, the setting fantastic, and the angling scenes are the stuff of our dreams.' *American Angler*

'It is the best fly-fishing book I have read this year.' Jeffrey Priest, *Trout Fisherman*, UK

'*The Trout Diaries* is a trophy catch that will satisfy angler, adventurer and philosopher alike.' Kennedy Warne, founding editor, *New Zealand Geographic*